Just The facts101 Textbook Key Facts

Equatorial Guinea Energy Policy, Laws and Regulations Handbook

by Cram101
Texbook NOT Included

Table of Contents

Index: Answers

Just The Facts101

Exam Prep for

Equatorial Guinea Energy Policy, Laws and Regulations Handbook

Just The Facts101 Exam Prep is your link from
the textbook and lecture to your exams.

Just The Facts101 Exam Preps are unauthorized and comprehensive reviews of your textbooks.

Just The Facts101 Exam Prep

eAIN 444696

Foundations of Business

A business, also known as an enterprise, agency or a firm, is an entity involved in the provision of goods and/or services to consumers. Businesses are prevalent in capitalist economies, where most of them are privately owned and provide goods and services to customers in exchange for other goods, services, or money.

:: Employment ::

__________ is a relationship between two parties, usually based on a contract where work is paid for, where one party, which may be a corporation, for profit, not-for-profit organization, co-operative or other entity is the employer and the other is the employee. Employees work in return for payment, which may be in the form of an hourly wage, by piecework or an annual salary, depending on the type of work an employee does or which sector she or he is working in. Employees in some fields or sectors may receive gratuities, bonus payment or stock options. In some types of __________ , employees may receive benefits in addition to payment. Benefits can include health insurance, housing, disability insurance or use of a gym. __________ is typically governed by __________ laws, regulations or legal contracts.

Exam Probability: **High**

1. *Answer choices:*

(see index for correct answer)

- a. Employment
- b. Workhaven
- c. Liaison job
- d. Timesheet

Guidance: level 1

:: Business law ::

__________ is where a person`s financial liability is limited to a fixed sum, most commonly the value of a person`s investment in a company or partnership. If a company with __________ is sued, then the claimants are suing the company, not its owners or investors. A shareholder in a limited company is not personally liable for any of the debts of the company, other than for the amount already invested in the company and for any unpaid amount on the shares in the company, if any. The same is true for the members of a __________ partnership and the limited partners in a limited partnership. By contrast, sole proprietors and partners in general partnerships are each liable for all the debts of the business .

Exam Probability: **Low**

2. *Answer choices:*

(see index for correct answer)

- a. Personal Property Security Act
- b. Family and Medical Leave Act of 1993
- c. Refusal to deal
- d. Financial Security Law of France

Guidance: level 1

:: Globalization-related theories ::

__________ is the process in which a nation is being improved in the sector of the economic, political, and social well-being of its people. The term has been used frequently by economists, politicians, and others in the 20th and 21st centuries. The concept, however, has been in existence in the West for centuries. "Modernization, "westernization", and especially "industrialization" are other terms often used while discussing __________ . __________ has a direct relationship with the environment and environmental issues. __________ is very often confused with industrial development, even in some academic sources.

Exam Probability: **High**

3. *Answer choices:*

(see index for correct answer)

- a. Capitalism
- b. post-industrial
- c. Economic Development

Guidance: level 1

:: Stock market ::

A _________ , equity market or share market is the aggregation of buyers and sellers of stocks , which represent ownership claims on businesses; these may include securities listed on a public stock exchange, as well as stock that is only traded privately. Examples of the latter include shares of private companies which are sold to investors through equity crowdfunding platforms. Stock exchanges list shares of common equity as well as other security types, e.g. corporate bonds and convertible bonds.

Exam Probability: **Low**

4. *Answer choices:*

(see index for correct answer)

- a. Volume-weighted average price
- b. Yellow strip
- c. Stock market
- d. P chip

Guidance: level 1

:: Television commercials ::

__________ is a characteristic that distinguishes physical entities that have biological processes, such as signaling and self-sustaining processes, from those that do not, either because such functions have ceased , or because they never had such functions and are classified as inanimate. Various forms of __________ exist, such as plants, animals, fungi, protists, archaea, and bacteria. The criteria can at times be ambiguous and may or may not define viruses, viroids, or potential synthetic __________ as "living". Biology is the science concerned with the study of __________ .

Exam Probability: **High**

5. *Answer choices:*

(see index for correct answer)

- a. The Pizza Head Show
- b. Life
- c. Godzilla vs. Charles Barkley
- d. The Force

Guidance: level 1

:: Marketing ::

A _________ is something that is necessary for an organism to live a healthy life. _________ s are distinguished from wants in that, in the case of a _________ , a deficiency causes a clear adverse outcome: a dysfunction or death. In other words, a _________ is something required for a safe, stable and healthy life while a want is a desire, wish or aspiration. When _________ s or wants are backed by purchasing power, they have the potential to become economic demands.

Exam Probability: **High**

6. *Answer choices:*

(see index for correct answer)

- a. Notability
- b. Competitor indexing
- c. Paddock girl
- d. Need

Guidance: level 1

:: Management ::

A _________ describes the rationale of how an organization creates, delivers, and captures value, in economic, social, cultural or other contexts. The process of _________ construction and modification is also called _________ innovation and forms a part of business strategy.

Exam Probability: **Medium**

7. *Answer choices:*

(see index for correct answer)

- a. Business process interoperability
- b. Private defense agency
- c. Management buyout
- d. Virtual customer environment

Guidance: level 1

:: Supply chain management terms ::

In business and finance, _________ is a system of organizations, people, activities, information, and resources involved inmoving a product or service from supplier to customer. _________ activities involve the transformation of natural resources, raw materials, and components into a finished product that is delivered to the end customer. In sophisticated _________ systems, used products may re-enter the _________ at any point where residual value is recyclable. _________ s link value chains.

Exam Probability: **Medium**

8. *Answer choices:*

(see index for correct answer)

- a. Overstock
- b. Price look-up code
- c. Final assembly schedule

- d. Supply chain

Guidance: level 1

:: Business ::

A _________ is a mathematical object used to count, measure, and label. The original examples are the natural _________ s 1, 2, 3, 4, and so forth. A written symbol like "5" that represents a _________ is called a numeral. A numeral system is an organized way to write and manipulate this type of symbol, for example the Hindu–Arabic numeral system allows combinations of numerical digits like "5" and "0" to represent larger _________ s like 50. A numeral in linguistics can refer to a symbol like 5, the words or phrase that names a _________ , like "five hundred", or other words that mean a specific _________ , like "dozen". In addition to their use in counting and measuring, numerals are often used for labels , for ordering , and for codes . In common usage, _________ may refer to a symbol, a word or phrase, or the mathematical object.

Exam Probability: **Low**

9. *Answer choices:*

(see index for correct answer)

- a. Ha Van Tham
- b. Business partnering
- c. Price adjustment
- d. Growth platform

Guidance: level 1

:: Foreign direct investment ::

A _________ is an investment in the form of a controlling ownership in a business in one country by an entity based in another country. It is thus distinguished from a foreign portfolio investment by a notion of direct control.

Exam Probability: **Low**

10. *Answer choices:*

(see index for correct answer)

- a. Oligopolistic reaction
- b. FDi magazine
- c. FDI stock
- d. Foreign direct investment

Guidance: level 1

:: Property ::

The right to property or right to own property is often classified as a human right for natural persons regarding their possessions. A general recognition of a right to private property is found more rarely and is typically heavily constrained insofar as property is owned by legal persons and where it is used for production rather than consumption.

Exam Probability: **Medium**

11. *Answer choices:*

(see index for correct answer)

- a. Intermediate rent
- b. MagicBricks
- c. Rack-rent
- d. Property rights

Guidance: level 1

:: Marketing ::

__________ is based on a marketing concept which can be adopted by an organization as a strategy for business expansion. Where implemented, a franchisor licenses its know-how, procedures, intellectual property, use of its business model, brand, and rights to sell its branded products and services to a franchisee. In return the franchisee pays certain fees and agrees to comply with certain obligations, typically set out in a Franchise Agreement.

Exam Probability: **High**

12. *Answer choices:*

(see index for correct answer)

- a. Franchising
- b. Market orientation

- c. Cause-related loyalty marketing
- d. Customer equity

Guidance: level 1

:: Strategic management ::

_________ is a strategic planning technique used to help a person or organization identify strengths, weaknesses, opportunities, and threats related to business competition or project planning. It is intended to specify the objectives of the business venture or project and identify the internal and external factors that are favorable and unfavorable to achieving those objectives. Users of a _________ often ask and answer questions to generate meaningful information for each category to make the tool useful and identify their competitive advantage. SWOT has been described as the tried-and-true tool of strategic analysis.

Exam Probability: **High**

13. *Answer choices:*

(see index for correct answer)

- a. Influencer
- b. forced distribution
- c. The New Age of Innovation
- d. First-mover advantage

Guidance: level 1

:: Management occupations ::

_________ is the process of designing, launching and running a new business, which is often initially a small business. The people who create these businesses are called entrepreneurs.

Exam Probability: **Medium**

14. *Answer choices:*

(see index for correct answer)

- a. City manager
- b. Chief sustainability officer
- c. Hayward
- d. Chief diversity officer

Guidance: level 1

:: Mereology ::

_________ , in the abstract, is what belongs to or with something, whether as an attribute or as a component of said thing. In the context of this article, it is one or more components , whether physical or incorporeal, of a person`s estate; or so belonging to, as in being owned by, a person or jointly a group of people or a legal entity like a corporation or even a society. Depending on the nature of the _________ , an owner of _________ has the right to consume, alter, share, redefine, rent, mortgage, pawn, sell, exchange, transfer, give away or destroy it, or to exclude others from doing these things, as well as to perhaps abandon it; whereas regardless of the nature of the _________ , the owner thereof has the right to properly use it , or at the very least exclusively keep it.

Exam Probability: **Low**

15. *Answer choices:*

(see index for correct answer)

- a. Mereological essentialism
- b. Non-wellfounded mereology
- c. Property
- d. Simple

Guidance: level 1

:: Production and manufacturing ::

_________ is a set of techniques and tools for process improvement. Though as a shortened form it may be found written as 6S, it should not be confused with the methodology known as 6S .

Exam Probability: **High**

16. *Answer choices:*

(see index for correct answer)

- a. Nuffield Tools and Gauges
- b. Six Sigma
- c. Hydrosila
- d. Memo motion

Guidance: level 1

:: Infographics ::

A __________ is a graphical representation of data, in which "the data is represented by symbols, such as bars in a bar __________ , lines in a line __________ , or slices in a pie __________ ". A __________ can represent tabular numeric data, functions or some kinds of qualitative structure and provides different info.

Exam Probability: **Medium**

17. *Answer choices:*

(see index for correct answer)

- a. Information visualization
- b. Funnel chart

- c. Treemapping
- d. Chart

Guidance: level 1

:: ::

A _________ is an organization, usually a group of people or a company, authorized to act as a single entity and recognized as such in law. Early incorporated entities were established by charter . Most jurisdictions now allow the creation of new _________ s through registration.

Exam Probability: **Low**

18. *Answer choices:*

(see index for correct answer)

- a. empathy
- b. co-culture
- c. Character
- d. information systems assessment

Guidance: level 1

:: Derivatives (finance) ::

_________ is any bodily activity that enhances or maintains physical fitness and overall health and wellness. It is performed for various reasons, to aid growth and improve strength, preventing aging, developing muscles and the cardiovascular system, honing athletic skills, weight loss or maintenance, improving health and also for enjoyment. Many individuals choose to _________ outdoors where they can congregate in groups, socialize, and enhance well-being.

Exam Probability: **Medium**

19. *Answer choices:*

(see index for correct answer)

- a. Option screener
- b. Iron butterfly
- c. Exercise
- d. Forward-forward agreement

Guidance: level 1

:: Legal terms ::

_________ , a form of alternative dispute resolution , is a way to resolve disputes outside the courts. The dispute will be decided by one or more persons , which renders the " _________ award". An _________ award is legally binding on both sides and enforceable in the courts.

Exam Probability: **Low**

20. *Answer choices:*

(see index for correct answer)

- a. Bodily harm
- b. Arbitration
- c. Crime against nature
- d. Frivolous or vexatious

Guidance: level 1

:: ::

Culture is the social behavior and norms found in human societies. Culture is considered a central concept in anthropology, encompassing the range of phenomena that are transmitted through social learning in human societies. _________ universals are found in all human societies; these include expressive forms like art, music, dance, ritual, religion, and technologies like tool usage, cooking, shelter, and clothing. The concept of material culture covers the physical expressions of culture, such as technology, architecture and art, whereas the immaterial aspects of culture such as principles of social organization , mythology, philosophy, literature , and science comprise the intangible _________ heritage of a society.

Exam Probability: **Low**

21. *Answer choices:*

(see index for correct answer)

- a. Sarbanes-Oxley act of 2002

- b. hierarchical perspective
- c. open system
- d. Cultural

Guidance: level 1

:: Monopoly (economics) ::

A __________ is a form of intellectual property that gives its owner the legal right to exclude others from making, using, selling, and importing an invention for a limited period of years, in exchange for publishing an enabling public disclosure of the invention. In most countries __________ rights fall under civil law and the __________ holder needs to sue someone infringing the __________ in order to enforce his or her rights. In some industries __________ s are an essential form of competitive advantage; in others they are irrelevant.

Exam Probability: **Medium**

22. *Answer choices:*

(see index for correct answer)

- a. Eisenkammer Pirna
- b. Patent
- c. Competition Commission
- d. Demonopolization

Guidance: level 1

:: Employment ::

The __________ is an individual`s metaphorical "journey" through learning, work and other aspects of life. There are a number of ways to define __________ and the term is used in a variety of ways.

Exam Probability: **Low**

23. *Answer choices:*

(see index for correct answer)

- a. Liaison job
- b. In-basket test
- c. Career
- d. Employment Development Department

Guidance: level 1

:: Management ::

__________ is a process by which entities review the quality of all factors involved in production. ISO 9000 defines __________ as "A part of quality management focused on fulfilling quality requirements".

Exam Probability: **Low**

24. *Answer choices:*

(see index for correct answer)

- a. Quality control
- b. Preventive action
- c. Process capability
- d. Strategic group

Guidance: level 1

:: Budgets ::

A __________ is a financial plan for a defined period, often one year. It may also include planned sales volumes and revenues, resource quantities, costs and expenses, assets, liabilities and cash flows. Companies, governments, families and other organizations use it to express strategic plans of activities or events in measurable terms.

Exam Probability: **Low**

25. *Answer choices:*

(see index for correct answer)

- a. Envelope system
- b. Budget
- c. Zero budget
- d. Film budgeting

Guidance: level 1

:: Export and import control ::

" _________ " means the Government Service which is responsible for the administration of _________ law and the collection of duties and taxes and which also has the responsibility for the application of other laws and regulations relating to the importation, exportation, movement or storage of goods.

Exam Probability: **Low**

26. *Answer choices:*

(see index for correct answer)

- a. Plant Protection and Quarantine
- b. CoCom
- c. Customs
- d. VNIIS Exemption Letter

Guidance: level 1

:: Strategic alliances ::

A _________ is an agreement between two or more parties to pursue a set of agreed upon objectives needed while remaining independent organizations. A _________ will usually fall short of a legal partnership entity, agency, or corporate affiliate relationship. Typically, two companies form a _________ when each possesses one or more business assets or have expertise that will help the other by enhancing their businesses. _________ s can develop in outsourcing relationships where the parties desire to achieve long-term win-win benefits and innovation based on mutually desired outcomes.

Exam Probability: **High**

27. *Answer choices:*

(see index for correct answer)

- a. International joint venture
- b. Cross-licensing
- c. Defensive termination
- d. Strategic alliance

Guidance: level 1

:: Consumer theory ::

A _________ is a technical term in psychology, economics and philosophy usually used in relation to choosing between alternatives. For example, someone prefers A over B if they would rather choose A than B.

Exam Probability: **High**

28. *Answer choices:*

(see index for correct answer)

- a. Preference
- b. Expenditure function
- c. Elasticity of intertemporal substitution
- d. Demand vacuum

Guidance: level 1

:: Generally Accepted Accounting Principles ::

An _________ or profit and loss account is one of the financial statements of a company and shows the company's revenues and expenses during a particular period.

Exam Probability: **Low**

29. *Answer choices:*

(see index for correct answer)

- a. Net income
- b. Revenue recognition
- c. Matching principle
- d. Income statement

Guidance: level 1

:: Corporate crime ::

_________ LLP, based in Chicago, was an American holding company. Formerly one of the "Big Five" accounting firms , the firm had provided auditing, tax, and consulting services to large corporations. By 2001, it had become one of the world`s largest multinational companies.

Exam Probability: **Medium**

30. *Answer choices:*

(see index for correct answer)

- a. Equity Funding
- b. Arthur Andersen
- c. Ovson Egg
- d. Corporate Manslaughter and Corporate Homicide Act 2007

Guidance: level 1

:: Information systems ::

_________ are formal, sociotechnical, organizational systems designed to collect, process, store, and distribute information. In a sociotechnical perspective, _________ are composed by four components: task, people, structure , and technology.

Exam Probability: **High**

31. *Answer choices:*

(see index for correct answer)

- a. Information systems
- b. Geographical Operations System
- c. Data system
- d. Field force automation

Guidance: level 1

:: Credit cards ::

A __________ is a payment card issued to users to enable the cardholder to pay a merchant for goods and services based on the cardholder`s promise to the card issuer to pay them for the amounts plus the other agreed charges. The card issuer creates a revolving account and grants a line of credit to the cardholder, from which the cardholder can borrow money for payment to a merchant or as a cash advance.

Exam Probability: **Medium**

32. *Answer choices:*

(see index for correct answer)

- a. Black Card
- b. Credit Saison

- c. Barclaycard
- d. Credit card

Guidance: level 1

:: Business ::

The seller, or the provider of the goods or services, completes a sale in response to an acquisition, appropriation, requisition or a direct interaction with the buyer at the point of sale. There is a passing of title of the item, and the settlement of a price, in which agreement is reached on a price for which transfer of ownership of the item will occur. The seller, not the purchaser typically executes the sale and it may be completed prior to the obligation of payment. In the case of indirect interaction, a person who sells goods or service on behalf of the owner is known as a _________ man or _________ woman or _________ person, but this often refers to someone selling goods in a store/shop, in which case other terms are also common, including _________ clerk, shop assistant, and retail clerk.

Exam Probability: **Medium**

33. *Answer choices:*

(see index for correct answer)

- a. Business as usual
- b. Vendor screening
- c. Sales
- d. Business tourism

Guidance: level 1

:: Management ::

A _________ is a method or technique that has been generally accepted as superior to any alternatives because it produces results that are superior to those achieved by other means or because it has become a standard way of doing things, e.g., a standard way of complying with legal or ethical requirements.

Exam Probability: **High**

34. *Answer choices:*

(see index for correct answer)

- a. Public sector consulting
- b. Business value
- c. Competitive advantage
- d. Business plan

Guidance: level 1

:: Marketing ::

A __________ is a group of customers within a business`s serviceable available market at which a business aims its marketing efforts and resources. A __________ is a subset of the total market for a product or service. The __________ typically consists of consumers who exhibit similar characteristics and are considered most likely to buy a business`s market offerings or are likely to be the most profitable segments for the business to service.

Exam Probability: **Medium**

35. *Answer choices:*

(see index for correct answer)

- a. Branded asset management
- b. Cyberdoc
- c. Lead generation
- d. Target market

Guidance: level 1

:: Business law ::

A __________ is a group of people who jointly supervise the activities of an organization, which can be either a for-profit business, nonprofit organization, or a government agency. Such a board`s powers, duties, and responsibilities are determined by government regulations and the organization`s own constitution and bylaws. These authorities may specify the number of members of the board, how they are to be chosen, and how often they are to meet.

Exam Probability: **High**

36. *Answer choices:*

(see index for correct answer)

- a. Board of directors
- b. Articles of partnership
- c. Process agent
- d. Ease of doing business index

Guidance: level 1

:: Statistical terminology ::

_________ is the magnitude or dimensions of a thing. _________ can be measured as length, width, height, diameter, perimeter, area, volume, or mass.

Exam Probability: **Medium**

37. *Answer choices:*

(see index for correct answer)

- a. Probability of error
- b. Size
- c. Stability
- d. Studentization

Guidance: level 1

:: Regression analysis ::

A _________ often refers to a set of documented requirements to be satisfied by a material, design, product, or service. A _________ is often a type of technical standard.

Exam Probability: **High**

38. *Answer choices:*

(see index for correct answer)

- a. Smearing retransformation
- b. Virtual sensing
- c. Residual sum of squares
- d. Component analysis

Guidance: level 1

:: Electronic feedback ::

_________ occurs when outputs of a system are routed back as inputs as part of a chain of cause-and-effect that forms a circuit or loop. The system can then be said to feed back into itself. The notion of cause-and-effect has to be handled carefully when applied to _________ systems.

Exam Probability: **Medium**

39. *Answer choices:*

(see index for correct answer)

- a. feedback loop
- b. Feedback

Guidance: level 1

:: Marketing ::

A _________ is an overall experience of a customer that distinguishes an organization or product from its rivals in the eyes of the customer. _________ s are used in business, marketing, and advertising. Name _________ s are sometimes distinguished from generic or store _________ s.

Exam Probability: **Medium**

40. *Answer choices:*

(see index for correct answer)

- a. MARC USA
- b. Brand
- c. Green market
- d. Object Value

Guidance: level 1

:: Quality management ::

_________ ensures that an organization, product or service is consistent. It has four main components: quality planning, quality assurance, quality control and quality improvement. _________ is focused not only on product and service quality, but also on the means to achieve it. _________ , therefore, uses quality assurance and control of processes as well as products to achieve more consistent quality.What a customer wants and is willing to pay for it determines quality. It is written or unwritten commitment to a known or unknown consumer in the market . Thus, quality can be defined as fitness for intended use or, in other words, how well the product performs its intended function

Exam Probability: **Medium**

41. *Answer choices:*

(see index for correct answer)

- a. Test bay
- b. Quality management
- c. PQASSO
- d. Dana Ulery

Guidance: level 1

:: Human resource management ::

_________ encompasses values and behaviors that contribute to the unique social and psychological environment of a business. The _________ influences the way people interact, the context within which knowledge is created, the resistance they will have towards certain changes, and ultimately the way they share knowledge. _________ represents the collective values, beliefs and principles of organizational members and is a product of factors such as history, product, market, technology, strategy, type of employees, management style, and national culture; culture includes the organization`s vision, values, norms, systems, symbols, language, assumptions, environment, location, beliefs and habits.

Exam Probability: **Medium**

42. *Answer choices:*

(see index for correct answer)

- a. Organizational culture
- b. Employeeship
- c. Progressive discipline
- d. Perceived organizational support

Guidance: level 1

:: Economic globalization ::

_________ is an agreement in which one company hires another company to be responsible for a planned or existing activity that is or could be done internally,and sometimes involves transferring employees and assets from one firm to another.

Exam Probability: **Medium**

43. *Answer choices:*

(see index for correct answer)

- a. reshoring
- b. global financial

Guidance: level 1

:: International trade ::

An _________ is a good brought into a jurisdiction, especially across a national border, from an external source. The party bringing in the good is called an _________ er. An _________ in the receiving country is an export from the sending country. _________ ation and exportation are the defining financial transactions of international trade.

Exam Probability: **Medium**

44. *Answer choices:*

(see index for correct answer)

- a. 2008 G-20 Washington summit
- b. Import
- c. Importation right
- d. Trade Agreements Act of 1979

Guidance: level 1

:: Unemployment ::

In economics, a _________ is a business cycle contraction when there is a general decline in economic activity. Macroeconomic indicators such as GDP , investment spending, capacity utilization, household income, business profits, and inflation fall, while bankruptcies and the unemployment rate rise. In the United Kingdom, it is defined as a negative economic growth for two consecutive quarters.

Exam Probability: **High**

45. *Answer choices:*

(see index for correct answer)

- a. Recession
- b. Misery index
- c. Mount Street Club
- d. Discouraged worker

Guidance: level 1

:: ::

An __________ is a contingent motivator. Traditional __________ s are extrinsic motivators which reward actions to yield a desired outcome. The effectiveness of traditional __________ s has changed as the needs of Western society have evolved. While the traditional __________ model is effective when there is a defined procedure and goal for a task, Western society started to require a higher volume of critical thinkers, so the traditional model became less effective. Institutions are now following a trend in implementing strategies that rely on intrinsic motivations rather than the extrinsic motivations that the traditional __________ s foster.

Exam Probability: **Medium**

46. *Answer choices:*

(see index for correct answer)

- a. Incentive
- b. levels of analysis
- c. functional perspective
- d. co-culture

Guidance: level 1

:: Business law ::

A __________ is an arrangement where parties, known as partners, agree to cooperate to advance their mutual interests. The partners in a __________ may be individuals, businesses, interest-based organizations, schools, governments or combinations. Organizations may partner to increase the likelihood of each achieving their mission and to amplify their reach. A __________ may result in issuing and holding equity or may be only governed by a contract.

Exam Probability: **Low**

47. *Answer choices:*

(see index for correct answer)

- a. Ladenschlussgesetz
- b. Refusal to deal
- c. Partnership
- d. Rules of origin

Guidance: level 1

:: Reputation management ::

__________ or image of a social entity is an opinion about that entity, typically as a result of social evaluation on a set of criteria.

Exam Probability: **High**

48. *Answer choices:*

(see index for correct answer)

- a. ClaimID
- b. Hilltop algorithm
- c. Conversocial
- d. Reputation

Guidance: level 1

:: Systems theory ::

A _________ is a set of policies, processes and procedures used by an organization to ensure that it can fulfill the tasks required to achieve its objectives. These objectives cover many aspects of the organization`s operations . For instance, an environmental _________ enables organizations to improve their environmental performance and an occupational health and safety _________ enables an organization to control its occupational health and safety risks, etc.

Exam Probability: **Low**

49. *Answer choices:*

(see index for correct answer)

- a. Management system
- b. transient state
- c. subsystem
- d. co-design

Guidance: level 1

:: ::

__________ is the collection of techniques, skills, methods, and processes used in the production of goods or services or in the accomplishment of objectives, such as scientific investigation. __________ can be the knowledge of techniques, processes, and the like, or it can be embedded in machines to allow for operation without detailed knowledge of their workings. Systems applying __________ by taking an input, changing it according to the system`s use, and then producing an outcome are referred to as __________ systems or technological systems.

Exam Probability: **High**

50. *Answer choices:*

(see index for correct answer)

- a. corporate values
- b. Technology
- c. interpersonal communication
- d. deep-level diversity

Guidance: level 1

:: Public relations ::

_________ is the public visibility or awareness for any product, service or company. It may also refer to the movement of information from its source to the general public, often but not always via the media. The subjects of _________ include people , goods and services, organizations, and works of art or entertainment.

Exam Probability: **High**

51. *Answer choices:*

(see index for correct answer)

- a. Publicity
- b. Vantage PR
- c. Upstate California
- d. Corporate website

Guidance: level 1

:: Competition (economics) ::

_________ arises whenever at least two parties strive for a goal which cannot be shared: where one`s gain is the other`s loss .

Exam Probability: **High**

52. *Answer choices:*

(see index for correct answer)

- a. Regulatory competition
- b. Competition
- c. Tax competition
- d. Blindspots analysis

Guidance: level 1

:: Data management ::

_________ is a form of intellectual property that grants the creator of an original creative work an exclusive legal right to determine whether and under what conditions this original work may be copied and used by others, usually for a limited term of years. The exclusive rights are not absolute but limited by limitations and exceptions to _________ law, including fair use. A major limitation on _________ on ideas is that _________ protects only the original expression of ideas, and not the underlying ideas themselves.

Exam Probability: **Low**

53. *Answer choices:*

(see index for correct answer)

- a. Concurrency control
- b. Machine-readable data
- c. Data grid
- d. Data discovery

Guidance: level 1

:: Social security ::

__________ is "any government system that provides monetary assistance to people with an inadequate or no income." In the United States, this is usually called welfare or a social safety net, especially when talking about Canada and European countries.

Exam Probability: **Low**

54. *Answer choices:*

(see index for correct answer)

- a. Social security
- b. Social Security Act 1938
- c. Intergenerational struggle
- d. Social Security Board

Guidance: level 1

:: Project management ::

Contemporary business and science treat as a _________ any undertaking, carried out individually or collaboratively and possibly involving research or design, that is carefully planned to achieve a particular aim.

Exam Probability: **High**

55. *Answer choices:*

(see index for correct answer)

- a. Feature-driven development
- b. RationalPlan
- c. Team performance management
- d. Project

Guidance: level 1

:: Marketing ::

_________ comes from the Latin neg and otsia referring to businessmen who, unlike the patricians, had no leisure time in their industriousness; it held the meaning of business until the 17th century when it took on the diplomatic connotation as a dialogue between two or more people or parties intended to reach a beneficial outcome over one or more issues where a conflict exists with respect to at least one of these issues. Thus, _________ is a process of combining divergent positions into a joint agreement under a decision rule of unanimity.

Exam Probability: **High**

56. *Answer choices:*

(see index for correct answer)

- a. Landing page
- b. Ben Franklin effect
- c. Negotiation
- d. Double-loop marketing

Guidance: level 1

:: Treaties ::

An __________ is a relationship among people, groups, or states that have joined together for mutual benefit or to achieve some common purpose, whether or not explicit agreement has been worked out among them. Members of an __________ are called allies. __________s form in many settings, including political __________s, military __________s, and business __________s. When the term is used in the context of war or armed struggle, such associations may also be called allied powers, especially when discussing World War I or World War II.

Exam Probability: **Medium**

57. *Answer choices:*

(see index for correct answer)

- a. Full Powers
- b. Investor state dispute settlement

- c. Alliance
- d. Secret treaty

Guidance: level 1

:: Non-profit technology ::

Instituto del Tercer Mundo is a Non-Governmental Organization that performs information, communication and education activities. __________ , which was established in 1989, shares the same secretariat and coordinating personnel as Social Watch and is based in Montevideo, Uruguay.

Exam Probability: **Medium**

58. *Answer choices:*

(see index for correct answer)

- a. Code for America Commons
- b. ITeM
- c. Action for Global Information Sharing
- d. DC Web Women

Guidance: level 1

:: Project management ::

__________ is the right to exercise power, which can be formalized by a state and exercised by way of judges, appointed executives of government, or the ecclesiastical or priestly appointed representatives of a God or other deities.

Exam Probability: **High**

59. *Answer choices:*

(see index for correct answer)

- a. Identifying and Managing Project Risk
- b. Time horizon
- c. Project Management South Africa
- d. Sustainable event management

Guidance: level 1

Management

Management is the administration of an organization, whether it is a business, a not-for-profit organization, or government body. Management includes the activities of setting the strategy of an organization and coordinating the efforts of its employees (or of volunteers) to accomplish its objectives through the application of available resources, such as financial, natural, technological, and human resources.

:: Types of marketing ::

In microeconomics and management, _________ is an arrangement in which the supply chain of a company is owned by that company. Usually each member of the supply chain produces a different product or service, and the products combine to satisfy a common need. It is contrasted with horizontal integration, wherein a company produces several items which are related to one another. _________ has also described management styles that bring large portions of the supply chain not only under a common ownership, but also into one corporation .

Exam Probability: **Medium**

1. *Answer choices:*

(see index for correct answer)

- a. Menu engineering
- b. Affinity marketing
- c. Vertical disintegration
- d. Relationship marketing

Guidance: level 1

:: ::

A _________ or GM is an executive who has overall responsibility for managing both the revenue and cost elements of a company`s income statement, known as profit & loss responsibility. A _________ usually oversees most or all of the firm`s marketing and sales functions as well as the day-to-day operations of the business. Frequently, the _________ is responsible for effective planning, delegating, coordinating, staffing, organizing, and decision making to attain desirable profit making results for an organization .

Exam Probability: **High**

2. *Answer choices:*

(see index for correct answer)

- a. Character
- b. corporate values
- c. process perspective
- d. functional perspective

Guidance: level 1

:: ::

A _________ is a fund into which a sum of money is added during an employee`s employment years, and from which payments are drawn to support the person`s retirement from work in the form of periodic payments. A _________ may be a "defined benefit plan" where a fixed sum is paid regularly to a person, or a "defined contribution plan" under which a fixed sum is invested and then becomes available at retirement age. _________ s should not be confused with severance pay; the former is usually paid in regular installments for life after retirement, while the latter is typically paid as a fixed amount after involuntary termination of employment prior to retirement.

Exam Probability: **Low**

3. *Answer choices:*

(see index for correct answer)

- a. Pension
- b. imperative
- c. Character
- d. interpersonal communication

Guidance: level 1

:: ::

__________ is a form of development in which a person called a coach supports a learner or client in achieving a specific personal or professional goal by providing training and guidance. The learner is sometimes called a coachee. Occasionally, __________ may mean an informal relationship between two people, of whom one has more experience and expertise than the other and offers advice and guidance as the latter learns; but __________ differs from mentoring in focusing on specific tasks or objectives, as opposed to more general goals or overall development.

Exam Probability: **High**

4. *Answer choices:*

(see index for correct answer)

- a. Character
- b. deep-level diversity
- c. levels of analysis
- d. Coaching

Guidance: level 1

:: ::

_________ is the practice of protecting the natural environment by individuals, organizations and governments. Its objectives are to conserve natural resources and the existing natural environment and, where possible, to repair damage and reverse trends.

Exam Probability: **High**

5. *Answer choices:*

(see index for correct answer)

- a. Character
- b. co-culture
- c. Environmental protection
- d. interpersonal communication

Guidance: level 1

:: Project management ::

A __________ is a source or supply from which a benefit is produced and it has some utility. __________s can broadly be classified upon their availability—they are classified into renewable and non-renewable __________s.Examples of non renewable __________s are coal ,crude oil natural gas nuclear energy etc. Examples of renewable __________s are air,water,wind,solar energy etc. They can also be classified as actual and potential on the basis of level of development and use, on the basis of origin they can be classified as biotic and abiotic, and on the basis of their distribution, as ubiquitous and localized . An item becomes a __________ with time and developing technology. Typically, __________s are materials, energy, services, staff, knowledge, or other assets that are transformed to produce benefit and in the process may be consumed or made unavailable. Benefits of __________ utilization may include increased wealth, proper functioning of a system, or enhanced well-being. From a human perspective a natural __________ is anything obtained from the environment to satisfy human needs and wants. From a broader biological or ecological perspective a __________ satisfies the needs of a living organism .

Exam Probability: **Low**

6. *Answer choices:*

(see index for correct answer)

- a. Resource
- b. Stages of project finance
- c. Scope statement
- d. Agile management

Guidance: level 1

:: Social psychology ::

In social psychology, _________ is the phenomenon of a person exerting less effort to achieve a goal when he or she works in a group than when working alone. This is seen as one of the main reasons groups are sometimes less productive than the combined performance of their members working as individuals, but should be distinguished from the accidental coordination problems that groups sometimes experience.

Exam Probability: **High**

7. *Answer choices:*

(see index for correct answer)

- a. Social penetration
- b. fear appeal
- c. thought control
- d. Social loafing

Guidance: level 1

:: ::

_________ is the moral stance, political philosophy, ideology, or social outlook that emphasizes the moral worth of the individual. Individualists promote the exercise of one`s goals and desires and so value independence and self-reliance and advocate that interests of the individual should achieve precedence over the state or a social group, while opposing external interference upon one`s own interests by society or institutions such as the government. _________ is often defined in contrast to totalitarianism, collectivism, and more corporate social forms.

Exam Probability: **High**

8. *Answer choices:*

(see index for correct answer)

- a. hierarchical perspective
- b. corporate values
- c. Individualism
- d. levels of analysis

Guidance: level 1

:: ::

The __________ is an intergovernmental organization that is concerned with the regulation of international trade between nations. The WTO officially commenced on 1 January 1995 under the Marrakesh Agreement, signed by 124 nations on 15 April 1994, replacing the General Agreement on Tariffs and Trade , which commenced in 1948. It is the largest international economic organization in the world.

Exam Probability: **Medium**

9. *Answer choices:*

(see index for correct answer)

- a. hierarchical
- b. empathy

- c. World Trade Organization
- d. interpersonal communication

Guidance: level 1

:: Human resource management ::

Frederick Herzberg, an American psychologist, originally developed the concept of ` _________ ` in 1968, in an article that he published on pioneering studies at A T&T. The concept stemmed from Herzberg`s motivator-hygiene theory, which is based on the premise that job attitude is a construct of two independent factors, namely job satisfaction and job dissatisfaction. Job satisfaction encompasses intrinsic factors that arise from the work itself, including achievement and advancement; whilst job dissatisfaction stems from factors external to the actual work, including company policy and the quality of supervision.

Exam Probability: **Low**

10. *Answer choices:*

(see index for correct answer)

- a. Chief human resources officer
- b. Corporate Equality Index
- c. Job enrichment
- d. Person specification

Guidance: level 1

:: Monopoly (economics) ::

A __________ is a form of intellectual property that gives its owner the legal right to exclude others from making, using, selling, and importing an invention for a limited period of years, in exchange for publishing an enabling public disclosure of the invention. In most countries __________ rights fall under civil law and the __________ holder needs to sue someone infringing the __________ in order to enforce his or her rights. In some industries __________ s are an essential form of competitive advantage; in others they are irrelevant.

Exam Probability: **High**

11. *Answer choices:*

(see index for correct answer)

- a. Government monopoly
- b. Bilateral monopoly
- c. Patent
- d. State monopoly capitalism

Guidance: level 1

:: ::

__________ is the consumption and saving opportunity gained by an entity within a specified timeframe, which is generally expressed in monetary terms. For households and individuals, " __________ is the sum of all the wages, salaries, profits, interest payments, rents, and other forms of earnings received in a given period of time."

Exam Probability: **Low**

12. *Answer choices:*

(see index for correct answer)

- a. information systems assessment
- b. Character
- c. similarity-attraction theory
- d. Income

Guidance: level 1

:: Income ::

__________ is a ratio between the net profit and cost of investment resulting from an investment of some resources. A high ROI means the investment`s gains favorably to its cost. As a performance measure, ROI is used to evaluate the efficiency of an investment or to compare the efficiencies of several different investments. In purely economic terms, it is one way of relating profits to capital invested. __________ is a performance measure used by businesses to identify the efficiency of an investment or number of different investments.

Exam Probability: **Medium**

13. *Answer choices:*

(see index for correct answer)

- a. Return of investment
- b. Return on investment
- c. Imputed income
- d. Windfall gain

Guidance: level 1

:: Teams ::

A _________ usually refers to a group of individuals who work together from different geographic locations and rely on communication technology such as email, FAX, and video or voice conferencing services in order to collaborate. The term can also refer to groups or teams that work together asynchronously or across organizational levels. Powell, Piccoli and Ives define _________ s as "groups of geographically, organizationally and/or time dispersed workers brought together by information and telecommunication technologies to accomplish one or more organizational tasks." According to Ale Ebrahim et. al. , _________ s can also be defined as "small temporary groups of geographically, organizationally and/or time dispersed knowledge workers who coordinate their work predominantly with electronic information and communication technologies in order to accomplish one or more organization tasks."

Exam Probability: **Medium**

14. *Answer choices:*

(see index for correct answer)

- a. Virtual team
- b. Team-building

Guidance: level 1

:: ::

The __________ or just chief executive , is the most senior corporate, executive, or administrative officer in charge of managing an organization especially an independent legal entity such as a company or nonprofit institution. CEOs lead a range of organizations, including public and private corporations, non-profit organizations and even some government organizations . The CEO of a corporation or company typically reports to the board of directors and is charged with maximizing the value of the entity, which may include maximizing the share price, market share, revenues or another element. In the non-profit and government sector, CEOs typically aim at achieving outcomes related to the organization`s mission, such as reducing poverty, increasing literacy, etc.

Exam Probability: **High**

15. *Answer choices:*

(see index for correct answer)

- a. imperative
- b. personal values

- c. Chief executive officer
- d. empathy

Guidance: level 1

:: ::

_________ involves the development of an action plan designed to motivate and guide a person or group toward a goal. _________ can be guided by goal-setting criteria such as SMART criteria. _________ is a major component of personal-development and management literature.

Exam Probability: **Low**

16. *Answer choices:*

(see index for correct answer)

- a. corporate values
- b. Goal setting
- c. process perspective
- d. levels of analysis

Guidance: level 1

:: Personality tests ::

The Myers–Briggs Type Indicator is an introspective self-report questionnaire with the purpose of indicating differing psychological preferences in how people perceive the world around them and make decisions. . Though the test superficially resembles some psychological theories it is commonly classified as pseudoscience, especially as pertains to its supposed predictive abilities.

Exam Probability: **Medium**

17. *Answer choices:*

(see index for correct answer)

- a. personality quiz
- b. Myers-Briggs type
- c. Myers-Briggs Type Indicator
- d. Keirsey Temperament Sorter

Guidance: level 1

:: Behaviorism ::

In behavioral psychology, _________ is a consequence applied that will strengthen an organism`s future behavior whenever that behavior is preceded by a specific antecedent stimulus. This strengthening effect may be measured as a higher frequency of behavior , longer duration , greater magnitude , or shorter latency . There are two types of _________ , known as positive _________ and negative _________ ; positive is where by a reward is offered on expression of the wanted behaviour and negative is taking away an undesirable element in the persons environment whenever the desired behaviour is achieved.

Exam Probability: **Medium**

18. *Answer choices:*

(see index for correct answer)

- a. Reinforcement
- b. Systematic desensitization
- c. Matching Law
- d. social facilitation

Guidance: level 1

:: Evaluation ::

__________ is the practice of being honest and showing a consistent and uncompromising adherence to strong moral and ethical principles and values.In ethics, __________ is regarded as the honesty and truthfulness or accuracy of one`s actions. __________ can stand in opposition to hypocrisy, in that judging with the standards of __________ involves regarding internal consistency as a virtue, and suggests that parties holding within themselves apparently conflicting values should account for the discrepancy or alter their beliefs. The word __________ evolved from the Latin adjective integer, meaning whole or complete. In this context, __________ is the inner sense of "wholeness" deriving from qualities such as honesty and consistency of character. As such, one may judge that others "have __________ " to the extent that they act according to the values, beliefs and principles they claim to hold.

Exam Probability: **Medium**

19. *Answer choices:*

(see index for correct answer)

- a. Integrity
- b. Transferable skills analysis
- c. Evaluation approaches
- d. Summative assessment

Guidance: level 1

:: Organizational structure ::

An _________ defines how activities such as task allocation, coordination, and supervision are directed toward the achievement of organizational aims.

Exam Probability: **High**

20. *Answer choices:*

(see index for correct answer)

- a. Unorganisation
- b. Organizational structure
- c. Automated Bureaucracy
- d. Blessed Unrest

Guidance: level 1

:: ::

In sales, commerce and economics, a _________ is the recipient of a good, service, product or an idea - obtained from a seller, vendor, or supplier via a financial transaction or exchange for money or some other valuable consideration.

Exam Probability: **Medium**

21. *Answer choices:*

(see index for correct answer)

- a. cultural
- b. Customer
- c. information systems assessment
- d. Character

Guidance: level 1

:: ::

In business strategy, _________ is establishing a competitive advantage by having the lowest cost of operation in the industry. _________ is often driven by company efficiency, size, scale, scope and cumulative experience .A _________ strategy aims to exploit scale of production, well-defined scope and other economies , producing highly standardized products, using advanced technology.In recent years, more and more companies have chosen a strategic mix to achieve market leadership. These patterns consist of simultaneous _________ , superior customer service and product leadership. Walmart has succeeded across the world due to its _________ strategy. The company has cut down on exesses at every point of production and thus are able to provide the consumers with quality products at low prices.

Exam Probability: **Low**

22. *Answer choices:*

(see index for correct answer)

- a. Cost leadership
- b. functional perspective
- c. similarity-attraction theory
- d. levels of analysis

Guidance: level 1

:: Human resource management ::

__________ involves improving the effectiveness of organizations and the individuals and teams within them. Training may be viewed as related to immediate changes in organizational effectiveness via organized instruction, while development is related to the progress of longer-term organizational and employee goals. While __________ technically have differing definitions, the two are oftentimes used interchangeably and/or together. __________ has historically been a topic within applied psychology but has within the last two decades become closely associated with human resources management, talent management, human resources development, instructional design, human factors, and knowledge management.

Exam Probability: **Low**

23. *Answer choices:*

(see index for correct answer)

- a. Competency-based recruitment
- b. Human resource accounting
- c. Training and development
- d. Mechanical aptitude

Guidance: level 1

:: Business ethics ::

__________ is a type of harassment technique that relates to a sexual nature and the unwelcome or inappropriate promise of rewards in exchange for sexual favors. __________ includes a range of actions from mild transgressions to sexual abuse or assault. Harassment can occur in many different social settings such as the workplace, the home, school, churches, etc. Harassers or victims may be of any gender.

Exam Probability: **High**

24. *Answer choices:*

(see index for correct answer)

- a. Corporate social responsibility
- b. Hostile work environment
- c. Sexual harassment
- d. Society for Business Ethics

Guidance: level 1

:: Problem solving ::

In other words, __________ is a situation where a group of people meet to generate new ideas and solutions around a specific domain of interest by removing inhibitions. People are able to think more freely and they suggest as many spontaneous new ideas as possible. All the ideas are noted down and those ideas are not criticized and after __________ session the ideas are evaluated.The term was popularized by Alex Faickney Osborn in the 1953 book Applied Imagination.

Exam Probability: **High**

25. *Answer choices:*

(see index for correct answer)

- a. Rogerian argument
- b. Problem finding
- c. Convergent and divergent production
- d. Brainstorming

Guidance: level 1

:: Legal terms ::

_________ , a form of alternative dispute resolution , is a way to resolve disputes outside the courts. The dispute will be decided by one or more persons , which renders the " _________ award". An _________ award is legally binding on both sides and enforceable in the courts.

Exam Probability: **Low**

26. *Answer choices:*

(see index for correct answer)

- a. Additur
- b. Fuero
- c. Abuse of process

- d. Partial verdict

Guidance: level 1

:: Production and manufacturing ::

Automatic _________ in continuous production processes is a combination of control engineering and chemical engineering disciplines that uses industrial control systems to achieve a production level of consistency, economy and safety which could not be achieved purely by human manual control. It is implemented widely in industries such as oil refining, pulp and paper manufacturing, chemical processing and power generating plants.

Exam Probability: **Low**

27. *Answer choices:*

(see index for correct answer)

- a. Hydrosila
- b. Reverse engineering
- c. Profibus
- d. Process control

Guidance: level 1

:: ::

A __________ is a professional who provides expert advice in a particular area such as security , management, education, accountancy, law, human resources, marketing , finance, engineering, science or any of many other specialized fields.

Exam Probability: **High**

28. *Answer choices:*

(see index for correct answer)

- a. information systems assessment
- b. Consultant
- c. open system
- d. Sarbanes-Oxley act of 2002

Guidance: level 1

:: ::

__________ or accountancy is the measurement, processing, and communication of financial information about economic entities such as businesses and corporations. The modern field was established by the Italian mathematician Luca Pacioli in 1494. __________ , which has been called the "language of business", measures the results of an organization`s economic activities and conveys this information to a variety of users, including investors, creditors, management, and regulators. Practitioners of __________ are known as accountants. The terms " __________ " and "financial reporting" are often used as synonyms.

Exam Probability: **Medium**

29. *Answer choices:*

(see index for correct answer)

- a. similarity-attraction theory
- b. co-culture
- c. Accounting
- d. surface-level diversity

Guidance: level 1

:: ::

_________ comprises all of the processes of governing – whether undertaken by the government of a state, by a market or by a network – over a social system and whether through the laws, norms, power or language of an organized society. It relates to "the processes of interaction and decision-making among the actors involved in a collective problem that lead to the creation, reinforcement, or reproduction of social norms and institutions".In lay terms, it could be described as the political processes that exist in and between formal institutions.

Exam Probability: **High**

30. *Answer choices:*

(see index for correct answer)

- a. Sarbanes-Oxley act of 2002
- b. interpersonal communication
- c. hierarchical perspective
- d. Governance

Guidance: level 1

:: ::

A _________ is a problem offering two possibilities, neither of which is unambiguously acceptable or preferable. The possibilities are termed the horns of the _________ , a clichéd usage, but distinguishing the _________ from other kinds of predicament as a matter of usage.

Exam Probability: **Low**

31. *Answer choices:*

(see index for correct answer)

- a. personal values
- b. interpersonal communication
- c. deep-level diversity
- d. Dilemma

Guidance: level 1

:: Majority–minority relations ::

_________ , also known as reservation in India and Nepal, positive discrimination / action in the United Kingdom, and employment equity in Canada and South Africa, is the policy of promoting the education and employment of members of groups that are known to have previously suffered from discrimination. Historically and internationally, support for _________ has sought to achieve goals such as bridging inequalities in employment and pay, increasing access to education, promoting diversity, and redressing apparent past wrongs, harms, or hindrances.

Exam Probability: **High**

32. *Answer choices:*

(see index for correct answer)

- a. cultural Relativism
- b. Affirmative action
- c. positive discrimination

Guidance: level 1

:: Credit cards ::

The _________ Company, also known as Amex, is an American multinational financial services corporation headquartered in Three World Financial Center in New York City. The company was founded in 1850 and is one of the 30 components of the Dow Jones Industrial Average. The company is best known for its charge card, credit card, and traveler`s cheque businesses.

Exam Probability: **High**

33. *Answer choices:*

(see index for correct answer)

- a. Netbanx
- b. Universal Air Travel Plan
- c. American Express
- d. SBI Cards

Guidance: level 1

:: ::

_________ Corporation was an American energy, commodities, and services company based in Houston, Texas. It was founded in 1985 as a merger between Houston Natural Gas and InterNorth, both relatively small regional companies. Before its bankruptcy on December 3, 2001, _________ employed approximately 29,000 staff and was a major electricity, natural gas, communications and pulp and paper company, with claimed revenues of nearly $101 billion during 2000. Fortune named _________ "America`s Most Innovative Company" for six consecutive years.

Exam Probability: **High**

34. *Answer choices:*

(see index for correct answer)

- a. process perspective
- b. personal values
- c. Enron
- d. similarity-attraction theory

Guidance: level 1

:: Production economics ::

_________ is the joint use of a resource or space. It is also the process of dividing and distributing. In its narrow sense, it refers to joint or alternating use of inherently finite goods, such as a common pasture or a shared residence. Still more loosely, " _________ " can actually mean giving something as an outright gift: for example, to "share" one`s food really means to give some of it as a gift. _________ is a basic component of human interaction, and is responsible for strengthening social ties and ensuring a person's well-being.

Exam Probability: **Low**

35. *Answer choices:*

(see index for correct answer)

- a. HMI quality
- b. Marginal product of labor
- c. Robinson Crusoe economy
- d. Factor price

Guidance: level 1

:: Materials ::

A _________ , also known as a feedstock, unprocessed material, or primary commodity, is a basic material that is used to produce goods, finished products, energy, or intermediate materials which are feedstock for future finished products. As feedstock, the term connotes these materials are bottleneck assets and are highly important with regard to producing other products. An example of this is crude oil, which is a _________ and a feedstock used in the production of industrial chemicals, fuels, plastics, and pharmaceutical goods; lumber is a _________ used to produce a variety of products including all types of furniture. The term " _________ " denotes materials in minimally processed or unprocessed in states; e.g., raw latex, crude oil, cotton, coal, raw biomass, iron ore, air, logs, or water i.e. "...any product of agriculture, forestry, fishing and any other mineral that is in its natural form or which has undergone the transformation required to prepare it for internationally marketing in substantial volumes."

Exam Probability: **Low**

36. *Answer choices:*

(see index for correct answer)

- a. Biocompatible material

- b. Raw material
- c. Tortoiseshell
- d. Diamondoid

Guidance: level 1

:: Game theory ::

To __________ is to make a deal between different parties where each party gives up part of their demand. In arguments, __________ is a concept of finding agreement through communication, through a mutual acceptance of terms—often involving variations from an original goal or desires.

Exam Probability: **Medium**

37. *Answer choices:*

(see index for correct answer)

- a. Compromise
- b. Linear production game
- c. Evolutionary game theory
- d. Uncorrelated asymmetry

Guidance: level 1

:: Quality management ::

A __________ or quality control circle is a group of workers who do the same or similar work, who meet regularly to identify, analyze and solve work-related problems. Normally small in size, the group is usually led by a supervisor or manager and presents its solutions to management; where possible, workers implement the solutions themselves in order to improve the performance of the organization and motivate employees. __________ s were at their most popular during the 1980s, but continue to exist in the form of Kaizen groups and similar worker participation schemes.

Exam Probability: **Low**

38. *Answer choices:*

(see index for correct answer)

- a. PQASSO
- b. European Quality in Social Services
- c. Management by wandering around
- d. TL 9000

Guidance: level 1

:: ::

_________ is the collection of mechanisms, processes and relations by which corporations are controlled and operated. Governance structures and principles identify the distribution of rights and responsibilities among different participants in the corporation and include the rules and procedures for making decisions in corporate affairs. _________ is necessary because of the possibility of conflicts of interests between stakeholders, primarily between shareholders and upper management or among shareholders.

Exam Probability: **Low**

39. *Answer choices:*

(see index for correct answer)

- a. levels of analysis
- b. corporate values
- c. Character
- d. hierarchical perspective

Guidance: level 1

:: ::

In organizational behavior and industrial/organizational psychology, proactivity or _________ behavior by individuals refers to anticipatory, change-oriented and self-initiated behavior in situations. _________ behavior involves acting in advance of a future situation, rather than just reacting. It means taking control and making things happen rather than just adjusting to a situation or waiting for something to happen. _________ employees generally do not need to be asked to act, nor do they require detailed instructions.

Exam Probability: **Low**

40. *Answer choices:*

(see index for correct answer)

- a. similarity-attraction theory
- b. corporate values
- c. imperative
- d. Proactive

Guidance: level 1

:: ::

A __________ is a research instrument consisting of a series of questions for the purpose of gathering information from respondents. The __________ was invented by the Statistical Society of London in 1838.

Exam Probability: **Low**

41. *Answer choices:*

(see index for correct answer)

- a. hierarchical
- b. deep-level diversity
- c. Questionnaire
- d. levels of analysis

Guidance: level 1

:: Critical thinking ::

An __________ is someone who has a prolonged or intense experience through practice and education in a particular field. Informally, an __________ is someone widely recognized as a reliable source of technique or skill whose faculty for judging or deciding rightly, justly, or wisely is accorded authority and status by peers or the public in a specific well-distinguished domain. An __________ , more generally, is a person with extensive knowledge or ability based on research, experience, or occupation and in a particular area of study. __________ s are called in for advice on their respective subject, but they do not always agree on the particulars of a field of study. An __________ can be believed, by virtue of credential, training, education, profession, publication or experience, to have special knowledge of a subject beyond that of the average person, sufficient that others may officially rely upon the individual`s opinion. Historically, an __________ was referred to as a sage . The individual was usually a profound thinker distinguished for wisdom and sound judgment.

Exam Probability: **High**

42. *Answer choices:*

(see index for correct answer)

- a. Fallacy
- b. Expert
- c. Proof
- d. Evidence

Guidance: level 1

:: Market research ::

_________ is an organized effort to gather information about target markets or customers. It is a very important component of business strategy. The term is commonly interchanged with marketing research; however, expert practitioners may wish to draw a distinction, in that marketing research is concerned specifically about marketing processes, while _________ is concerned specifically with markets.

Exam Probability: **High**

43. *Answer choices:*

(see index for correct answer)

- a. Market research
- b. Confidence interval
- c. Incite
- d. Voter News Service

Guidance: level 1

:: ::

__________ is a kind of action that occur as two or more objects have an effect upon one another. The idea of a two-way effect is essential in the concept of __________ , as opposed to a one-way causal effect. A closely related term is interconnectivity, which deals with the __________ s of __________ s within systems: combinations of many simple __________ s can lead to surprising emergent phenomena. __________ has different tailored meanings in various sciences. Changes can also involve __________ .

Exam Probability: **High**

44. *Answer choices:*

(see index for correct answer)

- a. open system
- b. personal values
- c. levels of analysis
- d. Interaction

Guidance: level 1

:: Project management ::

A __________ is a type of bar chart that illustrates a project schedule, named after its inventor, Henry Gantt , who designed such a chart around the years 1910–1915. Modern __________ s also show the dependency relationships between activities and current schedule status.

Exam Probability: **Low**

45. *Answer choices:*

(see index for correct answer)

- a. Organizational project management
- b. Gantt chart
- c. Graphical Evaluation and Review Technique
- d. Sustainable event management

Guidance: level 1

:: Labour relations ::

_________ is a field of study that can have different meanings depending on the context in which it is used. In an international context, it is a subfield of labor history that studies the human relations with regard to work – in its broadest sense – and how this connects to questions of social inequality. It explicitly encompasses unregulated, historical, and non-Western forms of labor. Here, _________ define "for or with whom one works and under what rules. These rules determine the type of work, type and amount of remuneration, working hours, degrees of physical and psychological strain, as well as the degree of freedom and autonomy associated with the work."

Exam Probability: **High**

46. *Answer choices:*

(see index for correct answer)

- a. Negotiated cartelism
- b. Union representative

- c. European Trade Union Confederation
- d. Two-tier system

Guidance: level 1

:: Project management ::

A __________ is a professional in the field of project management. __________ s have the responsibility of the planning, procurement and execution of a project, in any undertaking that has a defined scope, defined start and a defined finish; regardless of industry. __________ s are first point of contact for any issues or discrepancies arising from within the heads of various departments in an organization before the problem escalates to higher authorities. Project management is the responsibility of a __________ . This individual seldom participates directly in the activities that produce the end result, but rather strives to maintain the progress, mutual interaction and tasks of various parties in such a way that reduces the risk of overall failure, maximizes benefits, and minimizes costs.

Exam Probability: **High**

47. *Answer choices:*

(see index for correct answer)

- a. Project manager
- b. Scope
- c. Transport Initiatives Edinburgh
- d. overdue

Guidance: level 1

:: ::

The __________ or labour force is the labour pool in employment. It is generally used to describe those working for a single company or industry, but can also apply to a geographic region like a city, state, or country. Within a company, its value can be labelled as its " __________ in Place". The __________ of a country includes both the employed and the unemployed. The labour force participation rate, LFPR , is the ratio between the labour force and the overall size of their cohort . The term generally excludes the employers or management, and can imply those involved in manual labour. It may also mean all those who are available for work.

Exam Probability: **High**

48. *Answer choices:*

(see index for correct answer)

- a. surface-level diversity
- b. similarity-attraction theory
- c. imperative
- d. Workforce

Guidance: level 1

:: Electronic feedback ::

_________ occurs when outputs of a system are routed back as inputs as part of a chain of cause-and-effect that forms a circuit or loop. The system can then be said to feed back into itself. The notion of cause-and-effect has to be handled carefully when applied to _________ systems.

Exam Probability: **High**

49. *Answer choices:*

(see index for correct answer)

- a. Feedback
- b. Positive feedback

Guidance: level 1

:: ::

_________ involves decision making. It can include judging the merits of multiple options and selecting one or more of them. One can make a _________ between imagined options or between real options followed by the corresponding action. For example, a traveler might choose a route for a journey based on the preference of arriving at a given destination as soon as possible. The preferred route can then follow from information such as the length of each of the possible routes, traffic conditions, etc. The arrival at a _________ can include more complex motivators such as cognition, instinct, and feeling.

Exam Probability: **Low**

50. *Answer choices:*

(see index for correct answer)

- a. hierarchical
- b. information systems assessment
- c. personal values
- d. Choice

Guidance: level 1

:: Meetings ::

A _________ is a body of one or more persons that is subordinate to a deliberative assembly. Usually, the assembly sends matters into a _________ as a way to explore them more fully than would be possible if the assembly itself were considering them. _________ s may have different functions and their type of work differ depending on the type of the organization and its needs.

Exam Probability: **High**

51. *Answer choices:*

(see index for correct answer)

- a. Popular assembly
- b. Agenda
- c. Speed geeking
- d. Brown bag seminar

Guidance: level 1

:: Evaluation ::

A _________ is an evaluation of a publication, service, or company such as a movie , video game , musical composition , book ; a piece of hardware like a car, home appliance, or computer; or an event or performance, such as a live music concert, play, musical theater show, dance show, or art exhibition. In addition to a critical evaluation, the _________ `s author may assign the work a rating to indicate its relative merit. More loosely, an author may _________ current events, trends, or items in the news. A compilation of _________ s may itself be called a _________ . The New York _________ of Books, for instance, is a collection of essays on literature, culture, and current affairs. National _________ , founded by William F. Buckley, Jr., is an influential conservative magazine, and Monthly _________ is a long-running socialist periodical.

Exam Probability: **Low**

52. *Answer choices:*

(see index for correct answer)

- a. Shifting baseline
- b. Quality assurance
- c. Educational assessment
- d. Review

Guidance: level 1

:: Project management ::

_________ is a process of setting goals, planning and/or controlling the organizing and leading the execution of any type of activity, such as.

Exam Probability: **High**

53. *Answer choices:*

(see index for correct answer)

- a. Commissioning management systems
- b. Outcome mapping
- c. Indian Institute of Project Management
- d. Management process

Guidance: level 1

:: Organizational theory ::

_________ is the process of creating, retaining, and transferring knowledge within an organization. An organization improves over time as it gains experience. From this experience, it is able to create knowledge. This knowledge is broad, covering any topic that could better an organization. Examples may include ways to increase production efficiency or to develop beneficial investor relations. Knowledge is created at four different units: individual, group, organizational, and inter organizational.

Exam Probability: **Medium**

54. *Answer choices:*

(see index for correct answer)

- a. Performance problem
- b. Team effectiveness
- c. Linking pin model
- d. Organizational learning

Guidance: level 1

:: Information science ::

_________ is the resolution of uncertainty; it is that which answers the question of "what an entity is" and thus defines both its essence and nature of its characteristics. _________ relates to both data and knowledge, as data is meaningful _________ representing values attributed to parameters, and knowledge signifies understanding of a concept. _________ is uncoupled from an observer, which is an entity that can access _________ and thus discern what it specifies; _________ exists beyond an event horizon for example. In the case of knowledge, the _________ itself requires a cognitive observer to be obtained.

Exam Probability: **Medium**

55. *Answer choices:*

(see index for correct answer)

- a. Recording format
- b. Ontology alignment
- c. Patron-driven acquisition
- d. Information

Guidance: level 1

:: Management ::

_________ is the identification, evaluation, and prioritization of risks followed by coordinated and economical application of resources to minimize, monitor, and control the probability or impact of unfortunate events or to maximize the realization of opportunities.

Exam Probability: **Low**

56. *Answer choices:*

(see index for correct answer)

- a. Management cockpit
- b. Risk management
- c. Earned value management
- d. Scenario planning

Guidance: level 1

:: Classification systems ::

__________ is the practice of comparing business processes and performance metrics to industry bests and best practices from other companies. Dimensions typically measured are quality, time and cost.

Exam Probability: **Low**

57. *Answer choices:*

(see index for correct answer)

- a. Systematized Nomenclature of Medicine
- b. Galaxy morphological classification
- c. TUN
- d. Benchmarking

Guidance: level 1

:: Occupational safety and health ::

__________ is a chemical element with symbol Pb and atomic number 82. It is a heavy metal that is denser than most common materials. __________ is soft and malleable, and also has a relatively low melting point. When freshly cut, __________ is silvery with a hint of blue; it tarnishes to a dull gray color when exposed to air. __________ has the highest atomic number of any stable element and three of its isotopes are endpoints of major nuclear decay chains of heavier elements.

Exam Probability: **Medium**

58. *Answer choices:*

(see index for correct answer)

- a. Safe Work Procedure
- b. Prevention through design
- c. Helicopter Underwater Escape Training
- d. Code of safe working practices

Guidance: level 1

:: Product design ::

_________ as a verb is to create a new product to be sold by a business to its customers. A very broad coefficient and effective generation and development of ideas through a process that leads to new products. Thus, it is a major aspect of new product development.

Exam Probability: **High**

59. *Answer choices:*

(see index for correct answer)

- a. Beta Tank
- b. Crippleware
- c. Product design

- d. The Handle

Guidance: level 1

Business law

Corporate law (also known as business law) is the body of law governing the rights, relations, and conduct of persons, companies, organizations and businesses. It refers to the legal practice relating to, or the theory of corporations. Corporate law often describes the law relating to matters which derive directly from the life-cycle of a corporation. It thus encompasses the formation, funding, governance, and death of a corporation.

:: Real estate valuation ::

_________ or OMV is the price at which an asset would trade in a competitive auction setting. _________ is often used interchangeably with open _________ , fair value or fair _________ , although these terms have distinct definitions in different standards, and may or may not differ in some circumstances.

Exam Probability: **Low**

1. *Answer choices:*

(see index for correct answer)

- a. Royal Institution of Chartered Surveyors
- b. Broker%27s Price Opinion
- c. ZipRealty
- d. Real estate benchmarking

Guidance: level 1

:: ::

In logic and philosophy, an _________ is a series of statements , called the premises or premisses , intended to determine the degree of truth of another statement, the conclusion. The logical form of an _________ in a natural language can be represented in a symbolic formal language, and independently of natural language formally defined " _________ s" can be made in math and computer science.

Exam Probability: **High**

2. *Answer choices:*

(see index for correct answer)

- a. Character
- b. empathy
- c. corporate values
- d. imperative

Guidance: level 1

:: Contract law ::

In contract law, __________ is an excuse for the nonperformance of duties under a contract, based on a change in circumstances , the nonoccurrence of which was an underlying assumption of the contract, that makes performance of the contract literally impossible.

Exam Probability: **Low**

3. *Answer choices:*

(see index for correct answer)

- a. Community Benefits Agreement
- b. Unenforceable
- c. Quasi-contract
- d. Impossibility

Guidance: level 1

:: Legal procedure ::

An _________ is generally the first occasion that the trier of fact has to hear from a lawyer in a trial, aside possibly from questioning during voir dire. The _________ is generally constructed to serve as a "road map" for the fact-finder. This is especially essential, in many jury trials, since jurors know nothing at all about the case before the trial, . Though such statements may be dramatic and vivid, they must be limited to the evidence reasonably expected to be presented during the trial. Attorneys generally conclude _________ s with a reminder that at the conclusion of evidence, the attorney will return to ask the fact-finder to find in his or her client`s favor.

Exam Probability: **Medium**

4. *Answer choices:*

(see index for correct answer)

- a. Opening statement
- b. appellate
- c. civil procedure
- d. Procedural law

Guidance: level 1

:: Business ethics ::

__________ is a type of harassment technique that relates to a sexual nature and the unwelcome or inappropriate promise of rewards in exchange for sexual favors. __________ includes a range of actions from mild transgressions to sexual abuse or assault. Harassment can occur in many different social settings such as the workplace, the home, school, churches, etc. Harassers or victims may be of any gender.

Exam Probability: **Medium**

5. *Answer choices:*

(see index for correct answer)

- a. Sexual harassment
- b. Center for Adult Development
- c. Institute of Business Ethics
- d. Sustainability Accounting Standards Board

Guidance: level 1

:: Real property law ::

A __________ is the grant of authority or rights, stating that the granter formally recognizes the prerogative of the recipient to exercise the rights specified. It is implicit that the granter retains superiority , and that the recipient admits a limited status within the relationship, and it is within that sense that __________ s were historically granted, and that sense is retained in modern usage of the term.

Exam Probability: **High**

6. *Answer choices:*

(see index for correct answer)

- a. EULIS
- b. Habous
- c. Conveyancing
- d. Trespass to land

Guidance: level 1

:: ::

_________ is property that is movable. In common law systems, _________ may also be called chattels or personalty. In civil law systems, _________ is often called movable property or movables – any property that can be moved from one location to another.

Exam Probability: **High**

7. *Answer choices:*

(see index for correct answer)

- a. Personal property
- b. open system
- c. surface-level diversity

- d. empathy

Guidance: level 1

:: Real property law ::

_________ is an area of criminal law or tort law broadly divided into three groups: _________ to the person, _________ to chattels and _________ to land.

Exam Probability: **Low**

8. *Answer choices:*

(see index for correct answer)

- a. Ultimogeniture
- b. Open mines doctrine
- c. Trespass
- d. Townsite

Guidance: level 1

:: Labour relations ::

__________ is a field of study that can have different meanings depending on the context in which it is used. In an international context, it is a subfield of labor history that studies the human relations with regard to work – in its broadest sense – and how this connects to questions of social inequality. It explicitly encompasses unregulated, historical, and non-Western forms of labor. Here, __________ define "for or with whom one works and under what rules. These rules determine the type of work, type and amount of remuneration, working hours, degrees of physical and psychological strain, as well as the degree of freedom and autonomy associated with the work."

Exam Probability: **High**

9. *Answer choices:*

(see index for correct answer)

- a. Employee voice
- b. European Trade Union Confederation
- c. Labor relations
- d. Labour council

Guidance: level 1

:: Jurisdiction ::

In United States law, __________ jurisdiction is the subject-matter jurisdiction of United States federal courts to hear a civil case because the plaintiff has alleged a violation of the United States Constitution, federal law, or a treaty to which the United States is a party.

Exam Probability: **Low**

10. *Answer choices:*

(see index for correct answer)

- a. Jurisdiction in rem
- b. Removal jurisdiction
- c. General jurisdiction
- d. Appellate jurisdiction

Guidance: level 1

:: ::

_________ is the principled guide to action taken by the administrative executive branches of the state with regard to a class of issues, in a manner consistent with law and institutional customs.

Exam Probability: **Low**

11. *Answer choices:*

(see index for correct answer)

- a. co-culture
- b. Sarbanes-Oxley act of 2002
- c. corporate values
- d. Public policy

Guidance: level 1

:: Legal terms ::

_________ is the set of laws that governs how members of a society are to behave. It is contrasted with procedural law, which is the set of procedures for making, administering, and enforcing _________ . _________ defines rights and responsibilities in civil law, and crimes and punishments in criminal law. It may be codified in statutes or exist through precedent in common law.

Exam Probability: **Medium**

12. *Answer choices:*

(see index for correct answer)

- a. Form of action
- b. Abstract of judgment
- c. Force
- d. Substantive law

Guidance: level 1

:: ::

The words " _________ " and "testify" both derive from the Latin word testis, referring to the notion of a disinterested third-party witness.

Exam Probability: **Low**

13. *Answer choices:*

(see index for correct answer)

- a. corporate values
- b. Testimony
- c. cultural
- d. similarity-attraction theory

Guidance: level 1

:: Auctioneering ::

An __________ is a process of buying and selling goods or services by offering them up for bid, taking bids, and then selling the item to the highest bidder. The open ascending price __________ is arguably the most common form of __________ in use today. Participants bid openly against one another, with each subsequent bid required to be higher than the previous bid. An __________ eer may announce prices, bidders may call out their bids themselves , or bids may be submitted electronically with the highest current bid publicly displayed. In a Dutch __________ , the __________ eer begins with a high asking price for some quantity of like items; the price is lowered until a participant is willing to accept the __________ eer`s price for some quantity of the goods in the lot or until the seller`s reserve price is met. While __________ s are most associated in the public imagination with the sale of antiques, paintings, rare collectibles and expensive wines, __________ s are also used for commodities, livestock, radio spectrum and used cars. In economic theory, an __________ may refer to any mechanism or set of trading rules for exchange.

Exam Probability: **High**

14. *Answer choices:*

(see index for correct answer)

- a. Bidding fee auction
- b. Unique bid auction
- c. Auction
- d. Online travel auction

Guidance: level 1

:: ::

The Sherman Antitrust Act of 1890 was a United States antitrust law that regulates competition among enterprises, which was passed by Congress under the presidency of Benjamin Harrison.

Exam Probability: **Low**

15. *Answer choices:*

(see index for correct answer)

- a. deep-level diversity
- b. hierarchical
- c. open system
- d. Sherman Act

Guidance: level 1

:: ::

A _________ is monetary compensation paid by an employer to an employee in exchange for work done. Payment may be calculated as a fixed amount for each task completed , or at an hourly or daily rate , or based on an easily measured quantity of work done.

Exam Probability: **Low**

16. *Answer choices:*

(see index for correct answer)

- a. Sarbanes-Oxley act of 2002
- b. imperative
- c. corporate values
- d. Wage

Guidance: level 1

:: Treaties ::

A _________ is an agreement under international law entered into by actors in international law, namely sovereign states and international organizations. A _________ may also be known as an agreement, protocol, covenant, convention, pact, or exchange of letters, among other terms. Regardless of terminology, all of these forms of agreements are, under international law, equally considered treaties and the rules are the same.

Exam Probability: **High**

17. *Answer choices:*

(see index for correct answer)

- a. Multilateral treaty
- b. Bilateral treaty
- c. Treaty
- d. Subsidiary alliance

Guidance: level 1

:: Debt ::

A __________ is a party that has a claim on the services of a second party. It is a person or institution to whom money is owed. The first party, in general, has provided some property or service to the second party under the assumption that the second party will return an equivalent property and service. The second party is frequently called a debtor or borrower. The first party is called the __________, which is the lender of property, service, or money.

Exam Probability: **High**

18. *Answer choices:*

(see index for correct answer)

- a. Bailout
- b. Medical debt
- c. Cessio bonorum
- d. Creditor

Guidance: level 1

:: Parental leave ::

_________ is a type of employment discrimination that occurs when expectant women are fired, not hired, or otherwise discriminated against due to their pregnancy or intention to become pregnant. Common forms of _________ include not being hired due to visible pregnancy or likelihood of becoming pregnant, being fired after informing an employer of one`s pregnancy, being fired after maternity leave, and receiving a pay dock due to pregnancy. Convention on the Elimination of All Forms of Discrimination against Women prohibits dismissal on the grounds of maternity or pregnancy and ensures right to maternity leave or comparable social benefits. The Maternity Protection Convention C 183 proclaims adequate protection for pregnancy as well. Though women have some protection in the United States because of the _________ Act of 1978, it has not completely curbed the incidence of _________. The Equal Rights Amendment could ensure more robust sex equality ensuring that women and men could both work and have children at the same time.

Exam Probability: **Low**

19. *Answer choices:*

(see index for correct answer)

- a. Pregnant Workers Directive
- b. Sara Hlupekile Longwe
- c. Parental leave
- d. Cleveland Board of Education v. LaFleur

Guidance: level 1

:: Business law ::

An __________ is a natural person, business, or corporation that provides goods or services to another entity under terms specified in a contract or within a verbal agreement. Unlike an employee, an __________ does not work regularly for an employer but works as and when required, during which time they may be subject to law of agency. __________s are usually paid on a freelance basis. Contractors often work through a limited company or franchise, which they themselves own, or may work through an umbrella company.

Exam Probability: **Low**

20. *Answer choices:*

(see index for correct answer)

- a. Economic torts
- b. Ease of doing business index
- c. Business valuation
- d. Independent contractor

Guidance: level 1

:: Contract law ::

__________ are damages whose amount the parties designate during the formation of a contract for the injured party to collect as compensation upon a specific breach .

Exam Probability: **High**

21. *Answer choices:*

(see index for correct answer)

- a. Peppercorn
- b. Liquidated damages
- c. Contra proferentem
- d. Revocation

Guidance: level 1

:: Contract law ::

_________ is a legal process for collecting a monetary judgment on behalf of a plaintiff from a defendant. _________ allows the plaintiff to take the money or property of the debtor from the person or institution that holds that property . A similar legal mechanism called execution allows the seizure of money or property held directly by the debtor.

Exam Probability: **High**

22. *Answer choices:*

(see index for correct answer)

- a. Invitation to treat
- b. Garnishment
- c. Retainer agreement
- d. Forum selection clause

Guidance: level 1

:: Writs ::

In common law, a _________ is a formal _________ ten order issued by a body with administrative or judicial jurisdiction; in modern usage, this body is generally a court. Warrants, prerogative _________ s, and subpoenas are common types of _________ , but many forms exist and have existed.

Exam Probability: **Low**

23. *Answer choices:*

(see index for correct answer)

- a. Writ of assistance
- b. Writ
- c. Writ of execution

Guidance: level 1

:: Business law ::

A _________ is a form of partnership similar to a general partnership except that while a general partnership must have at least two general partners , a _________ must have at least one GP and at least one limited partner.

Exam Probability: **High**

24. *Answer choices:*

(see index for correct answer)

- a. Partnership
- b. Security interest
- c. Limited partnership
- d. Ladenschlussgesetz

Guidance: level 1

:: Real property law ::

A _________ is any legal instrument in writing which passes, affirms or confirms an interest, right, or property and that is signed, attested, delivered, and in some jurisdictions, sealed. It is commonly associated with transferring title to property. The _________ has a greater presumption of validity and is less rebuttable than an instrument signed by the party to the _________ . A _________ can be unilateral or bilateral. _________ s include conveyances, commissions, licenses, patents, diplomas, and conditionally powers of attorney if executed as _________ s. The _________ is the modern descendant of the medieval charter, and delivery is thought to symbolically replace the ancient ceremony of livery of seisin.

Exam Probability: **Medium**

25. *Answer choices:*

(see index for correct answer)

- a. Manorial roll
- b. Nonpossessory interest in land
- c. Exaction
- d. Deed

Guidance: level 1

:: ::

Employment is a relationship between two parties, usually based on a contract where work is paid for, where one party, which may be a corporation, for profit, not-for-profit organization, co-operative or other entity is the employer and the other is the employee. Employees work in return for payment, which may be in the form of an hourly wage, by piecework or an annual salary, depending on the type of work an employee does or which sector she or he is working in. Employees in some fields or sectors may receive gratuities, bonus payment or stock options. In some types of employment, employees may receive benefits in addition to payment. Benefits can include health insurance, housing, disability insurance or use of a gym. Employment is typically governed by employment laws, regulations or legal contracts.

Exam Probability: **Low**

26. *Answer choices:*

(see index for correct answer)

- a. corporate values
- b. surface-level diversity
- c. Personnel

- d. Character

Guidance: level 1

:: ::

In contract law, rescission is an equitable remedy which allows a contractual party to cancel the contract. Parties may _________ if they are the victims of a vitiating factor, such as misrepresentation, mistake, duress, or undue influence. Rescission is the unwinding of a transaction. This is done to bring the parties, as far as possible, back to the position in which they were before they entered into a contract .

Exam Probability: **Medium**

27. *Answer choices:*

(see index for correct answer)

- a. information systems assessment
- b. Rescind
- c. imperative
- d. Character

Guidance: level 1

:: ::

In the law of evidence, a _________ of a particular fact can be made without the aid of proof in some situations. The invocation of a _________ shifts the burden of proof from one party to the opposing party in a court trial.

Exam Probability: **High**

28. *Answer choices:*

(see index for correct answer)

- a. process perspective
- b. Presumption
- c. interpersonal communication
- d. personal values

Guidance: level 1

:: Legal doctrines and principles ::

_________ is a failure to exercise appropriate and or ethical ruled care expected to be exercised amongst specified circumstances. The area of tort law known as _________ involves harm caused by failing to act as a form of carelessness possibly with extenuating circumstances. The core concept of _________ is that people should exercise reasonable care in their actions, by taking account of the potential harm that they might foreseeably cause to other people or property.

Exam Probability: **Low**

29. *Answer choices:*

(see index for correct answer)

- a. Assumption of risk
- b. Negligence
- c. Proximate cause
- d. Exclusionary rule

Guidance: level 1

:: Legal doctrines and principles ::

_________ is a defense in the law of torts, which bars or reduces a plaintiff's right to recovery against a negligent tortfeasor if the defendant can demonstrate that the plaintiff voluntarily and knowingly assumed the risks at issue inherent to the dangerous activity in which he was participating at the time of his or her injury.

Exam Probability: **Medium**

30. *Answer choices:*

(see index for correct answer)

- a. Assumption of risk
- b. negligence
- c. Attractive nuisance
- d. Mutual assent

Guidance: level 1

:: Contract law ::

Offer and acceptance analysis is a traditional approach in contract law. The offer and acceptance formula, developed in the 19th century, identifies a moment of formation when the parties are of one mind. This classical approach to contract formation has been modified by developments in the law of estoppel, misleading conduct, misrepresentation and unjust enrichment.

Exam Probability: **Medium**

31. *Answer choices:*

(see index for correct answer)

- a. Contract lifecycle management
- b. Offeree
- c. Scots contract law
- d. Impracticability

Guidance: level 1

:: Commerce ::

_________ relates to "the exchange of goods and services, especially on a large scale". It includes legal, economic, political, social, cultural and technological systems that operate in a country or in international trade.

Exam Probability: **Medium**

32. *Answer choices:*

(see index for correct answer)

- a. Commerce
- b. Organ trade
- c. Staple right
- d. Card association

Guidance: level 1

:: ::

_________ or accountancy is the measurement, processing, and communication of financial information about economic entities such as businesses and corporations. The modern field was established by the Italian mathematician Luca Pacioli in 1494. _________ , which has been called the "language of business", measures the results of an organization`s economic activities and conveys this information to a variety of users, including investors, creditors, management, and regulators. Practitioners of _________ are known as accountants. The terms " _________ " and "financial reporting" are often used as synonyms.

Exam Probability: **Medium**

33. *Answer choices:*

(see index for correct answer)

- a. empathy
- b. information systems assessment
- c. Accounting
- d. surface-level diversity

Guidance: level 1

:: Personal property law ::

Bailment describes a legal relationship in common law where physical possession of personal property, or a chattel, is transferred from one person to another person who subsequently has possession of the property. It arises when a person gives property to someone else for safekeeping, and is a cause of action independent of contract or tort.

Exam Probability: **High**

34. *Answer choices:*

(see index for correct answer)

- a. bailor
- b. Bailee

Guidance: level 1

:: Business law ::

A _________ is a contractual arrangement calling for the lessee to pay the lessor for use of an asset. Property, buildings and vehicles are common assets that are _________ d. Industrial or business equipment is also _________ d.

Exam Probability: **Low**

35. *Answer choices:*

(see index for correct answer)

- a. Unfair Commercial Practices Directive
- b. Lease
- c. Forged endorsement
- d. Fraud deterrence

Guidance: level 1

:: Marketing ::

A _________ is an overall experience of a customer that distinguishes an organization or product from its rivals in the eyes of the customer. _________ s are used in business, marketing, and advertising. Name _________ s are sometimes distinguished from generic or store _________ s.

Exam Probability: **High**

36. *Answer choices:*

(see index for correct answer)

- a. Brand
- b. Online research community
- c. Kano model
- d. Analyst relations

Guidance: level 1

:: White-collar criminals ::

_________ refers to financially motivated, nonviolent crime committed by businesses and government professionals. It was first defined by the sociologist Edwin Sutherland in 1939 as "a crime committed by a person of respectability and high social status in the course of their occupation". Typical _________ s could include wage theft, fraud, bribery, Ponzi schemes, insider trading, labor racketeering, embezzlement, cybercrime, copyright infringement, money laundering, identity theft, and forgery. Lawyers can specialize in _________ .

Exam Probability: **Low**

37. *Answer choices:*

(see index for correct answer)

- a. White-collar crime
- b. Tongsun Park

Guidance: level 1

:: Corporate finance ::

__________ is a contract law concept about the purchase of the release from a debt obligation. It is one of the methods by which parties to a contract may terminate their agreement. The release is completed by the transfer of valuable consideration that must not be the actual performance of the obligation itself. The accord is the agreement to discharge the obligation and the satisfaction is the legal "consideration" which binds the parties to the agreement. A valid accord does not discharge the prior contract; instead it suspends the right to enforce it in accordance with the terms of the accord contract, in which satisfaction, or performance of the contract will discharge both contracts . If the creditor breaches the accord, then the debtor will be able to bring up the existence of the accord in order to enjoin any action against him.

Exam Probability: **High**

38. *Answer choices:*

(see index for correct answer)

- a. Tender offer
- b. Liquidity forecast
- c. Commercial finance
- d. Accord and satisfaction

Guidance: level 1

:: Contract law ::

At common law, __________ is an alternative principle to the perfect tender rule. It allows a court to imply a term that allows a partial or substantially similar performance to stand in for the performance specified in the contract.

Exam Probability: **Medium**

39. *Answer choices:*

(see index for correct answer)

- a. first refusal
- b. Neo-classical contract
- c. Implied warranty
- d. Substantial performance

Guidance: level 1

:: ::

According to the philosopher Piyush Mathur , "Tangibility is the property that a phenomenon exhibits if it has and/or transports mass and/or energy and/or momentum".

Exam Probability: **Low**

40. *Answer choices:*

(see index for correct answer)

- a. interpersonal communication
- b. hierarchical
- c. information systems assessment
- d. process perspective

Guidance: level 1

:: Notes (finance) ::

A __________ , sometimes referred to as a note payable, is a legal instrument , in which one party promises in writing to pay a determinate sum of money to the other , either at a fixed or determinable future time or on demand of the payee, under specific terms.

Exam Probability: **Medium**

41. *Answer choices:*

(see index for correct answer)

- a. A notes
- b. Promissory note
- c. Federal Reserve Note
- d. Demand Note

Guidance: level 1

:: International trade ::

A _________ is a document issued by a carrier to acknowledge receipt of cargo for shipment. Although the term historically related only to carriage by sea, a _________ may today be used for any type of carriage of goods.

Exam Probability: **High**

42. *Answer choices:*

(see index for correct answer)

- a. Bill of lading
- b. Agency for International Trade Information and Co-operation
- c. Import
- d. Organisation for Economic Co-operation and Development

Guidance: level 1

:: ::

In common law legal systems, __________ is a principle or rule established in a previous legal case that is either binding on or persuasive for a court or other tribunal when deciding subsequent cases with similar issues or facts. Common-law legal systems place great value on deciding cases according to consistent principled rules, so that similar facts will yield similar and predictable outcomes, and observance of __________ is the mechanism by which that goal is attained. The principle by which judges are bound to __________ s is known as stare decisis. Common-law __________ is a third kind of law, on equal footing with statutory law and delegated legislation or regulatory law

.

Exam Probability: **High**

43. *Answer choices:*

(see index for correct answer)

- a. Precedent
- b. information systems assessment
- c. cultural
- d. co-culture

Guidance: level 1

:: Criminal law ::

__________ is the body of law that relates to crime. It proscribes conduct perceived as threatening, harmful, or otherwise endangering to the property, health, safety, and moral welfare of people inclusive of one`s self. Most __________ is established by statute, which is to say that the laws are enacted by a legislature. __________ includes the punishment and rehabilitation of people who violate such laws. __________ varies according to jurisdiction, and differs from civil law, where emphasis is more on dispute resolution and victim compensation, rather than on punishment or rehabilitation. Criminal procedure is a formalized official activity that authenticates the fact of commission of a crime and authorizes punitive or rehabilitative treatment of the offender.

Exam Probability: **High**

44. *Answer choices:*

(see index for correct answer)

- a. Mala prohibita
- b. Criminal law
- c. complicit
- d. Self-incrimination

Guidance: level 1

:: Contract law ::

In contract law, a _________ is a promise which is not a condition of the contract or an innominate term: it is a term "not going to the root of the contract", and which only entitles the innocent party to damages if it is breached: i.e. the _________ is not true or the defaulting party does not perform the contract in accordance with the terms of the _________. A _________ is not guarantee. It is a mere promise. It may be enforced if it is breached by an award for the legal remedy of damages.

Exam Probability: **Medium**

45. *Answer choices:*

(see index for correct answer)

- a. Handshake deal
- b. Warranty
- c. Culpa in contrahendo
- d. Pact ink

Guidance: level 1

:: Business models ::

A _________, _________ company or daughter company is a company that is owned or controlled by another company, which is called the parent company, parent, or holding company. The _________ can be a company, corporation, or limited liability company. In some cases it is a government or state-owned enterprise. In some cases, particularly in the music and book publishing industries, subsidiaries are referred to as imprints.

Exam Probability: **Medium**

46. *Answer choices:*

(see index for correct answer)

- a. Premium business model
- b. One stop shop
- c. Subsidiary
- d. Subscription business model

Guidance: level 1

:: Ethically disputed business practices ::

__________ is the trading of a public company`s stock or other securities by individuals with access to nonpublic information about the company. In various countries, some kinds of trading based on insider information is illegal. This is because it is seen as unfair to other investors who do not have access to the information, as the investor with insider information could potentially make larger profits than a typical investor could make. The rules governing __________ are complex and vary significantly from country to country. The extent of enforcement also varies from one country to another. The definition of insider in one jurisdiction can be broad, and may cover not only insiders themselves but also any persons related to them, such as brokers, associates and even family members. A person who becomes aware of non-public information and trades on that basis may be guilty of a crime.

Exam Probability: **Medium**

47. *Answer choices:*

(see index for correct answer)

- a. Insider trading
- b. Market abuse
- c. Conflict of interest
- d. Trademark troll

Guidance: level 1

:: Contract law ::

__________ is an equitable remedy in the law of contract, whereby a court issues an order requiring a party to perform a specific act, such as to complete performance of the contract. It is typically available in the sale of land, but otherwise is not generally available if damages are an appropriate alternative. __________ is almost never available for contracts of personal service, although performance may also be ensured through the threat of proceedings for contempt of court.

Exam Probability: **High**

48. *Answer choices:*

(see index for correct answer)

- a. Specific performance
- b. Anticipatory repudiation
- c. Synallagmatic contract

- d. Reciprocal obligation

Guidance: level 1

:: Anti-competitive behaviour ::

Restraints of trade is a common law doctrine relating to the enforceability of contractual restrictions on freedom to conduct business. It is a precursor of modern competition law. In an old leading case of Mitchel v Reynolds Lord Smith LC said,

Exam Probability: **High**

49. *Answer choices:*

(see index for correct answer)

- a. Resale price maintenance
- b. Restraint of trade
- c. Fixed book price agreement
- d. American Antitrust Institute

Guidance: level 1

:: Criminal procedure ::

In law, a verdict is the formal finding of fact made by a jury on matters or questions submitted to the jury by a judge. In a bench trial, the judge`s decision near the end of the trial is simply referred to as a finding. In England and Wales, a coroner`s findings are called verdicts .

Exam Probability: **Low**

50. *Answer choices:*

(see index for correct answer)

- a. Exoneration
- b. criminal procedure

Guidance: level 1

:: Contract law ::

Offer and acceptance analysis is a traditional approach in contract law. The offer and acceptance formula, developed in the 19th century, identifies a moment of formation when the parties are of one mind. This classical approach to contract formation has been modified by developments in the law of estoppel, misleading conduct, misrepresentation and unjust enrichment.

Exam Probability: **Low**

51. *Answer choices:*

(see index for correct answer)

- a. Redhibition
- b. Offeror
- c. Rescission
- d. Pre-existing duty rule

Guidance: level 1

:: Insolvency ::

_________ is a legal process through which people or other entities who cannot repay debts to creditors may seek relief from some or all of their debts. In most jurisdictions, _________ is imposed by a court order, often initiated by the debtor.

Exam Probability: **High**

52. *Answer choices:*

(see index for correct answer)

- a. Conservatorship
- b. Insolvency law of Russia
- c. Personal Insolvency Arrangement
- d. Financial distress

Guidance: level 1

:: ::

A __________ loan or, simply, __________ is used either by purchasers of real property to raise funds to buy real estate, or alternatively by existing property owners to raise funds for any purpose, while putting a lien on the property being __________d. The loan is "secured" on the borrower`s property through a process known as __________ origination. This means that a legal mechanism is put into place which allows the lender to take possession and sell the secured property to pay off the loan in the event the borrower defaults on the loan or otherwise fails to abide by its terms. The word __________ is derived from a Law French term used in Britain in the Middle Ages meaning "death pledge" and refers to the pledge ending when either the obligation is fulfilled or the property is taken through foreclosure. A __________ can also be described as "a borrower giving consideration in the form of a collateral for a benefit ".

Exam Probability: **High**

53. *Answer choices:*

(see index for correct answer)

- a. open system
- b. Mortgage
- c. process perspective
- d. empathy

Guidance: level 1

:: ::

_________ , often abbreviated cert. in the United States, is a process for seeking judicial review and a writ issued by a court that agrees to review. A _________ is issued by a superior court, directing an inferior court, tribunal, or other public authority to send the record of a proceeding for review.

Exam Probability: **Medium**

54. *Answer choices:*

(see index for correct answer)

- a. deep-level diversity
- b. Character
- c. Certiorari
- d. corporate values

Guidance: level 1

:: Employment discrimination ::

_________ is a form of discrimination based on race, gender, religion, national origin, physical or mental disability, age, sexual orientation, and gender identity by employers. Earnings differentials or occupational differentiation—where differences in pay come from differences in qualifications or responsibilities—should not be confused with _________ . Discrimination can be intended and involve disparate treatment of a group or be unintended, yet create disparate impact for a group.

Exam Probability: **Low**

55. *Answer choices:*

(see index for correct answer)

- a. Employment discrimination
- b. Employment Non-Discrimination Act
- c. United Kingdom employment equality law
- d. New South Wales selection bias

Guidance: level 1

:: ::

_________ , or auditory perception, is the ability to perceive sounds by detecting vibrations, changes in the pressure of the surrounding medium through time, through an organ such as the ear. The academic field concerned with _________ is auditory science.

Exam Probability: **Low**

56. *Answer choices:*

(see index for correct answer)

- a. hierarchical
- b. personal values
- c. cultural

- d. imperative

Guidance: level 1

:: Business models ::

A __________ is "an autonomous association of persons united voluntarily to meet their common economic, social, and cultural needs and aspirations through a jointly-owned and democratically-controlled enterprise". __________ s may include.

Exam Probability: **High**

57. *Answer choices:*

(see index for correct answer)

- a. Cooperative
- b. Legacy carrier
- c. Copy to China
- d. Praenumeration

Guidance: level 1

:: Manufacturing ::

A _________ is a building for storing goods. _________ s are used by manufacturers, importers, exporters, wholesalers, transport businesses, customs, etc. They are usually large plain buildings in industrial parks on the outskirts of cities, towns or villages.

Exam Probability: **High**

58. *Answer choices:*

(see index for correct answer)

- a. Warehouse
- b. Obeya
- c. Greatpac
- d. Manufacturing Readiness Level

Guidance: level 1

:: Commercial crimes ::

_________ is the process of concealing the origins of money obtained illegally by passing it through a complex sequence of banking transfers or commercial transactions. The overall scheme of this process returns the money to the launderer in an obscure and indirect way.

Exam Probability: **Medium**

59. *Answer choices:*

(see index for correct answer)

- a. Money laundering
- b. Shanzhai
- c. Late trading
- d. Pranknet

Guidance: level 1

Finance

Finance is a field that is concerned with the allocation (investment) of assets and liabilities over space and time, often under conditions of risk or uncertainty. Finance can also be defined as the science of money management. Participants in the market aim to price assets based on their risk level, fundamental value, and their expected rate of return. Finance can be split into three sub-categories: public finance, corporate finance and personal finance.

:: Data management ::

__________ is a form of intellectual property that grants the creator of an original creative work an exclusive legal right to determine whether and under what conditions this original work may be copied and used by others, usually for a limited term of years. The exclusive rights are not absolute but limited by limitations and exceptions to __________ law, including fair use. A major limitation on __________ on ideas is that __________ protects only the original expression of ideas, and not the underlying ideas themselves.

Exam Probability: **High**

1. *Answer choices:*

(see index for correct answer)

- a. Copyright
- b. ROOT
- c. Navigational database
- d. Isolation

Guidance: level 1

:: Generally Accepted Accounting Principles ::

__________, also referred to as the bottom line, net income, or net earnings is a measure of the profitability of a venture after accounting for all costs and taxes. It is the actual profit, and includes the operating expenses that are excluded from gross profit.

Exam Probability: **Low**

2. *Answer choices:*

(see index for correct answer)

- a. Net profit
- b. Shares outstanding
- c. Cost principle
- d. Indian Accounting Standards

Guidance: level 1

:: Accounting ::

__________ is a process of providing relief to shared service organization`s cost centers that provide a product or service. In turn, the associated expense is assigned to internal clients` cost centers that consume the products and services. For example, the CIO may provide all IT services within the company and assign the costs back to the business units that consume each offering.

Exam Probability: **Medium**

3. *Answer choices:*

(see index for correct answer)

- a. History of accounting
- b. FreeAgent
- c. Cost allocation
- d. INPACT International

Guidance: level 1

:: ::

In marketing, a _________ is a ticket or document that can be redeemed for a financial discount or rebate when purchasing a product.

Exam Probability: **High**

4. *Answer choices:*

(see index for correct answer)

- a. similarity-attraction theory
- b. functional perspective
- c. deep-level diversity
- d. hierarchical perspective

Guidance: level 1

:: Mathematical finance ::

_________ is the value of an asset at a specific date. It measures the nominal future sum of money that a given sum of money is "worth" at a specified time in the future assuming a certain interest rate, or more generally, rate of return; it is the present value multiplied by the accumulation function. The value does not include corrections for inflation or other factors that affect the true value of money in the future. This is used in time value of money calculations.

Exam Probability: **Low**

5. *Answer choices:*

(see index for correct answer)

- a. Weighted average return on assets
- b. QuantLib
- c. Alternative beta
- d. ExMark

Guidance: level 1

:: Contract law ::

A _________ is a legally-binding agreement which recognises and governs the rights and duties of the parties to the agreement. A _________ is legally enforceable because it meets the requirements and approval of the law. An agreement typically involves the exchange of goods, services, money, or promises of any of those. In the event of breach of _________, the law awards the injured party access to legal remedies such as damages and cancellation.

Exam Probability: **Low**

6. *Answer choices:*

(see index for correct answer)

- a. Illusory promise
- b. Unjust enrichment
- c. Mistake
- d. Contract

Guidance: level 1

:: ::

A __________ is the process of presenting a topic to an audience. It is typically a demonstration, introduction, lecture, or speech meant to inform, persuade, inspire, motivate, or to build good will or to present a new idea or product. The term can also be used for a formal or ritualized introduction or offering, as with the __________ of a debutante. __________ s in certain formats are also known as keynote address.

Exam Probability: **High**

7. *Answer choices:*

(see index for correct answer)

- a. interpersonal communication
- b. levels of analysis

- c. hierarchical perspective
- d. Presentation

Guidance: level 1

:: Generally Accepted Accounting Principles ::

Expenditure is an outflow of money to another person or group to pay for an item or service, or for a category of costs. For a tenant, rent is an _________ . For students or parents, tuition is an _________ . Buying food, clothing, furniture or an automobile is often referred to as an _________ . An _________ is a cost that is "paid" or "remitted", usually in exchange for something of value. Something that seems to cost a great deal is "expensive". Something that seems to cost little is "inexpensive". " _________ s of the table" are _________ s of dining, refreshments, a feast, etc.

Exam Probability: **Medium**

8. *Answer choices:*

(see index for correct answer)

- a. Long-term liabilities
- b. Completed-contract method
- c. Goodwill
- d. Earnings before interest, taxes and depreciation

Guidance: level 1

:: Actuarial science ::

The __________ is the greater benefit of receiving money now rather than an identical sum later. It is founded on time preference.

Exam Probability: **Low**

9. *Answer choices:*

(see index for correct answer)

- a. Time value of money
- b. Risk
- c. Esscher principle
- d. SWAG

Guidance: level 1

:: Personal finance ::

__________ is income not spent, or deferred consumption. Methods of __________ include putting money aside in, for example, a deposit account, a pension account, an investment fund, or as cash. __________ also involves reducing expenditures, such as recurring costs. In terms of personal finance, __________ generally specifies low-risk preservation of money, as in a deposit account, versus investment, wherein risk is a lot higher; in economics more broadly, it refers to any income not used for immediate consumption.

Exam Probability: **High**

10. *Answer choices:*

(see index for correct answer)

- a. App-o-rama
- b. Saving
- c. Custodial account
- d. Individual Development Account

Guidance: level 1

:: ::

_________ is a marketing communication that employs an openly sponsored, non-personal message to promote or sell a product, service or idea. Sponsors of _________ are typically businesses wishing to promote their products or services. _________ is differentiated from public relations in that an advertiser pays for and has control over the message. It differs from personal selling in that the message is non-personal, i.e., not directed to a particular individual. _________ is communicated through various mass media, including traditional media such as newspapers, magazines, television, radio, outdoor _________ or direct mail; and new media such as search results, blogs, social media, websites or text messages. The actual presentation of the message in a medium is referred to as an advertisement, or "ad" or advert for short.

Exam Probability: **Low**

11. *Answer choices:*

(see index for correct answer)

- a. hierarchical perspective
- b. Character
- c. functional perspective
- d. Advertising

Guidance: level 1

:: Financial risk ::

__________ is the risk that arises for bond owners from fluctuating interest rates. How much __________ a bond has depends on how sensitive its price is to interest rate changes in the market. The sensitivity depends on two things, the bond`s time to maturity, and the coupon rate of the bond.

Exam Probability: **Low**

12. *Answer choices:*

(see index for correct answer)

- a. Risk neutral
- b. ITGC
- c. Specific risk
- d. Interest rate risk

Guidance: level 1

:: Real estate ::

Amortisation is paying off an amount owed over time by making planned, incremental payments of principal and interest. To amortise a loan means "to kill it off". In accounting, amortisation refers to charging or writing off an intangible asset`s cost as an operational expense over its estimated useful life to reduce a company`s taxable income.

Exam Probability: **Low**

13. *Answer choices:*

(see index for correct answer)

- a. Bundle of rights
- b. Estate agent
- c. CMC Group
- d. Amortization

Guidance: level 1

:: Business economics ::

In finance, _________ is the risk of losses caused by interest rate changes. The prices of most financial instruments, such as stocks and bonds move inversely with interest rates, so investors are subject to capital loss when rates rise.

Exam Probability: **Low**

14. *Answer choices:*

(see index for correct answer)

- a. Business ecosystem
- b. Willingness to pay
- c. Rate risk
- d. Seasonal industry

Guidance: level 1

:: Inventory ::

In business and accounting/accountancy, _________ or continuous inventory describes systems of inventory where information on inventory quantity and availability is updated on a continuous basis as a function of doing business. Generally this is accomplished by connecting the inventory system with order entry and in retail the point of sale system. In this case, book inventory would be exactly the same as, or almost the same, as the real inventory.

Exam Probability: **Medium**

15. *Answer choices:*

(see index for correct answer)

- a. just-in-time manufacturing
- b. Decomposition

- c. Perpetual inventory
- d. Safety stock

Guidance: level 1

:: Management accounting ::

" _________ s are the structural determinants of the cost of an activity, reflecting any linkages or interrelationships that affect it". Therefore we could assume that the _________ s determine the cost behavior within the activities, reflecting the links that these have with other activities and relationships that affect them.

Exam Probability: **Medium**

16. *Answer choices:*

(see index for correct answer)

- a. Cost driver
- b. Inventory valuation
- c. Dual overhead rate
- d. Process costing

Guidance: level 1

:: ::

In the broadest sense, _________ is any practice which contributes to the sale of products to a retail consumer. At a retail in-store level, _________ refers to the variety of products available for sale and the display of those products in such a way that it stimulates interest and entices customers to make a purchase.

Exam Probability: **Low**

17. *Answer choices:*

(see index for correct answer)

- a. interpersonal communication
- b. Merchandising
- c. deep-level diversity
- d. functional perspective

Guidance: level 1

:: ::

A tax is a compulsory financial charge or some other type of levy imposed upon a taxpayer by a governmental organization in order to fund various public expenditures. A failure to pay, along with evasion of or resistance to _________, is punishable by law. Taxes consist of direct or indirect taxes and may be paid in money or as its labour equivalent.

Exam Probability: **Medium**

18. *Answer choices:*

(see index for correct answer)

- a. co-culture
- b. personal values
- c. interpersonal communication
- d. surface-level diversity

Guidance: level 1

:: Basel II ::

A _________ is the risk of default on a debt that may arise from a borrower failing to make required payments. In the first resort, the risk is that of the lender and includes lost principal and interest, disruption to cash flows, and increased collection costs. The loss may be complete or partial. In an efficient market, higher levels of _________ will be associated with higher borrowing costs. Because of this, measures of borrowing costs such as yield spreads can be used to infer _________ levels based on assessments by market participants.

Exam Probability: **Medium**

19. *Answer choices:*

(see index for correct answer)

- a. Market risk
- b. Advanced IRB

- c. Foundation IRB
- d. Basel II

Guidance: level 1

:: Auditing ::

_________ , as defined by accounting and auditing, is a process for assuring of an organization`s objectives in operational effectiveness and efficiency, reliable financial reporting, and compliance with laws, regulations and policies. A broad concept, _________ involves everything that controls risks to an organization.

Exam Probability: **Low**

20. *Answer choices:*

(see index for correct answer)

- a. Management audit
- b. International Association of Airline Internal Auditors
- c. Internal control
- d. Legal auditing

Guidance: level 1

:: Accounting journals and ledgers ::

_________ is a daybook or journal which is used to record transactions relating to adjustment entries, opening stock, accounting errors etc. The source documents of this prime entry book are journal voucher, copy of management reports and invoices.

Exam Probability: **Medium**

21. *Answer choices:*

(see index for correct answer)

- a. Journal entry
- b. Subledger
- c. Check register
- d. General journal

Guidance: level 1

:: Marketing ::

A _________ is something that is necessary for an organism to live a healthy life. _________ s are distinguished from wants in that, in the case of a _________ , a deficiency causes a clear adverse outcome: a dysfunction or death. In other words, a _________ is something required for a safe, stable and healthy life while a want is a desire, wish or aspiration. When _________ s or wants are backed by purchasing power, they have the potential to become economic demands.

Exam Probability: **High**

22. *Answer choices:*

(see index for correct answer)

- a. Advertising media selection
- b. Need
- c. Marketing communications planning framework
- d. Marketspace

Guidance: level 1

:: ::

A __________ is an entity that owes a debt to another entity. The entity may be an individual, a firm, a government, a company or other legal person. The counterparty is called a creditor. When the counterpart of this debt arrangement is a bank, the __________ is more often referred to as a borrower.

Exam Probability: **High**

23. *Answer choices:*

(see index for correct answer)

- a. Debtor
- b. Sarbanes-Oxley act of 2002
- c. surface-level diversity
- d. open system

Guidance: level 1

:: Mereology ::

__________ , in the abstract, is what belongs to or with something, whether as an attribute or as a component of said thing. In the context of this article, it is one or more components , whether physical or incorporeal, of a person's estate; or so belonging to, as in being owned by, a person or jointly a group of people or a legal entity like a corporation or even a society. Depending on the nature of the __________ , an owner of __________ has the right to consume, alter, share, redefine, rent, mortgage, pawn, sell, exchange, transfer, give away or destroy it, or to exclude others from doing these things, as well as to perhaps abandon it; whereas regardless of the nature of the __________ , the owner thereof has the right to properly use it , or at the very least exclusively keep it.

Exam Probability: **Medium**

24. *Answer choices:*

(see index for correct answer)

- a. Mereological nihilism
- b. Simple
- c. Mereotopology
- d. Property

Guidance: level 1

:: ::

From an accounting perspective, _________ is crucial because _________ and _________ taxes considerably affect the net income of most companies and because they are subject to laws and regulations .

Exam Probability: **Low**

25. *Answer choices:*

(see index for correct answer)

- a. levels of analysis
- b. Payroll
- c. personal values
- d. hierarchical

Guidance: level 1

:: Public finance ::

_________ is the process by which the monetary authority of a country, typically the central bank or currency board, controls either the cost of very short-term borrowing or the money supply, often targeting inflation rate or interest rate to ensure price stability and general trust in the currency.

Exam Probability: **Medium**

26. *Answer choices:*

(see index for correct answer)

- a. Monetary policy
- b. Preference revelation
- c. California Municipal Treasurers Association
- d. Budget Day

Guidance: level 1

:: Business law ::

A __________ is a group of people who jointly supervise the activities of an organization, which can be either a for-profit business, nonprofit organization, or a government agency. Such a board`s powers, duties, and responsibilities are determined by government regulations and the organization`s own constitution and bylaws. These authorities may specify the number of members of the board, how they are to be chosen, and how often they are to meet.

Exam Probability: **High**

27. *Answer choices:*

(see index for correct answer)

- a. Board of directors
- b. Bulk sale
- c. Managed service company

- d. Arbitration clause

Guidance: level 1

:: Loans ::

In corporate finance, a _________ is a medium- to long-term debt instrument used by large companies to borrow money, at a fixed rate of interest. The legal term " _________ " originally referred to a document that either creates a debt or acknowledges it, but in some countries the term is now used interchangeably with bond, loan stock or note. A _________ is thus like a certificate of loan or a loan bond evidencing the fact that the company is liable to pay a specified amount with interest and although the money raised by the _________ s becomes a part of the company`s capital structure, it does not become share capital. Senior _________ s get paid before subordinate _________ s, and there are varying rates of risk and payoff for these categories.

Exam Probability: **High**

28. *Answer choices:*

(see index for correct answer)

- a. VA loan
- b. Debenture
- c. Construction loan
- d. Loan shark

Guidance: level 1

:: ::

_________ is a concept of English common law and is a necessity for simple contracts but not for special contracts . The concept has been adopted by other common law jurisdictions, including the US.

Exam Probability: **High**

29. *Answer choices:*

(see index for correct answer)

- a. Consideration
- b. open system
- c. corporate values
- d. interpersonal communication

Guidance: level 1

:: Commerce ::

Continuation of an entity as a _________ is presumed as the basis for financial reporting unless and until the entity`s liquidation becomes imminent. Preparation of financial statements under this presumption is commonly referred to as the _________ basis of accounting. If and when an entity`s liquidation becomes imminent, financial statements are prepared under the liquidation basis of accounting .

Exam Probability: **High**

30. *Answer choices:*

(see index for correct answer)

- a. Statutory holdback
- b. Shipping list
- c. Bunker adjustment factor
- d. Going concern

Guidance: level 1

:: Payments ::

A __________ is the trade of value from one party to another for goods, or services, or to fulfill a legal obligation.

Exam Probability: **Medium**

31. *Answer choices:*

(see index for correct answer)

- a. Payment
- b. County payments
- c. Thirty pieces of silver
- d. Market transition payments

Guidance: level 1

:: Elementary geometry ::

The __________ is the front of an animal`s head that features three of the head`s sense organs, the eyes, nose, and mouth, and through which animals express many of their emotions. The __________ is crucial for human identity, and damage such as scarring or developmental deformities affects the psyche adversely.

Exam Probability: **High**

32. *Answer choices:*

(see index for correct answer)

- a. Parallel postulate
- b. Transversal
- c. Golden angle
- d. Tangent

Guidance: level 1

:: Interest ::

In finance, _________ is the interest on a bond or loan that has accumulated since the principal investment, or since the previous coupon payment if there has been one already.

Exam Probability: **High**

33. *Answer choices:*

(see index for correct answer)

- a. Vix Pervenit
- b. Penal interest
- c. Usury
- d. Interest sensitivity gap

Guidance: level 1

:: Generally Accepted Accounting Principles ::

In accounting, an economic item`s _________ is the original nominal monetary value of that item. _________ accounting involves reporting assets and liabilities at their _________ s, which are not updated for changes in the items` values. Consequently, the amounts reported for these balance sheet items often differ from their current economic or market values.

Exam Probability: **Low**

34. *Answer choices:*

(see index for correct answer)

- a. Operating statement
- b. Historical cost
- c. Long-term liabilities
- d. Profit

Guidance: level 1

:: Generally Accepted Accounting Principles ::

In accounting and finance, earnings before interest and taxes is a measure of a firm`s profit that includes all incomes and expenses except interest expenses and income tax expenses.

Exam Probability: **High**

35. *Answer choices:*

(see index for correct answer)

- a. Operating Income
- b. Generally accepted accounting principles
- c. Engagement letter
- d. Standard Business Reporting

Guidance: level 1

:: Cash flow ::

In corporate finance, _________ or _________ to firm is a way of looking at a business`s cash flow to see what is available for distribution among all the securities holders of a corporate entity. This may be useful to parties such as equity holders, debt holders, preferred stock holders, and convertible security holders when they want to see how much cash can be extracted from a company without causing issues to its operations.

Exam Probability: **Low**

36. *Answer choices:*

(see index for correct answer)

- a. Cash carrier
- b. Propequity
- c. Cash flow loan
- d. Free cash flow

Guidance: level 1

:: Business law ::

__________ is where a person's financial liability is limited to a fixed sum, most commonly the value of a person's investment in a company or partnership. If a company with __________ is sued, then the claimants are suing the company, not its owners or investors. A shareholder in a limited company is not personally liable for any of the debts of the company, other than for the amount already invested in the company and for any unpaid amount on the shares in the company, if any. The same is true for the members of a __________ partnership and the limited partners in a limited partnership. By contrast, sole proprietors and partners in general partnerships are each liable for all the debts of the business .

Exam Probability: **High**

37. *Answer choices:*

(see index for correct answer)

- a. Examinership
- b. WIPO Copyright Treaty
- c. Sole proprietorship
- d. Whitewash waiver

Guidance: level 1

:: Generally Accepted Accounting Principles ::

In accounting, __________ is the income that a business have from its normal business activities, usually from the sale of goods and services to customers. __________ is also referred to as sales or turnover.Some companies receive __________ from interest, royalties, or other fees. __________ may refer to business income in general, or it may refer to the amount, in a monetary unit, earned during a period of time, as in "Last year, Company X had __________ of $42 million". Profits or net income generally imply total __________ minus total expenses in a given period. In accounting, in the balance statement it is a subsection of the Equity section and __________ increases equity, it is often referred to as the "top line" due to its position on the income statement at the very top. This is to be contrasted with the "bottom line" which denotes net income .

Exam Probability: **Medium**

38. *Answer choices:*

(see index for correct answer)

- a. Consolidation
- b. Operating income
- c. Revenue
- d. Gross income

Guidance: level 1

:: Pharmaceutical industry ::

A __________ is a document in which data collected for a clinical trial is first recorded. This data is usually later entered in the case report form. The International Conference on Harmonisation of Technical Requirements for Registration of Pharmaceuticals for Human Use guidelines define __________ s as "original documents, data, and records." __________ s contain source data, which is defined as "all information in original records and certified copies of original records of clinical findings, observations, or other activities in a clinical trial necessary for the reconstruction and evaluation of the trial."

Exam Probability: **Low**

39. *Answer choices:*

(see index for correct answer)

- a. Good manufacturing practice
- b. Bad Pharma
- c. Blister pack
- d. Source document

Guidance: level 1

:: Stock market ::

A __________ or stock divide increases the number of shares in a company. The price is adjusted such that the before and after market capitalization of the company remains the same and dilution does not occur. Options and warrants are included.

Exam Probability: **Low**

40. *Answer choices:*

(see index for correct answer)

- a. Underweight
- b. Secondary shares
- c. Stock market data systems
- d. Lock-up period

Guidance: level 1

:: Accounting terminology ::

__________ of something is, in finance, the adding together of interest or different investments over a period of time. It holds specific meanings in accounting, where it can refer to accounts on a balance sheet that represent liabilities and non-cash-based assets used in __________ -based accounting. These types of accounts include, among others, accounts payable, accounts receivable, goodwill, deferred tax liability and future interest expense.

Exam Probability: **Low**

41. *Answer choices:*

(see index for correct answer)

- a. Double-entry accounting
- b. General ledger

- c. Accrual
- d. Accrued liabilities

Guidance: level 1

:: ::

In production, research, retail, and accounting, a __________ is the value of money that has been used up to produce something or deliver a service, and hence is not available for use anymore. In business, the __________ may be one of acquisition, in which case the amount of money expended to acquire it is counted as __________. In this case, money is the input that is gone in order to acquire the thing. This acquisition __________ may be the sum of the __________ of production as incurred by the original producer, and further __________ s of transaction as incurred by the acquirer over and above the price paid to the producer. Usually, the price also includes a mark-up for profit over the __________ of production.

Exam Probability: **Low**

42. *Answer choices:*

(see index for correct answer)

- a. imperative
- b. deep-level diversity
- c. co-culture
- d. Cost

Guidance: level 1

:: Asset ::

In accounting, a __________ is any asset which can reasonably be expected to be sold, consumed, or exhausted through the normal operations of a business within the current fiscal year or operating cycle . Typical __________ s include cash, cash equivalents, short-term investments , accounts receivable, stock inventory, supplies, and the portion of prepaid liabilities which will be paid within a year.In simple words, assets which are held for a short period are known as __________ s. Such assets are expected to be realised in cash or consumed during the normal operating cycle of the business.

Exam Probability: **High**

43. *Answer choices:*

(see index for correct answer)

- a. Fixed asset
- b. Current asset

Guidance: level 1

:: Shareholders ::

A __________ is a payment made by a corporation to its shareholders, usually as a distribution of profits. When a corporation earns a profit or surplus, the corporation is able to re-invest the profit in the business and pay a proportion of the profit as a __________ to shareholders. Distribution to shareholders may be in cash or, if the corporation has a __________ reinvestment plan, the amount can be paid by the issue of further shares or share repurchase. When __________s are paid, shareholders typically must pay income taxes, and the corporation does not receive a corporate income tax deduction for the __________ payments.

Exam Probability: **Medium**

44. *Answer choices:*

(see index for correct answer)

- a. Shotgun clause
- b. Dividend
- c. Shareholder ownership value
- d. Activist shareholder

Guidance: level 1

:: Fixed income market ::

In finance, the __________ is a curve showing several yields or interest rates across different contract lengths for a similar debt contract. The curve shows the relation between the interest rate and the time to maturity, known as the "term", of the debt for a given borrower in a given currency. For example, the U.S. dollar interest rates paid on U.S. Treasury securities for various maturities are closely watched by many traders, and are commonly plotted on a graph such as the one on the right which is informally called "the __________ ". More formal mathematical descriptions of this relation are often called the term structure of interest rates.

Exam Probability: **Low**

45. *Answer choices:*

(see index for correct answer)

- a. Inter-dealer broker
- b. Fixed-income attribution
- c. Bond market
- d. Yield curve

Guidance: level 1

:: Debt ::

__________ , in finance and economics, is payment from a borrower or deposit-taking financial institution to a lender or depositor of an amount above repayment of the principal sum , at a particular rate. It is distinct from a fee which the borrower may pay the lender or some third party. It is also distinct from dividend which is paid by a company to its shareholders from its profit or reserve, but not at a particular rate decided beforehand, rather on a pro rata basis as a share in the reward gained by risk taking entrepreneurs when the revenue earned exceeds the total costs.

Exam Probability: **High**

46. *Answer choices:*

(see index for correct answer)

- a. Phantom debt
- b. Extendible bond
- c. Asset protection
- d. Interest

Guidance: level 1

:: ::

In accounting, the __________ is a measure of the number of times inventory is sold or used in a time period such as a year. It is calculated to see if a business has an excessive inventory in comparison to its sales level. The equation for __________ equals the cost of goods sold divided by the average inventory. __________ is also known as inventory turns, merchandise turnover, stockturn, stock turns, turns, and stock turnover.

Exam Probability: **Medium**

47. *Answer choices:*

(see index for correct answer)

- a. information systems assessment
- b. open system
- c. co-culture
- d. Inventory turnover

Guidance: level 1

:: Financial markets ::

In economics and finance, _________ is the practice of taking advantage of a price difference between two or more markets: striking a combination of matching deals that capitalize upon the imbalance, the profit being the difference between the market prices. When used by academics, an _________ is a transaction that involves no negative cash flow at any probabilistic or temporal state and a positive cash flow in at least one state; in simple terms, it is the possibility of a risk-free profit after transaction costs. For example, an _________ opportunity is present when there is the opportunity to instantaneously buy something for a low price and sell it for a higher price.

Exam Probability: **High**

48. *Answer choices:*

(see index for correct answer)

- a. Financial market
- b. Noise trader
- c. Payment schedule
- d. dark pool

Guidance: level 1

:: Inventory ::

It requires a detailed physical count, so that the company knows exactly how many of each goods brought on specific dates remained at year end inventory. When this information is found, the amount of goods are multiplied by their purchase cost at their purchase date, to get a number for the ending inventory cost.

Exam Probability: **High**

49. *Answer choices:*

(see index for correct answer)

- a. Specific identification
- b. Stock obsolescence
- c. Lower of cost or market
- d. Stock keeping unit

Guidance: level 1

:: ::

_________ is a means of protection from financial loss. It is a form of risk management, primarily used to hedge against the risk of a contingent or uncertain loss

Exam Probability: **Medium**

50. *Answer choices:*

(see index for correct answer)

- a. levels of analysis
- b. imperative
- c. Insurance
- d. interpersonal communication

Guidance: level 1

:: ::

An _________, for United States federal income tax, is a closely held corporation that makes a valid election to be taxed under Subchapter S of Chapter 1 of the Internal Revenue Code. In general, _________ s do not pay any income taxes. Instead, the corporation`s income or losses are divided among and passed through to its shareholders. The shareholders must then report the income or loss on their own individual income tax returns.

Exam Probability: **Medium**

51. *Answer choices:*

(see index for correct answer)

- a. hierarchical
- b. imperative
- c. information systems assessment
- d. corporate values

Guidance: level 1

:: ::

A _________ , in the word`s original meaning, is a sheet of paper on which one performs work. They come in many forms, most commonly associated with children`s school work assignments, tax forms, and accounting or other business environments. Software is increasingly taking over the paper-based _________ .

Exam Probability: **Medium**

52. *Answer choices:*

(see index for correct answer)

- a. Worksheet
- b. co-culture
- c. surface-level diversity

- d. similarity-attraction theory

Guidance: level 1

:: Pension funds ::

__________ s typically have large amounts of money to invest and are the major investors in listed and private companies. They are especially important to the stock market where large institutional investors dominate. The largest 300 __________ s collectively hold about $6 trillion in assets. In January 2008, The Economist reported that Morgan Stanley estimates that __________ s worldwide hold over US$20 trillion in assets, the largest for any category of investor ahead of mutual funds, insurance companies, currency reserves, sovereign wealth funds, hedge funds, or private equity.

Exam Probability: **High**

53. *Answer choices:*

(see index for correct answer)

- a. Pension led funding
- b. Pension buyout
- c. Texas Municipal Retirement System

Guidance: level 1

:: Credit cards ::

A __________ is a payment card issued to users to enable the cardholder to pay a merchant for goods and services based on the cardholder`s promise to the card issuer to pay them for the amounts plus the other agreed charges. The card issuer creates a revolving account and grants a line of credit to the cardholder, from which the cardholder can borrow money for payment to a merchant or as a cash advance.

Exam Probability: **Low**

54. *Answer choices:*

(see index for correct answer)

- a. Credit card
- b. Rail travel card
- c. Payments as a service
- d. Cashplus

Guidance: level 1

:: Generally Accepted Accounting Principles ::

A __________ , in accrual accounting, is any account where the asset or liability is not realized until a future date , e.g. annuities, charges, taxes, income, etc. The deferred item may be carried, dependent on type of __________ , as either an asset or liability. See also accrual.

Exam Probability: **Low**

55. *Answer choices:*

(see index for correct answer)

- a. Write-off
- b. Indian Accounting Standards
- c. Matching principle
- d. Deferral

Guidance: level 1

:: Money ::

Cash and _________ s are the most liquid current assets found on a business`s balance sheet. _________ s are short-term commitments "with temporarily idle cash and easily convertible into a known cash amount". An investment normally counts to be a _________ when it has a short maturity period of 90 days or less, and can be included in the cash and _________ s balance from the date of acquisition when it carries an insignificant risk of changes in the asset value; with more than 90 days maturity, the asset is not considered as cash and _________ s. Equity investments mostly are excluded from _________ s, unless they are essentially _________ s, for instance, if the preferred shares acquired within a short maturity period and with specified recovery date.

Exam Probability: **Low**

56. *Answer choices:*

(see index for correct answer)

- a. Purse bid
- b. Metallism
- c. Cash equivalent
- d. Ideal money

Guidance: level 1

:: Financial ratios ::

A _________ or accounting ratio is a relative magnitude of two selected numerical values taken from an enterprise's financial statements. Often used in accounting, there are many standard ratios used to try to evaluate the overall financial condition of a corporation or other organization. _________ s may be used by managers within a firm, by current and potential shareholders of a firm, and by a firm's creditors. Financial analysts use _________ s to compare the strengths and weaknesses in various companies. If shares in a company are traded in a financial market, the market price of the shares is used in certain _________ s.

Exam Probability: **Medium**

57. *Answer choices:*

(see index for correct answer)

- a. Asset turnover
- b. Social return on investment
- c. Financial ratio
- d. Return on assets

Guidance: level 1

:: Derivatives (finance) ::

A __________ or __________ row is a line of closely spaced shrubs and sometimes trees, planted and trained to form a barrier or to mark the boundary of an area, such as between neighbouring properties. __________ s used to separate a road from adjoining fields or one field from another, and of sufficient age to incorporate larger trees, are known as __________ rows. Often they serve as windbreaks to improve conditions for the adjacent crops, as in bocage country. When clipped and maintained, __________ s are also a simple form of topiary.

Exam Probability: **Medium**

58. *Answer choices:*

(see index for correct answer)

- a. Forward-forward agreement
- b. Triple witching
- c. Package unit
- d. Hedge

Guidance: level 1

:: Investment ::

The __________ is a measure of an investment's rate of return. The term internal refers to the fact that the calculation excludes external factors, such as the risk-free rate, inflation, the cost of capital, or various financial risks.

Exam Probability: **Low**

59. *Answer choices:*

(see index for correct answer)

- a. Enterprise Investment Scheme
- b. Index fund
- c. Internal rate of return
- d. Value Research

Guidance: level 1

Human resource management

Human resource (HR) management is the strategic approach to the effective management of organization workers so that they help the business gain a competitive advantage. It is designed to maximize employee performance in service of an employer's strategic objectives. HR is primarily concerned with the management of people within organizations, focusing on policies and on systems. HR departments are responsible for overseeing employee-benefits design, employee recruitment, training and development, performance appraisal, and rewarding (e.g., managing pay and benefit systems). HR also concerns itself with organizational change and industrial relations, that is, the balancing of organizational practices with requirements arising from collective bargaining and from governmental laws.

:: Offshoring ::

Outsourcing is an agreement in which one company hires another company to be responsible for a planned or existing activity that is or could be done internally,and sometimes involves transferring employees and assets from one firm to another.

Exam Probability: **High**

1. *Answer choices:*

(see index for correct answer)

- a. American Jobs
- b. Layoff
- c. TeleTech
- d. Nearshoring

Guidance: level 1

:: Employee relations ::

_________ ownership, or employee share ownership, is an ownership interest in a company held by the company`s workforce. The ownership interest may be facilitated by the company as part of employees` remuneration or incentive compensation for work performed, or the company itself may be employee owned.

Exam Probability: **Medium**

2. *Answer choices:*

(see index for correct answer)

- a. Employee morale
- b. Employee handbook
- c. Employee stock
- d. Industry Federation of the State of Rio de Janeiro

Guidance: level 1

:: Organizational behavior ::

__________ is the act of matching attitudes, beliefs, and behaviors to group norms or politics. Norms are implicit, specific rules, shared by a group of individuals, that guide their interactions with others. People often choose to conform to society rather than to pursue personal desires because it is often easier to follow the path others have made already, rather than creating a new one. This tendency to conform occurs in small groups and/or society as a whole, and may result from subtle unconscious influences , or direct and overt social pressure. __________ can occur in the presence of others, or when an individual is alone. For example, people tend to follow social norms when eating or watching television, even when alone.

Exam Probability: **Low**

3. *Answer choices:*

(see index for correct answer)

- a. Conformity
- b. Span of control

- c. Managerial grid model
- d. Burnout

Guidance: level 1

:: Human resource management ::

_________ , Inc. is an American office staffing company that operates globally. The company places employees at all levels in various sectors including financial services, information technology, and law. Also, its professional services include human resource and management consulting, outsourcing, recruitment, career transition, and vendor management. _________ was founded by William Russell Kelly in 1946 and is headquartered in Troy, Michigan. In 2015, the company reported 8,100 employees, $5.5 billion in revenue, and placed 550,000 employees to work in positions in various sectors, making it one of the world`s largest staffing firms.

Exam Probability: **Medium**

4. *Answer choices:*

(see index for correct answer)

- a. Continuing professional development
- b. Corporate Equality Index
- c. Mechanical aptitude
- d. Kelly Services

Guidance: level 1

:: Labour relations ::

_________ is the practice of hiring more workers than are needed to perform a given job, or to adopt work procedures which appear pointless, complex and time-consuming merely to employ additional workers. The term "make-work" is sometimes used as a synonym for _________ .

Exam Probability: **High**

5. *Answer choices:*

(see index for correct answer)

- a. Comprehensive campaign
- b. Jesse Simons
- c. Disciplinary counseling
- d. Featherbedding

Guidance: level 1

:: Labour relations ::

A bargaining _________ occurs when the two sides negotiating an agreement are unable to reach an agreement and become deadlocked. An _________ is almost invariably mutually harmful, either as a result of direct action which may be taken such as a strike in employment negotiation or sanctions/military action in international relations, or simply due to the resulting delay in negotiating a mutually beneficial agreement. The word _________ may also refer to any situation in which no progress can be made. _________s provide opportunities for problem solving to provide an insight that leads to progress.

Exam Probability: **Low**

6. *Answer choices:*

(see index for correct answer)

- a. Impasse
- b. Delta Board Council
- c. Merit shop
- d. Eurocadres

Guidance: level 1

:: Workplace ::

A __________ is a process through which feedback from an employee`s subordinates, colleagues, and supervisor, as well as a self-evaluation by the employee themselves is gathered. Such feedback can also include, when relevant, feedback from external sources who interact with the employee, such as customers and suppliers or other interested stakeholders. __________ is so named because it solicits feedback regarding an employee`s behavior from a variety of points of view . It therefore may be contrasted with "downward feedback" , or "upward feedback" delivered to supervisory or management employees by subordinates only.

Exam Probability: **Medium**

7. *Answer choices:*

(see index for correct answer)

- a. Feminisation of the workplace
- b. Workplace relationships
- c. Workplace spirituality
- d. Workplace romance

Guidance: level 1

:: ::

On December 31, 2016, Xerox separated its business process service operations into a new publicly traded company, Conduent. Xerox focuses on its document technology and document outsourcing business, and continues to trade on the NYSE. On January 31, 2018, Xerox announced that it would sell a controlling stake to Fujifilm, which has maintained a joint venture in the Asia-Pacific region known as Fuji Xerox.

Exam Probability: **Low**

8. *Answer choices:*

(see index for correct answer)

- a. empathy
- b. Xerox Corporation
- c. surface-level diversity
- d. corporate values

Guidance: level 1

:: Management ::

The __________ is a strategy performance management tool – a semi-standard structured report, that can be used by managers to keep track of the execution of activities by the staff within their control and to monitor the consequences arising from these actions.

Exam Probability: **Medium**

9. *Answer choices:*

(see index for correct answer)

- a. Organizational space
- b. Supply network
- c. Quick response manufacturing
- d. Balanced scorecard

Guidance: level 1

:: Human resource management ::

An _________ is a diagram that shows the structure of an organization and the relationships and relative ranks of its parts and positions/jobs. The term is also used for similar diagrams, for example ones showing the different elements of a field of knowledge or a group of languages.

Exam Probability: **Medium**

10. *Answer choices:*

(see index for correct answer)

- a. ROWE
- b. The war for talent
- c. Administrative services organization
- d. Health human resources

Guidance: level 1

:: Human resource management ::

Frederick Herzberg, an American psychologist, originally developed the concept of ` _________ ` in 1968, in an article that he published on pioneering studies at A T&T. The concept stemmed from Herzberg`s motivator-hygiene theory, which is based on the premise that job attitude is a construct of two independent factors, namely job satisfaction and job dissatisfaction. Job satisfaction encompasses intrinsic factors that arise from the work itself, including achievement and advancement; whilst job dissatisfaction stems from factors external to the actual work, including company policy and the quality of supervision.

Exam Probability: **High**

11. *Answer choices:*

(see index for correct answer)

- a. Organizational chart
- b. Open plan
- c. Induction training
- d. Job enrichment

Guidance: level 1

:: Types of marketing ::

In microeconomics and management, _________ is an arrangement in which the supply chain of a company is owned by that company. Usually each member of the supply chain produces a different product or service, and the products combine to satisfy a common need. It is contrasted with horizontal integration, wherein a company produces several items which are related to one another. _________ has also described management styles that bring large portions of the supply chain not only under a common ownership, but also into one corporation .

Exam Probability: **Medium**

12. *Answer choices:*

(see index for correct answer)

- a. Vertical disintegration
- b. Relationship marketing
- c. Close Range Marketing
- d. Global marketing

Guidance: level 1

:: Validity (statistics) ::

In psychometrics, _________ refers to the extent to which a measure represents all facets of a given construct. For example, a depression scale may lack _________ if it only assesses the affective dimension of depression but fails to take into account the behavioral dimension. An element of subjectivity exists in relation to determining _________ , which requires a degree of agreement about what a particular personality trait such as extraversion represents. A disagreement about a personality trait will prevent the gain of a high _________ .

Exam Probability: **Low**

13. *Answer choices:*

(see index for correct answer)

- a. Content validity
- b. Nomological network
- c. Validation
- d. Face validity

Guidance: level 1

:: Developmental psychology ::

_________ behavior refers to behavior that enables a person to get along in his or her environment with greatest success and least conflict with others. This is a term used in the areas of psychology and special education. _________ behavior relates to every day skills or tasks that the average person is able to complete, similar to the term life skills.

Exam Probability: **Low**

14. *Answer choices:*

(see index for correct answer)

- a. Cognitive development
- b. Adult development

Guidance: level 1

:: Stochastic processes ::

_________ in its modern meaning is a "new idea, creative thoughts, new imaginations in form of device or method". _________ is often also viewed as the application of better solutions that meet new requirements, unarticulated needs, or existing market needs. Such _________ takes place through the provision of more-effective products, processes, services, technologies, or business models that are made available to markets, governments and society. An _________ is something original and more effective and, as a consequence, new, that "breaks into" the market or society. _________ is related to, but not the same as, invention, as _________ is more apt to involve the practical implementation of an invention to make a meaningful impact in the market or society, and not all _________ s require an invention. _________ often manifests itself via the engineering process, when the problem being solved is of a technical or scientific nature. The opposite of _________ is exnovation.

Exam Probability: **High**

15. *Answer choices:*

(see index for correct answer)

- a. Self-similar process
- b. Brownian excursion
- c. Innovation
- d. Hurst exponent

Guidance: level 1

:: Management ::

__________ is a set of activities that ensure goals are met in an effective and efficient manner. __________ can focus on the performance of an organization, a department, an employee, or the processes in place to manage particular tasks. __________ standards are generally organized and disseminated by senior leadership at an organization, and by task owners.

Exam Probability: **Low**

16. *Answer choices:*

(see index for correct answer)

- a. Performance management
- b. Corporate transparency
- c. Intelligent customer
- d. Scenario planning

Guidance: level 1

:: Business ethics cases ::

_________ , 477 U.S. 57 , is a US labor law case, where the United States Supreme Court, in a 9-0 decision, recognized sexual harassment as a violation of Title VII of the Civil Rights Act of 1964. The case was the first of its kind to reach the Supreme Court and would redefine sexual harassment in the workplace.

Exam Probability: **Low**

17. *Answer choices:*

(see index for correct answer)

- a. Libor scandal
- b. Sandstorm report
- c. Meritor Savings Bank v. Vinson
- d. Jenson v. Eveleth Taconite Co.

Guidance: level 1

:: Human resource management ::

A __________ is a form of payment from an employer to an employee, which may be specified in an employment contract. It is contrasted with piece wages, where each job, hour or other unit is paid separately, rather than on a periodic basis.From the point of view of running a business, __________ can also be viewed as the cost of acquiring and retaining human resources for running operations, and is then termed personnel expense or __________ expense. In accounting, salaries are recorded in payroll accounts.

Exam Probability: **Low**

18. *Answer choices:*

(see index for correct answer)

- a. CEO succession
- b. Talascend
- c. Resource-based view
- d. Upward communication

Guidance: level 1

:: Employment ::

A flat organization has an organizational structure with few or no levels of middle management between staff and executives. An organization`s structure refers to the nature of the distribution of the units and positions within it, also to the nature of the relationships among those units and positions. Tall and flat organizations differ based on how many levels of management are present in the organization, and how much control managers are endowed with.

Exam Probability: **High**

19. *Answer choices:*

(see index for correct answer)

- a. Jobless claims
- b. Delayering
- c. Local hiring
- d. Transformation in economics

Guidance: level 1

:: Employment compensation ::

A __________ is the minimum income necessary for a worker to meet their basic needs. Needs are defined to include food, housing, and other essential needs such as clothing. The goal of a __________ is to allow a worker to afford a basic but decent standard of living. Due to the flexible nature of the term "needs", there is not one universally accepted measure of what a __________ is and as such it varies by location and household type.

Exam Probability: **Medium**

20. *Answer choices:*

(see index for correct answer)

- a. Golden boot compensation
- b. Living wage

- c. Employee stock purchase plan
- d. Equal Pay Act of 1963

Guidance: level 1

:: Design of experiments ::

In the design of experiments, treatments are applied to experimental units in the treatment group. In comparative experiments, members of the complementary group, the _________ , receive either no treatment or a standard treatment.

Exam Probability: **Medium**

21. *Answer choices:*

(see index for correct answer)

- a. Association scheme
- b. Control group
- c. Latin square
- d. Provocation test

Guidance: level 1

:: United States employment discrimination case law ::

__________, 524 U.S. 775 , is a US labor law case of the United States Supreme Court in which the Court identified the circumstances under which an employer may be held liable under Title VII of the Civil Rights Act of 1964 for the acts of a supervisory employee whose sexual harassment of subordinates has created a hostile work environment amounting to employment discrimination. The court held that "an employer is vicariously liable for actionable discrimination caused by a supervisor, but subject to an affirmative defense looking to the reasonableness of the employer`s conduct as well as that of a plaintiff victim."

Exam Probability: **Medium**

22. *Answer choices:*

(see index for correct answer)

- a. Griggs v. Duke Power Co.
- b. Gross v. FBL Financial Services, Inc.
- c. Bundy v. Jackson
- d. Price Waterhouse v. Hopkins

Guidance: level 1

:: ::

In production, research, retail, and accounting, a _________ is the value of money that has been used up to produce something or deliver a service, and hence is not available for use anymore. In business, the _________ may be one of acquisition, in which case the amount of money expended to acquire it is counted as _________. In this case, money is the input that is gone in order to acquire the thing. This acquisition _________ may be the sum of the _________ of production as incurred by the original producer, and further _________s of transaction as incurred by the acquirer over and above the price paid to the producer. Usually, the price also includes a mark-up for profit over the _________ of production.

Exam Probability: **Medium**

23. *Answer choices:*

(see index for correct answer)

- a. Cost
- b. personal values
- c. similarity-attraction theory
- d. levels of analysis

Guidance: level 1

:: Occupational safety and health ::

Note: Parts of this article are written from the perspective of aircraft safety analysis techniques and definitions; these may not represent current best practice and the article needs to be updated to represent a more generic description of _________ and discussion of more modern standards and techniques.

Exam Probability: **Low**

24. *Answer choices:*

(see index for correct answer)

- a. National Day of Mourning
- b. Electric shock
- c. Hazard analysis
- d. Manganese

Guidance: level 1

:: Hazard analysis ::

A _________ is an agent which has the potential to cause harm to a vulnerable target. The terms " _________ " and "risk" are often used interchangeably. However, in terms of risk assessment, they are two very distinct terms. A _________ is any agent that can cause harm or damage to humans, property, or the environment. Risk is defined as the probability that exposure to a _________ will lead to a negative consequence, or more simply, a _________ poses no risk if there is no exposure to that _________ .

Exam Probability: **Medium**

25. *Answer choices:*

(see index for correct answer)

- a. Swiss cheese model
- b. Hazard
- c. Risk assessment
- d. Hazard identification

Guidance: level 1

:: ::

_________ refers to the overall process of attracting, shortlisting, selecting and appointing suitable candidates for jobs within an organization. _________ can also refer to processes involved in choosing individuals for unpaid roles. Managers, human resource generalists and _________ specialists may be tasked with carrying out _________, but in some cases public-sector employment agencies, commercial _________ agencies, or specialist search consultancies are used to undertake parts of the process. Internet-based technologies which support all aspects of _________ have become widespread.

Exam Probability: **Low**

26. *Answer choices:*

(see index for correct answer)

- a. Recruitment
- b. functional perspective
- c. open system
- d. cultural

Guidance: level 1

:: Human resource management ::

__________ is a method of job analysis that was developed by the Employment and Training Administration of the United States Department of Labor. FJA produces standardized occupational information specific to the performance of the work and the performer.

Exam Probability: **Low**

27. *Answer choices:*

(see index for correct answer)

- a. Job performance
- b. Competency-based management
- c. Functional job analysis
- d. Performance domain

Guidance: level 1

:: Employment compensation ::

_________ is time off from work that workers can use to stay home to address their health and safety needs without losing pay. Paid _________ is a statutory requirement in many nations. Most European, many Latin American, a few African and a few Asian countries have legal requirements for paid _________ .

Exam Probability: **Medium**

28. *Answer choices:*

(see index for correct answer)

- a. Employee assistance program
- b. Pay scale
- c. Maximum wage
- d. Workers Compensation Act 1987

Guidance: level 1

:: Employment compensation ::

Employee stock ownership, or employee share ownership, is an ownership interest in a company held by the company`s workforce. The ownership interest may be facilitated by the company as part of employees` remuneration or incentive compensation for work performed, or the company itself may be employee owned.

Exam Probability: **High**

29. *Answer choices:*

(see index for correct answer)

- a. Golden boot compensation
- b. Employee stock ownership plan
- c. Health Reimbursement Account
- d. Compa-ratio

Guidance: level 1

:: Power (social and political) ::

In a notable study of power conducted by social psychologists John R. P. French and Bertram Raven in 1959, power is divided into five separate and distinct forms. In 1965 Raven revised this model to include a sixth form by separating the informational power base as distinct from the _________ base.

Exam Probability: **High**

30. *Answer choices:*

(see index for correct answer)

- a. Hard power
- b. need for power
- c. Referent power

Guidance: level 1

:: Trade unions ::

A __________ is an association of workers forming a legal unit or legal personhood, usually called a "bargaining unit", which acts as bargaining agent and legal representative for a unit of employees in all matters of law or right arising from or in the administration of a collective agreement. Labour unions typically fund the formal organisation, head office, and legal team functions of the labour union through regular fees or union dues. The delegate staff of the labour union representation in the workforce are made up of workplace volunteers who are appointed by members in democratic elections.

Exam Probability: **Medium**

31. *Answer choices:*

(see index for correct answer)

- a. International Labour Sports Federation
- b. Union democracy
- c. TU
- d. Trade union

Guidance: level 1

:: Management ::

A _________ describes the rationale of how an organization creates, delivers, and captures value, in economic, social, cultural or other contexts. The process of _________ construction and modification is also called _________ innovation and forms a part of business strategy.

Exam Probability: **High**

32. *Answer choices:*

(see index for correct answer)

- a. Inside job
- b. Flat organization
- c. Managerial economics
- d. Quality

Guidance: level 1

:: ::

_________ is the process of collecting, analyzing and/or reporting information regarding the performance of an individual, group, organization, system or component. _________ is not a new concept, some of the earliest records of human activity relate to the counting or recording of activities.

Exam Probability: **Medium**

33. *Answer choices:*

(see index for correct answer)

- a. interpersonal communication
- b. surface-level diversity
- c. levels of analysis
- d. Performance measurement

Guidance: level 1

:: Unemployment by country ::

Unemployment benefits are payments made by back authorized bodies to unemployed people. In the United States, benefits are funded by a compulsory governmental insurance system, not taxes on individual citizens. Depending on the jurisdiction and the status of the person, those sums may be small, covering only basic needs, or may compensate the lost time proportionally to the previous earned salary.

Exam Probability: **High**

34. *Answer choices:*

(see index for correct answer)

- a. Unemployment in Brazil
- b. Unemployment in Spain
- c. Unemployment insurance

Guidance: level 1

:: ::

A _________ is a systematic way of determining the value/worth of a job in relation to other jobs in an organization. It tries to make a systematic comparison between jobs to assess their relative worth for the purpose of establishing a rational pay structure. _________ needs to be differentiated from job analysis. Job analysis is a systematic way of gathering information about a job. Every _________ method requires at least some basic job analysis in order to provide factual information about the jobs concerned. Thus, _________ begins with job analysis and ends at that point where the worth of a job is ascertained for achieving pay equity between jobs and different roles.

Exam Probability: **High**

35. *Answer choices:*

(see index for correct answer)

- a. personal values
- b. Job evaluation
- c. cultural
- d. empathy

Guidance: level 1

:: Psychometrics ::

A _________ is a set of categories designed to elicit information about a quantitative or a qualitative attribute. In the social sciences, particularly psychology, common examples are the Likert response scale and 1-10 _________ s in which a person selects the number which is considered to reflect the perceived quality of a product.

Exam Probability: **Medium**

36. *Answer choices:*

(see index for correct answer)

- a. Thurstone scale
- b. Rating scale
- c. Multistage testing
- d. Mokken scale

Guidance: level 1

:: Project management ::

_________ is a name for various theories of human motivation built on Douglas McGregor`s Theory X and Theory Y. Theories X, Y and various versions of Z have been used in human resource management, organizational behavior, organizational communication and organizational development.

Exam Probability: **Low**

37. *Answer choices:*

(see index for correct answer)

- a. Goodwerp
- b. Theory Z
- c. Stakeholder analysis
- d. Code name

Guidance: level 1

:: Fundamental analysis ::

__________ , also known as letter stock or restricted securities, is stock of a company that is not fully transferable until certain conditions have been met. Upon satisfaction of those conditions, the stock is no longer restricted, and becomes transferable to the person holding the award. __________ is often used as a form of employee compensation, in which case it typically becomes transferrable upon the satisfaction of certain conditions, such as continued employment for a period of time or the achievement of particular product-development milestones, earnings per share goals or other financial targets. __________ is a popular alternative to stock options, particularly for executives, due to favorable accounting rules and income tax treatment.

Exam Probability: **High**

38. *Answer choices:*

(see index for correct answer)

- a. Enterprise value

- b. Economic Value Added
- c. Trading Advantage
- d. Equity value

Guidance: level 1

:: ::

A __________ is monetary compensation paid by an employer to an employee in exchange for work done. Payment may be calculated as a fixed amount for each task completed , or at an hourly or daily rate , or based on an easily measured quantity of work done.

Exam Probability: **High**

39. *Answer choices:*

(see index for correct answer)

- a. imperative
- b. Sarbanes-Oxley act of 2002
- c. surface-level diversity
- d. hierarchical

Guidance: level 1

:: Human resource management ::

_________ refers to the ratio of the number of job positions to the number of job applicants and is used in the context of selection and recruitment.

Exam Probability: **Low**

40. *Answer choices:*

(see index for correct answer)

- a. Selection ratio
- b. Management by objectives
- c. Internal communications
- d. Occupational Information Network

Guidance: level 1

:: Business ethics ::

_________ is a type of harassment technique that relates to a sexual nature and the unwelcome or inappropriate promise of rewards in exchange for sexual favors. _________ includes a range of actions from mild transgressions to sexual abuse or assault. Harassment can occur in many different social settings such as the workplace, the home, school, churches, etc. Harassers or victims may be of any gender.

Exam Probability: **Medium**

41. *Answer choices:*

(see index for correct answer)

- a. Altruistic corporate social responsibility
- b. Corporate Knights
- c. Third-party technique
- d. Cost the limit of price

Guidance: level 1

:: ::

Educational technology is "the study and ethical practice of facilitating learning and improving performance by creating, using, and managing appropriate technological processes and resources".

Exam Probability: **Low**

42. *Answer choices:*

(see index for correct answer)

- a. cultural
- b. Character
- c. E-learning
- d. corporate values

Guidance: level 1

:: Project management ::

Some scenarios associate "this kind of planning" with learning "life skills". _________ s are necessary, or at least useful, in situations where individuals need to know what time they must be at a specific location to receive a specific service, and where people need to accomplish a set of goals within a set time period.

Exam Probability: **Medium**

43. *Answer choices:*

(see index for correct answer)

- a. Project portfolio management
- b. Hart Mason Index
- c. Transfer of Burden
- d. Theory Z of Ouchi

Guidance: level 1

:: Sociological terminology ::

In moral and political philosophy, the _________ is a theory or model that originated during the Age of Enlightenment and usually concerns the legitimacy of the authority of the state over the individual. _________ arguments typically posit that individuals have consented, either explicitly or tacitly, to surrender some of their freedoms and submit to the authority in exchange for protection of their remaining rights or maintenance of the social order. The relation between natural and legal rights is often a topic of _________ theory. The term takes its name from The _________, a 1762 book by Jean-Jacques Rousseau that discussed this concept. Although the antecedents of _________ theory are found in antiquity, in Greek and Stoic philosophy and Roman and Canon Law, the heyday of the _________ was the mid-17th to early 19th centuries, when it emerged as the leading doctrine of political legitimacy.

Exam Probability: **Low**

44. *Answer choices:*

(see index for correct answer)

- a. Typification
- b. social conditioning
- c. McDonaldization
- d. institutional racism

Guidance: level 1

:: Training ::

_________ is teaching, or developing in oneself or others, any skills and knowledge that relate to specific useful competencies. _________ has specific goals of improving one`s capability, capacity, productivity and performance. It forms the core of apprenticeships and provides the backbone of content at institutes of technology . In addition to the basic _________ required for a trade, occupation or profession, observers of the labor-market recognize as of 2008 the need to continue _________ beyond initial qualifications: to maintain, upgrade and update skills throughout working life. People within many professions and occupations may refer to this sort of _________ as professional development.

Exam Probability: **Medium**

45. *Answer choices:*

(see index for correct answer)

- a. Voluntary Protection Program
- b. Officer training
- c. G-learning
- d. Training

Guidance: level 1

:: Job interview ::

An __________ is a survey conducted with an individual who is separating from an organization or relationship. Most commonly, this occurs between an employee and an organization, a student and an educational institution, or a member and an association. An organization can use the information gained from an __________ to assess what should be improved, changed, or remain intact. More so, an organization can use the results from __________ s to reduce employee, student, or member turnover and increase productivity and engagement, thus reducing the high costs associated with turnover. Some examples of the value of conducting __________ s include shortening the recruiting and hiring process, reducing absenteeism, improving innovation, sustaining performance, and reducing possible litigation if issues mentioned in the __________ are addressed. It is important for each organization to customize its own __________ in order to maintain the highest levels of survey validity and reliability.

Exam Probability: **High**

46. *Answer choices:*

(see index for correct answer)

- a. Microsoft interview
- b. Mock interview
- c. Exit interview
- d. Case interview

Guidance: level 1

:: Human resource management ::

_________ assesses whether a person performs a job well. _________ , studied academically as part of industrial and organizational psychology, also forms a part of human resources management. Performance is an important criterion for organizational outcomes and success. John P. Campbell describes _________ as an individual-level variable, or something a single person does. This differentiates it from more encompassing constructs such as organizational performance or national performance, which are higher-level variables.

Exam Probability: **High**

47. *Answer choices:*

(see index for correct answer)

- a. Job performance
- b. Parallel running
- c. Job design
- d. Salary

Guidance: level 1

:: Persuasion techniques ::

_________ is a psychological technique in which an individual attempts to influence another person by becoming more likeable to their target. This term was coined by social psychologist Edward E. Jones, who further defined _________ as "a class of strategic behaviors illicitly designed to influence a particular other person concerning the attractiveness of one`s personal qualities." _________ research has identified some specific tactics of employing _________ .

Exam Probability: **Low**

48. *Answer choices:*

(see index for correct answer)

- a. Kolakeia
- b. Ingratiation
- c. Foot-in-the-door technique
- d. Modes of persuasion

Guidance: level 1

:: Human resource management ::

__________ , also known as management by results , was first popularized by Peter Drucker in his 1954 book The Practice of Management. __________ is the process of defining specific objectives within an organization that management can convey to organization members, then deciding on how to achieve each objective in sequence. This process allows managers to take work that needs to be done one step at a time to allow for a calm, yet productive work environment. This process also helps organization members to see their accomplishments as they achieve each objective, which reinforces a positive work environment and a sense of achievement. An important part of MBO is the measurement and comparison of an employee`s actual performance with the standards set. Ideally, when employees themselves have been involved with the goal-setting and choosing the course of action to be followed by them, they are more likely to fulfill their responsibilities.According to George S. Odiorne, the system of __________ can be described as a process whereby the superior and subordinate jointly identify common goals, define each individual`s major areas of responsibility in terms of the results expected of him or her, and use these measures as guides for operating the unit and assessing the contribution of each of its members.

Exam Probability: **Medium**

49. *Answer choices:*

(see index for correct answer)

- a. Organizational culture
- b. Mechanical aptitude
- c. Formal organization
- d. Management by objectives

Guidance: level 1

:: Trade unions ::

A __________ , in North America, or union branch , in the United Kingdom and other countries, is a local branch of a usually national trade union. The terms used for sub-branches of __________ s vary from country to country and include "shop committee", "shop floor committee", "board of control", "chapel", and others.

Exam Probability: **Low**

50. *Answer choices:*

(see index for correct answer)

- a. Public-sector trade union
- b. Local union
- c. Ghent system
- d. Craft unionism

Guidance: level 1

:: Human resource management ::

This term is often used in an employment or human resources context where rather than terminating employees for first or minor infractions, there is a system of escalating responses intended to correct the negative behavior rather than to punish the employee.

Exam Probability: **Medium**

51. *Answer choices:*

(see index for correct answer)

- a. TPI-theory
- b. Management by objectives
- c. Senior management
- d. Progressive discipline

Guidance: level 1

:: Industrial engineering ::

__________ is the formal process that sits alongside Requirements analysis and focuses on the human elements of the requirements.

Exam Probability: **Low**

52. *Answer choices:*

(see index for correct answer)

- a. Industrial ecology
- b. Needs analysis
- c. Package testing
- d. Human factors and ergonomics

Guidance: level 1

:: United States employment discrimination case law ::

_________ , 490 U.S. 228 , was an important decision by the United States Supreme Court on the issues of prescriptive sex discrimination and employer liability for sex discrimination. The employee, Ann Hopkins, sued her former employer, the accounting firm Price Waterhouse. She argued that the firm denied her partnership because she didn`t fit the partners` idea of what a female employee should look like and act like. The employer failed to prove that it would have denied her partnership anyway, and the Court held that constituted sex discrimination under Title VII of the Civil Rights Act of 1964. The significance of the Supreme Court`s ruling was twofold. First, it established that gender stereotyping is actionable as sex discrimination. Second, it established the mixed-motive framework that enables employees to prove discrimination when other, lawful reasons for the adverse employment action exist alongside discriminatory motivations or reasons.

Exam Probability: **Medium**

53. *Answer choices:*

(see index for correct answer)

- a. Glenn v. Brumby
- b. Hosanna-Tabor Evangelical Lutheran Church and School v. Equal Employment Opportunity Commission
- c. Price Waterhouse v. Hopkins
- d. Executive Order 11375

Guidance: level 1

:: Business ethics ::

_________ is a pejorative term for a workplace that has very poor, socially unacceptable working conditions. The work may be difficult, dangerous, climatically challenged or underpaid. Workers in _________ s may work long hours with low pay, regardless of laws mandating overtime pay or a minimum wage; child labor laws may also be violated. The Fair Labor Association`s "2006 Annual Public Report" inspected factories for FLA compliance in 18 countries including Bangladesh, El Salvador, Colombia, Guatemala, Malaysia, Thailand, Tunisia, Turkey, China, India, Vietnam, Honduras, Indonesia, Brazil, Mexico, and the US. The U.S. Department of Labor`s "2015 Findings on the Worst Forms of Child Labor" found that "18 countries did not meet the International Labour Organization`s recommendation for an adequate number of inspectors."

Exam Probability: **Low**

54. *Answer choices:*

(see index for correct answer)

- a. Eating your own dog food
- b. Sweatshop
- c. Earnings quality
- d. Jewish business ethics

Guidance: level 1

:: Employment compensation ::

_________ is a notional derivative of a Health Reimbursement Arrangement , a type of US employer-funded health benefit plan that reimburses employees for out-of-pocket medical expenses and, in limited cases, to pay for health insurance plan premiums.

Exam Probability: **Low**

55. *Answer choices:*

(see index for correct answer)

- a. Protection of Wages Convention, 1949
- b. Annual leave
- c. Basic Income Earth Network
- d. Health Reimbursement Account

Guidance: level 1

:: Outsourcing ::

_________ is the practice of sourcing from the global market for goods and services across geopolitical boundaries. _________ often aims to exploit global efficiencies in the delivery of a product or service. These efficiencies include low cost skilled labor, low cost raw material and other economic factors like tax breaks and low trade tariffs. A large number of Information Technology projects and Services, including IS Applications and Mobile Apps and database services are outsourced globally to countries like Pakistan and India for more economical pricing.

Exam Probability: **Low**

56. *Answer choices:*

(see index for correct answer)

- a. Application Management Services Framework
- b. IGATE
- c. Strategic sourcing
- d. Transition methodology

Guidance: level 1

:: Legal terms ::

_________ , a form of alternative dispute resolution , is a way to resolve disputes outside the courts. The dispute will be decided by one or more persons , which renders the " _________ award". An _________ award is legally binding on both sides and enforceable in the courts.

Exam Probability: **High**

57. *Answer choices:*

(see index for correct answer)

- a. Arbitration
- b. Objection
- c. Prejudice

- d. European Authorized Representative

Guidance: level 1

:: Survey methodology ::

A _________ is the procedure of systematically acquiring and recording information about the members of a given population. The term is used mostly in connection with national population and housing _________ es; other common _________ es include agriculture, business, and traffic _________ es. The United Nations defines the essential features of population and housing _________ es as "individual enumeration, universality within a defined territory, simultaneity and defined periodicity", and recommends that population _________ es be taken at least every 10 years. United Nations recommendations also cover _________ topics to be collected, official definitions, classifications and other useful information to co-ordinate international practice.

Exam Probability: **Low**

58. *Answer choices:*

(see index for correct answer)

- a. Census
- b. Survey sampling
- c. Enterprise feedback management
- d. National Health Interview Survey

Guidance: level 1

:: Analysis ::

__________ is the process of breaking a complex topic or substance into smaller parts in order to gain a better understanding of it. The technique has been applied in the study of mathematics and logic since before Aristotle , though __________ as a formal concept is a relatively recent development.

Exam Probability: **Medium**

59. *Answer choices:*

(see index for correct answer)

- a. Pinch analysis
- b. Analysis
- c. EATPUT
- d. Water pinch analysis

Guidance: level 1

Information systems

Information systems (IS) are formal, sociotechnical, organizational systems designed to collect, process, store, and distribute information. In a sociotechnical perspective Information Systems are composed by four components: technology, process, people and organizational structure.

:: Business process ::

A __________ or business method is a collection of related, structured activities or tasks by people or equipment which in a specific sequence produce a service or product for a particular customer or customers. __________ es occur at all organizational levels and may or may not be visible to the customers. A __________ may often be visualized as a flowchart of a sequence of activities with interleaving decision points or as a process matrix of a sequence of activities with relevance rules based on data in the process. The benefits of using __________ es include improved customer satisfaction and improved agility for reacting to rapid market change. Process-oriented organizations break down the barriers of structural departments and try to avoid functional silos.

Exam Probability: **Medium**

1. *Answer choices:*

(see index for correct answer)

- a. Real-time enterprise
- b. Hi-tech export
- c. Business Motivation Model
- d. PNMsoft

Guidance: level 1

:: Google services ::

_________ is a web mapping service developed by Google. It offers satellite imagery, aerial photography, street maps, 360° panoramic views of streets , real-time traffic conditions, and route planning for traveling by foot, car, bicycle and air , or public transportation.

Exam Probability: **High**

2. *Answer choices:*

(see index for correct answer)

- a. Google Art Project
- b. Google Translator Toolkit
- c. Google Videos
- d. Google Audio Indexing

Guidance: level 1

:: Data management ::

_________ is a data management concept concerning the capability that enables an organization to ensure that high data quality exists throughout the complete lifecycle of the data. The key focus areas of _________ include availability, usability, consistency, data integrity and data security and includes establishing processes to ensure effective data management throughout the enterprise such as accountability for the adverse effects of poor data quality and ensuring that the data which an enterprise has can be used by the entire organization.

Exam Probability: **High**

3. *Answer choices:*

(see index for correct answer)

- a. Data governance
- b. Client-side persistent data
- c. Rainbow Storage
- d. Storage model

Guidance: level 1

:: ::

A _________ is a computer network that interconnects computers within a limited area such as a residence, school, laboratory, university campus or office building. By contrast, a wide area network not only covers a larger geographic distance, but also generally involves leased telecommunication circuits.

Exam Probability: **Low**

4. *Answer choices:*

(see index for correct answer)

- a. imperative
- b. co-culture

- c. Local Area Network
- d. hierarchical

Guidance: level 1

:: Internet governance ::

A _________ is one of the domains at the highest level in the hierarchical Domain Name System of the Internet. The _________ names are installed in the root zone of the name space. For all domains in lower levels, it is the last part of the domain name, that is, the last label of a fully qualified domain name. For example, in the domain name www.example.com, the _________ is com. Responsibility for management of most _________ s is delegated to specific organizations by the Internet Corporation for Assigned Names and Numbers , which operates the Internet Assigned Numbers Authority , and is in charge of maintaining the DNS root zone.

Exam Probability: **High**

5. *Answer choices:*

(see index for correct answer)

- a. Routing Assets Database
- b. Q-CERT
- c. Top-level domain
- d. Foretec Seminars

Guidance: level 1

:: Service-oriented (business computing) ::

__________ is a software licensing and delivery model in which software is licensed on a subscription basis and is centrally hosted. It is sometimes referred to as "on-demand software", and was formerly referred to as "software plus services" by Microsoft. SaaS is typically accessed by users using a thin client, e.g. via a web browser. SaaS has become a common delivery model for many business applications, including office software, messaging software, payroll processing software, DBMS software, management software, CAD software, development software, gamification, virtualization, accounting, collaboration, customer relationship management , Management Information Systems , enterprise resource planning , invoicing, human resource management , talent acquisition, learning management systems, content management , Geographic Information Systems , and service desk management. SaaS has been incorporated into the strategy of nearly all leading enterprise software companies.

Exam Probability: **High**

6. *Answer choices:*

(see index for correct answer)

- a. Service-oriented architecture
- b. Barracuda Networks
- c. Contact Telecom
- d. Software as a service

Guidance: level 1

:: E-commerce ::

__________ , cybersecurity or information technology security is the protection of computer systems from theft or damage to their hardware, software or electronic data, as well as from disruption or misdirection of the services they provide.

Exam Probability: **High**

7. *Answer choices:*

(see index for correct answer)

- a. Computer security
- b. United Nations Convention on the Use of Electronic Communications in International Contracts
- c. The Cluetrain Manifesto
- d. TXT402

Guidance: level 1

:: Information technology management ::

B2B is often contrasted with business-to-consumer . In B2B commerce, it is often the case that the parties to the relationship have comparable negotiating power, and even when they do not, each party typically involves professional staff and legal counsel in the negotiation of terms, whereas B2C is shaped to a far greater degree by economic implications of information asymmetry. However, within a B2B context, large companies may have many commercial, resource and information advantages over smaller businesses. The United Kingdom government, for example, created the post of Small Business Commissioner under the Enterprise Act 2016 to "enable small businesses to resolve disputes" and "consider complaints by small business suppliers about payment issues with larger businesses that they supply."

Exam Probability: **Medium**

8. *Answer choices:*

(see index for correct answer)

- a. Business Information Services Library
- b. Business transaction performance
- c. Novo Solutions
- d. Infoblox

Guidance: level 1

:: Internet privacy ::

An __________ is a private network accessible only to an organization`s staff. Often, a wide range of information and services are available on an organization`s internal __________ that are unavailable to the public, unlike the Internet. A company-wide __________ can constitute an important focal point of internal communication and collaboration, and provide a single starting point to access internal and external resources. In its simplest form, an __________ is established with the technologies for local area networks and wide area networks . Many modern __________ s have search engines, user profiles, blogs, mobile apps with notifications, and events planning within their infrastructure.

Exam Probability: **High**

9. *Answer choices:*

(see index for correct answer)

- a. Opportunistic encryption
- b. Intranet
- c. Anonymous web browsing
- d. 2010 Duke University faux sex thesis controversy

Guidance: level 1

:: Confidence tricks ::

__________ is the fraudulent attempt to obtain sensitive information such as usernames, passwords and credit card details by disguising oneself as a trustworthy entity in an electronic communication. Typically carried out by email spoofing or instant messaging, it often directs users to enter personal information at a fake website which matches the look and feel of the legitimate site.

Exam Probability: **Medium**

10. *Answer choices:*

(see index for correct answer)

- a. Shyster
- b. Badger game
- c. Scams in intellectual property
- d. Phishing

Guidance: level 1

:: Global Positioning System ::

The __________ , originally Navstar GPS, is a satellite-based radionavigation system owned by the United States government and operated by the United States Air Force. It is a global navigation satellite system that provides geolocation and time information to a GPS receiver anywhere on or near the Earth where there is an unobstructed line of sight to four or more GPS satellites. Obstacles such as mountains and buildings block the relatively weak GPS signals.

Exam Probability: **High**

11. *Answer choices:*

(see index for correct answer)

- a. Waypoint
- b. GTX Corp
- c. GeoSpy
- d. Global Positioning System

Guidance: level 1

:: Marketing ::

__________ is a business model in which consumers create value and businesses consume that value. For example, when a consumer writes reviews or when a consumer gives a useful idea for new product development then that consumer is creating value for the business if the business adopts the input. In the C2B model, a reverse auction or demand collection model, enables buyers to name or demand their own price, which is often binding, for a specific good or service. Inside of a consumer to business market the roles involved in the transaction must be established and the consumer must offer something of value to the business.

Exam Probability: **Low**

12. *Answer choices:*

(see index for correct answer)

- a. Pick and pack
- b. Consumer-to-business
- c. Pricing strategies
- d. Product planning

Guidance: level 1

:: Digital rights management ::

_________ tools or technological protection measures are a set of access control technologies for restricting the use of proprietary hardware and copyrighted works. DRM technologies try to control the use, modification, and distribution of copyrighted works , as well as systems within devices that enforce these policies.

Exam Probability: **Low**

13. *Answer choices:*

(see index for correct answer)

- a. Digital rights management
- b. Always-on DRM
- c. Conditional access
- d. Software protection dongle

Guidance: level 1

:: Virtual reality ::

_________ is an experience taking place within simulated and immersive environments that can be similar to or completely different from the real world. Applications of _________ can include entertainment and educational purposes . Other, distinct types of VR style technology include augmented reality and mixed reality.

Exam Probability: **Low**

14. *Answer choices:*

(see index for correct answer)

- a. Amateur flight simulation
- b. Virtual reality
- c. MotionVR
- d. Imagination age

Guidance: level 1

:: Policy ::

A _________ is a statement or a legal document that discloses some or all of the ways a party gathers, uses, discloses, and manages a customer or client`s data. It fulfills a legal requirement to protect a customer or client`s privacy. Personal information can be anything that can be used to identify an individual, not limited to the person`s name, address, date of birth, marital status, contact information, ID issue, and expiry date, financial records, credit information, medical history, where one travels, and intentions to acquire goods and services. In the case of a business it is often a statement that declares a party`s policy on how it collects, stores, and releases personal information it collects. It informs the client what specific information is collected, and whether it is kept confidential, shared with partners, or sold to other firms or enterprises. Privacy policies typically represent a broader, more generalized treatment, as opposed to data use statements, which tend to be more detailed and specific.

Exam Probability: **High**

15. *Answer choices:*

(see index for correct answer)

- a. Privacy policy
- b. Multifunctionality in agriculture
- c. Veterinary Feed Directive
- d. Overton window

Guidance: level 1

:: Survey methodology ::

A _________ is the procedure of systematically acquiring and recording information about the members of a given population. The term is used mostly in connection with national population and housing _________ es; other common _________ es include agriculture, business, and traffic _________ es. The United Nations defines the essential features of population and housing _________ es as "individual enumeration, universality within a defined territory, simultaneity and defined periodicity", and recommends that population _________ es be taken at least every 10 years. United Nations recommendations also cover _________ topics to be collected, official definitions, classifications and other useful information to co-ordinate international practice.

Exam Probability: **High**

16. *Answer choices:*

(see index for correct answer)

- a. Self-report
- b. Survey sampling
- c. Public opinion
- d. Census

Guidance: level 1

:: Information technology ::

__________ is the use of computers to store, retrieve, transmit, and manipulate data, or information, often in the context of a business or other enterprise. IT is considered to be a subset of information and communications technology . An __________ system is generally an information system, a communications system or, more specifically speaking, a computer system – including all hardware, software and peripheral equipment – operated by a limited group of users.

Exam Probability: **Medium**

17. *Answer choices:*

(see index for correct answer)

- a. Omniview technology
- b. Design for All
- c. Information society
- d. Information technology

Guidance: level 1

:: E-commerce ::

__________ is a method of e-commerce where shoppers` friends become involved in the shopping experience. __________ attempts to use technology to mimic the social interactions found in physical malls and stores. With the rise of mobile devices, __________ is now extending beyond the online world and into the offline world of shopping.

Exam Probability: **Medium**

18. *Answer choices:*

(see index for correct answer)

- a. Helpling
- b. Transactional Link
- c. Social shopping
- d. EPAS

Guidance: level 1

:: Data management ::

__________ involves combining data residing in different sources and providing users with a unified view of them. This process becomes significant in a variety of situations, which include both commercial and scientific domains. __________ appears with increasing frequency as the volume and the need to share existing data explodes. It has become the focus of extensive theoretical work, and numerous open problems remain unsolved. __________ encourages collaboration between internal as well as external users

Exam Probability: **Low**

19. *Answer choices:*

(see index for correct answer)

- a. Operational system

- b. Data integration
- c. Data bank
- d. CERF

Guidance: level 1

:: ::

The __________ is a unit of digital information that most commonly consists of eight bits, representing a binary number. Historically, the __________ was the number of bits used to encode a single character of text in a computer and for this reason it is the smallest addressable unit of memory in many computer architectures.

Exam Probability: **Low**

20. *Answer choices:*

(see index for correct answer)

- a. Character
- b. Byte
- c. levels of analysis
- d. co-culture

Guidance: level 1

:: Internet marketing ::

_________ is the measurement, collection, analysis and reporting of web data for purposes of understanding and optimizing web usage. However, _________ is not just a process for measuring web traffic but can be used as a tool for business and market research, and to assess and improve the effectiveness of a website. _________ applications can also help companies measure the results of traditional print or broadcast advertising campaigns. It helps one to estimate how traffic to a website changes after the launch of a new advertising campaign. _________ provides information about the number of visitors to a website and the number of page views. It helps gauge traffic and popularity trends which is useful for market research.

Exam Probability: **Low**

21. *Answer choices:*

(see index for correct answer)

- a. Web analytics
- b. Ad text optimization
- c. Micro content
- d. Crown Partners

Guidance: level 1

:: Information systems ::

A __________ is an information system used for decision-making, and for the coordination, control, analysis, and visualization of information in an organization; especially in a company.

Exam Probability: **High**

22. *Answer choices:*

(see index for correct answer)

- a. Self-service software vendors
- b. Electronic Case Filing System
- c. Management information system
- d. Content management system

Guidance: level 1

:: Web security exploits ::

A __________ is a baked or cooked food that is small, flat and sweet. It usually contains flour, sugar and some type of oil or fat. It may include other ingredients such as raisins, oats, chocolate chips, nuts, etc.

Exam Probability: **High**

23. *Answer choices:*

(see index for correct answer)

- a. Cookie
- b. Browser exploit
- c. HTTP header injection
- d. HTTP response splitting

Guidance: level 1

:: Systems theory ::

A _________ is a group of interacting or interrelated entities that form a unified whole. A _________ is delineated by its spatial and temporal boundaries, surrounded and influenced by its environment, described by its structure and purpose and expressed in its functioning.

Exam Probability: **Low**

24. *Answer choices:*

(see index for correct answer)

- a. process system
- b. decentralized system
- c. subsystem
- d. management system

Guidance: level 1

:: Finance ::

_________ is a financial estimate intended to help buyers and owners determine the direct and indirect costs of a product or system. It is a management accounting concept that can be used in full cost accounting or even ecological economics where it includes social costs.

Exam Probability: **High**

25. *Answer choices:*

(see index for correct answer)

- a. XBRLS
- b. Total cost of ownership
- c. Liquid Tradable Securities
- d. Reverse greenshoe

Guidance: level 1

:: Management ::

In business, a _________ is the attribute that allows an organization to outperform its competitors. A _________ may include access to natural resources, such as high-grade ores or a low-cost power source, highly skilled labor, geographic location, high entry barriers, and access to new technology.

Exam Probability: **High**

26. *Answer choices:*

(see index for correct answer)

- a. Context analysis
- b. Design management
- c. Managerial economics
- d. Competitive advantage

Guidance: level 1

:: Computer security standards ::

The _________ for Information Technology Security Evaluation is an international standard for computer security certification. It is currently in version 3.1 revision 5.

Exam Probability: **Medium**

27. *Answer choices:*

(see index for correct answer)

- a. IEC 60870-6
- b. Blacker
- c. S/MIME
- d. Common Criteria

Guidance: level 1

:: Identity management ::

_________ is the ability of an individual or group to seclude themselves, or information about themselves, and thereby express themselves selectively. The boundaries and content of what is considered private differ among cultures and individuals, but share common themes. When something is private to a person, it usually means that something is inherently special or sensitive to them. The domain of _________ partially overlaps with security , which can include the concepts of appropriate use, as well as protection of information. _________ may also take the form of bodily integrity.

Exam Probability: **Medium**

28. *Answer choices:*

(see index for correct answer)

- a. Scott Mitic
- b. Privacy
- c. Credential
- d. Common Indexing Protocol

Guidance: level 1

:: E-commerce ::

Customer to customer markets provide an innovative way to allow customers to interact with each other. Traditional markets require business to customer relationships, in which a customer goes to the business in order to purchase a product or service. In customer to customer markets, the business facilitates an environment where customers can sell goods or services to each other. Other types of markets include business to business and business to customer .

Exam Probability: **Medium**

29. *Answer choices:*

(see index for correct answer)

- a. Consumer-to-consumer
- b. Cart32
- c. Scriptlance
- d. Digital distribution

Guidance: level 1

:: Big data ::

_________ is the discovery, interpretation, and communication of meaningful patterns in data; and the process of applying those patterns towards effective decision making. In other words, _________ can be understood as the connective tissue between data and effective decision making, within an organization. Especially valuable in areas rich with recorded information, _________ relies on the simultaneous application of statistics, computer programming and operations research to quantify performance.

Exam Probability: **High**

30. *Answer choices:*

(see index for correct answer)

- a. SAP HANA
- b. Analytics
- c. CloverETL
- d. Sogamo

Guidance: level 1

:: ::

In communications and information processing, _________ is a system of rules to convert information—such as a letter, word, sound, image, or gesture—into another form or representation, sometimes shortened or secret, for communication through a communication channel or storage in a storage medium. An early example is the invention of language, which enabled a person, through speech, to communicate what they saw, heard, felt, or thought to others. But speech limits the range of communication to the distance a voice can carry, and limits the audience to those present when the speech is uttered. The invention of writing, which converted spoken language into visual symbols, extended the range of communication across space and time.

Exam Probability: **Low**

31. *Answer choices:*

(see index for correct answer)

- a. Code
- b. levels of analysis
- c. hierarchical perspective
- d. Sarbanes-Oxley act of 2002

Guidance: level 1

:: Management ::

A __________ defines or constrains some aspect of business and always resolves to either true or false. __________ s are intended to assert business structure or to control or influence the behavior of the business. __________ s describe the operations, definitions and constraints that apply to an organization. __________ s can apply to people, processes, corporate behavior and computing systems in an organization, and are put in place to help the organization achieve its goals.

Exam Probability: **High**

32. *Answer choices:*

(see index for correct answer)

- a. Business rule
- b. Matrix management
- c. Concept of operations
- d. The Toyota Way

Guidance: level 1

:: Market structure and pricing ::

_________ is a term denoting that a product includes permission to use its source code, design documents, or content. It most commonly refers to the open-source model, in which open-source software or other products are released under an open-source license as part of the open-source-software movement. Use of the term originated with software, but has expanded beyond the software sector to cover other open content and forms of open collaboration.

Exam Probability: **Medium**

33. *Answer choices:*

(see index for correct answer)

- a. industry concentration
- b. Open-source economics
- c. Installed base
- d. Open source

Guidance: level 1

:: Transaction processing ::

In _________ , information systems typically facilitate and manage transaction-oriented applications.

Exam Probability: **Low**

34. *Answer choices:*

(see index for correct answer)

- a. Transactions per second
- b. In-database processing
- c. Consistency model
- d. CloudTran

Guidance: level 1

:: Management ::

_________ is the identification of an organization`s assets , followed by the development, documentation, and implementation of policies and procedures for protecting these assets.

Exam Probability: **High**

35. *Answer choices:*

(see index for correct answer)

- a. Managerial Psychology
- b. Business-oriented architecture
- c. Security management
- d. Managerial economics

Guidance: level 1

:: Knowledge engineering ::

The _________ is an extension of the World Wide Web through standards by the World Wide Web Consortium . The standards promote common data formats and exchange protocols on the Web, most fundamentally the Resource Description Framework . According to the W3C, "The _________ provides a common framework that allows data to be shared and reused across application, enterprise, and community boundaries". The _________ is therefore regarded as an integrator across different content, information applications and systems.

Exam Probability: **Low**

36. *Answer choices:*

(see index for correct answer)

- a. Semantic Web
- b. Collaborative innovation network
- c. DriveWorks
- d. Information Routing Group

Guidance: level 1

:: Sound recording ::

__________ is a medium for magnetic recording, made of a thin, magnetizable coating on a long, narrow strip of plastic film. It was developed in Germany in 1928, based on magnetic wire recording. Devices that record and play back audio and video using __________ are tape recorders and video tape recorders respectively. A device that stores computer data on __________ is known as a tape drive.

Exam Probability: **High**

37. *Answer choices:*

(see index for correct answer)

- a. Magnetic tape
- b. Flanging
- c. Pitch shift
- d. Holophonics

Guidance: level 1

:: Computer file formats ::

__________ is a communication protocol for peer-to-peer file sharing which is used to distribute data and electronic files over the Internet.

Exam Probability: **Low**

38. *Answer choices:*

(see index for correct answer)

- a. IGES
- b. Secure Digital Container
- c. BAI
- d. IMelody

Guidance: level 1

:: ::

_________ is software designed to provide a platform for other software. Examples of _________ include operating systems like macOS, Ubuntu and Microsoft Windows, computational science software, game engines, industrial automation, and software as a service applications.

Exam Probability: **Medium**

39. *Answer choices:*

(see index for correct answer)

- a. empathy
- b. interpersonal communication
- c. cultural
- d. Sarbanes-Oxley act of 2002

Guidance: level 1

:: Knowledge representation ::

_________ is the system in which users apply public tags to online items, typically to make those items easier for themselves or others to find later. Over time, this can give rise to a classification system based on those tags and how often they are applied or searched for, in contrast to a taxonomic classification designed by the owners of the content and specified when it is published. This practice is also known as collaborative tagging, social classification, social indexing, and social tagging. _________ was originally "the result of personal free tagging of information [...] for one`s own retrieval", but online sharing and interaction expanded it into collaborative forms. Social tagging is the application of tags in an open online environment where the tags of other users are available to others. Collaborative tagging is tagging performed by a group of users. This type of _________ is commonly used in cooperative and collaborative projects such as research, content repositories, and social bookmarking.

Exam Probability: **Medium**

40. *Answer choices:*

(see index for correct answer)

- a. Open world assumption
- b. User modeling
- c. Semantic similarity network
- d. Visual hierarchy

Guidance: level 1

:: Data management ::

A _________ is a place where you can store data. Commonly used to refer to a column in a database or a field in a data entry form or web form.

Exam Probability: **Medium**

41. *Answer choices:*

(see index for correct answer)

- a. Data field
- b. Hierarchical classifier
- c. Asset Description Metadata Schema
- d. Match report

Guidance: level 1

:: Virtual economies ::

_________ is an online virtual world, developed and owned by the San Francisco-based firm Linden Lab and launched on June 23, 2003. By 2013, _________ had approximately one million regular users; at the end of 2017 active user count totals "between 800,000 and 900,000". In many ways, _________ is similar to massively multiplayer online role-playing games; however, Linden Lab is emphatic that their creation is not a game: "There is no manufactured conflict, no set objective".

Exam Probability: **Low**

42. *Answer choices:*

(see index for correct answer)

- a. Virtual economy
- b. Final Fantasy XI
- c. Gaia Online
- d. Pardus

Guidance: level 1

:: ::

A _________ is the event in which two or more bodies exert forces on each other in about a relatively short time. Although the most common use of the word _________ refers to incidents in which two or more objects collide with great force, the scientific use of the term implies nothing about the magnitude of the force.

Exam Probability: **High**

43. *Answer choices:*

(see index for correct answer)

- a. co-culture
- b. open system

- c. Collision
- d. personal values

Guidance: level 1

:: ::

A ________ or data centre is a building, dedicated space within a building, or a group of buildings used to house computer systems and associated components, such as telecommunications and storage systems.

Exam Probability: **High**

44. *Answer choices:*

(see index for correct answer)

- a. Data center
- b. Sarbanes-Oxley act of 2002
- c. Character
- d. information systems assessment

Guidance: level 1

:: ::

_________ is a set of values of subjects with respect to qualitative or quantitative variables.

Exam Probability: **Low**

45. *Answer choices:*

(see index for correct answer)

- a. empathy
- b. Character
- c. open system
- d. levels of analysis

Guidance: level 1

:: Business process ::

Business process re-engineering is a business management strategy, originally pioneered in the early 1990s, focusing on the analysis and design of workflows and business processes within an organization. BPR aimed to help organizations fundamentally rethink how they do their work in order to improve customer service, cut operational costs, and become world-class competitors.

Exam Probability: **Low**

46. *Answer choices:*

(see index for correct answer)

- a. Software ecosystem
- b. Business process reengineering
- c. ProcessEdge
- d. Subject-oriented business process management

Guidance: level 1

:: Virtual economies ::

_________ Inc. is an American social game developer running social video game services founded in April 2007 and headquartered in San Francisco, California, United States. The company primarily focuses on mobile and social networking platforms. _________ states its mission as "connecting the world through games."

Exam Probability: **High**

47. *Answer choices:*

(see index for correct answer)

- a. Viximo
- b. Gold farming
- c. Elite: Dangerous
- d. Zynga

Guidance: level 1

:: Transaction processing ::

Transaction processing is information processing in computer science that is divided into individual, indivisible operations called transactions. Each transaction must succeed or fail as a complete unit; it can never be only partially complete.

Exam Probability: **Low**

48. *Answer choices:*

(see index for correct answer)

- a. CloudTran
- b. Transaction processing
- c. Online transaction processing
- d. Transaction server

Guidance: level 1

:: Critical thinking ::

In psychology, _________ is regarded as the cognitive process resulting in the selection of a belief or a course of action among several alternative possibilities. Every _________ process produces a final choice, which may or may not prompt action.

Exam Probability: **Low**

49. *Answer choices:*

(see index for correct answer)

- a. Decision-making
- b. Moral reasoning
- c. Higher-order thinking
- d. Attacking Faulty Reasoning

Guidance: level 1

:: Payment systems ::

__________ s are part of a payment system issued by financial institutions, such as a bank, to a customer that enables its owner to access the funds in the customer`s designated bank accounts, or through a credit account and make payments by electronic funds transfer and access automated teller machines . Such cards are known by a variety of names including bank cards, ATM cards, MAC , client cards, key cards or cash cards.

Exam Probability: **High**

50. *Answer choices:*

(see index for correct answer)

- a. Payment card
- b. PesaDroid

- c. Net Element
- d. Immediate Payment Service

Guidance: level 1

:: Information retrieval ::

_________ is the practice of making content from multiple enterprise-type sources, such as databases and intranets, searchable to a defined audience .

Exam Probability: **High**

51. *Answer choices:*

(see index for correct answer)

- a. Concept Searching Limited
- b. Scientific data archiving
- c. Enterprise search
- d. Globrix

Guidance: level 1

:: Credit cards ::

The _________ Company, also known as Amex, is an American multinational financial services corporation headquartered in Three World Financial Center in New York City. The company was founded in 1850 and is one of the 30 components of the Dow Jones Industrial Average. The company is best known for its charge card, credit card, and traveler's cheque businesses.

Exam Probability: **High**

52. *Answer choices:*

(see index for correct answer)

- a. Accolades Card
- b. American Express
- c. Diners Club International
- d. NexG PrePaid

Guidance: level 1

:: ::

Within the Internet, _________ s are formed by the rules and procedures of the _________ System . Any name registered in the DNS is a _________ . _________ s are used in various networking contexts and for application-specific naming and addressing purposes. In general, a _________ represents an Internet Protocol resource, such as a personal computer used to access the Internet, a server computer hosting a web site, or the web site itself or any other service communicated via the Internet. In 2017, 330.6 million _________ s had been registered.

Exam Probability: **Medium**

53. *Answer choices:*

(see index for correct answer)

- a. Domain name
- b. levels of analysis
- c. interpersonal communication
- d. similarity-attraction theory

Guidance: level 1

:: E-commerce ::

Electronic governance or e-governance is the application of information and communication technology for delivering government services, exchange of information, communication transactions, integration of various stand-alone systems and services between government-to-citizen , government-to-business , __________ , government-to-employees as well as back-office processes and interactions within the entire government framework. Through e-governance, government services are made available to citizens in a convenient, efficient, and transparent manner. The three main target groups that can be distinguished in governance concepts are government, citizens, andbusinesses/interest groups. In e-governance, there are no distinct boundaries.

Exam Probability: **High**

54. *Answer choices:*

(see index for correct answer)

- a. Open Market
- b. Online wallet
- c. Electronic Payment Services
- d. Government-to-government

Guidance: level 1

:: SQL ::

SQL is a domain-specific language used in programming and designed for managing data held in a relational database management system , or for stream processing in a relational data stream management system . It is particularly useful in handling structured data where there are relations between different entities/variables of the data. SQL offers two main advantages over older read/write APIs like ISAM or VSAM. First, it introduced the concept of accessing many records with one single command; and second, it eliminates the need to specify how to reach a record, e.g. with or without an index.

Exam Probability: **Low**

55. *Answer choices:*

(see index for correct answer)

- a. Check constraint
- b. SQL Access Group
- c. Structured query language
- d. Call Level Interface

Guidance: level 1

:: ::

A ________ is a computer file which stores data to be used by a computer application or system, including input and output data. A ________ usually does not contain instructions or code to be executed .

Exam Probability: **Medium**

56. *Answer choices:*

(see index for correct answer)

- a. hierarchical perspective
- b. Data file
- c. process perspective
- d. co-culture

Guidance: level 1

:: Data management ::

__________ , or IG, is the management of information at an organization. __________ balances the use and security of information. __________ helps with legal compliance, operational transparency, and reducing expenditures associated with legal discovery. An organization can establish a consistent and logical framework for employees to handle data through their __________ policies and procedures. These policies guide proper behavior regarding how organizations and their employees handle electronically stored information .

Exam Probability: **High**

57. *Answer choices:*

(see index for correct answer)

- a. NewSQL
- b. Asset Description Metadata Schema
- c. VMDS
- d. Information governance

Guidance: level 1

:: Industrial automation ::

__________ is the technology by which a process or procedure is performed with minimal human assistance. __________ or automatic control is the use of various control systems for operating equipment such as machinery, processes in factories, boilers and heat treating ovens, switching on telephone networks, steering and stabilization of ships, aircraft and other applications and vehicles with minimal or reduced human intervention.

Exam Probability: **Medium**

58. *Answer choices:*

(see index for correct answer)

- a. Advanced Plant Management System
- b. RAPIEnet
- c. CANopen
- d. EtherCAT

Guidance: level 1

:: Process management ::

When used in the context of communication networks, such as Ethernet or packet radio, _________ or network _________ is the rate of successful message delivery over a communication channel. The data these messages belong to may be delivered over a physical or logical link, or it can pass through a certain network node. _________ is usually measured in bits per second , and sometimes in data packets per second or data packets per time slot.

Exam Probability: **Low**

59. *Answer choices:*

(see index for correct answer)

- a. Business process orientation
- b. Contingency allowance

- c. Process specification
- d. Throughput

Guidance: level 1

Marketing

Marketing is the study and management of exchange relationships. Marketing is the business process of creating relationships with and satisfying customers. With its focus on the customer, marketing is one of the premier components of business management.

Marketing is defined by the American Marketing Association as "the activity, set of institutions, and processes for creating, communicating, delivering, and exchanging offerings that have value for customers, clients, partners, and society at large."

:: Trade associations ::

A __________ , also known as an industry trade group, business association, sector association or industry body, is an organization founded and funded by businesses that operate in a specific industry. An industry __________ participates in public relations activities such as advertising, education, political donations, lobbying and publishing, but its focus is collaboration between companies. Associations may offer other services, such as producing conferences, networking or charitable events or offering classes or educational materials. Many associations are non-profit organizations governed by bylaws and directed by officers who are also members.

Exam Probability: **Low**

1. *Answer choices:*

(see index for correct answer)

- a. Intellectual Property Committee
- b. Futures Industry Association
- c. UFFA
- d. Open Access Scholarly Publishers Association

Guidance: level 1

:: Brand management ::

__________ refers to the extent to which customers are able to recall or recognise a brand. __________ is a key consideration in consumer behavior, advertising management, brand management and strategy development. The consumer`s ability to recognise or recall a brand is central to purchasing decision-making. Purchasing cannot proceed unless a consumer is first aware of a product category and a brand within that category. Awareness does not necessarily mean that the consumer must be able to recall a specific brand name, but he or she must be able to recall sufficient distinguishing features for purchasing to proceed. For instance, if a consumer asks her friend to buy her some gum in a "blue pack", the friend would be expected to know which gum to buy, even though neither friend can recall the precise brand name at the time.

Exam Probability: **Low**

2. *Answer choices:*

(see index for correct answer)

- a. Brand preference
- b. Branded content
- c. Brand awareness
- d. Brand culture

Guidance: level 1

:: Business ::

The seller, or the provider of the goods or services, completes a sale in response to an acquisition, appropriation, requisition or a direct interaction with the buyer at the point of sale. There is a passing of title of the item, and the settlement of a price, in which agreement is reached on a price for which transfer of ownership of the item will occur. The seller, not the purchaser typically executes the sale and it may be completed prior to the obligation of payment. In the case of indirect interaction, a person who sells goods or service on behalf of the owner is known as a salesman or saleswoman or salesperson, but this often refers to someone _________ goods in a store/shop, in which case other terms are also common, including salesclerk, shop assistant, and retail clerk.

Exam Probability: **High**

3. *Answer choices:*

(see index for correct answer)

- a. Gray ceiling
- b. Business interoperability interface
- c. Selling
- d. First party leads

Guidance: level 1

:: Belief ::

__________ is an umbrella term of influence. __________ can attempt to influence a person`s beliefs, attitudes, intentions, motivations, or behaviors. In business, __________ is a process aimed at changing a person`s attitude or behavior toward some event, idea, object, or other person, by using written, spoken words or visual tools to convey information, feelings, or reasoning, or a combination thereof. __________ is also an often used tool in the pursuit of personal gain, such as election campaigning, giving a sales pitch, or in trial advocacy. __________ can also be interpreted as using one`s personal or positional resources to change people`s behaviors or attitudes.Systematic __________ is the process through which attitudes or beliefs are leveraged by appeals to logic and reason. Heuristic __________ on the other hand is the process through which attitudes or beliefs are leveraged by appeals to habit or emotion.

Exam Probability: **Medium**

4. *Answer choices:*

(see index for correct answer)

- a. Persuasion
- b. Fides et Ratio
- c. Anthropocentrism
- d. Sententia fidei proxima

Guidance: level 1

:: ::

Retail is the process of selling consumer goods or services to customers through multiple channels of distribution to earn a profit. Retailers satisfy demand identified through a supply chain. The term "retailer" is typically applied where a service provider fills the small orders of a large number of individuals, who are end-users, rather than large orders of a small number of wholesale, corporate or government clientele. Shopping generally refers to the act of buying products. Sometimes this is done to obtain final goods, including necessities such as food and clothing; sometimes it takes place as a recreational activity. Recreational shopping often involves window shopping and browsing: it does not always result in a purchase.

Exam Probability: **High**

5. *Answer choices:*

(see index for correct answer)

- a. Sarbanes-Oxley act of 2002
- b. open system
- c. Character
- d. similarity-attraction theory

Guidance: level 1

:: Marketing ::

__________ is the marketing of products that are presumed to be environmentally safe. It incorporates a broad range of activities, including product modification, changes to the production process, sustainable packaging, as well as modifying advertising. Yet defining __________ is not a simple task where several meanings intersect and contradict each other; an example of this will be the existence of varying social, environmental and retail definitions attached to this term. Other similar terms used are environmental marketing and ecological marketing.

Exam Probability: **Medium**

6. *Answer choices:*

(see index for correct answer)

- a. Promo
- b. Price war
- c. National brand
- d. Green marketing

Guidance: level 1

:: Marketing ::

__________ or stock is the goods and materials that a business holds for the ultimate goal of resale .

Exam Probability: **High**

7. *Answer choices:*

(see index for correct answer)

- a. Product churning
- b. reverse marketing
- c. Inventory
- d. Consumer-to-business

Guidance: level 1

:: ::

__________ , in general use, is a devotion and faithfulness to a nation, cause, philosophy, country, group, or person. Philosophers disagree on what can be an object of __________ , as some argue that __________ is strictly interpersonal and only another human being can be the object of __________ . The definition of __________ in law and political science is the fidelity of an individual to a nation, either one`s nation of birth, or one`s declared home nation by oath .

Exam Probability: **High**

8. *Answer choices:*

(see index for correct answer)

- a. Loyalty
- b. functional perspective
- c. interpersonal communication

- d. surface-level diversity

Guidance: level 1

:: Consumer behaviour ::

__________ refers to the ability of a company or product to retain its customers over some specified period. High __________ means customers of the product or business tend to return to, continue to buy or in some other way not defect to another product or business, or to non-use entirely. Selling organizations generally attempt to reduce customer defections. __________ starts with the first contact an organization has with a customer and continues throughout the entire lifetime of a relationship and successful retention efforts take this entire lifecycle into account. A company`s ability to attract and retain new customers is related not only to its product or services, but also to the way it services its existing customers, the value the customers actually generate as a result of utilizing the solutions, and the reputation it creates within and across the marketplace.

Exam Probability: **Low**

9. *Answer choices:*

(see index for correct answer)

- a. Shopping Neutral
- b. University of Michigan Consumer Sentiment Index
- c. Customer retention
- d. Canadian Index of Consumer Confidence

Guidance: level 1

:: ::

A _________ consists of one people who live in the same dwelling and share meals. It may also consist of a single family or another group of people. A dwelling is considered to contain multiple _________ s if meals or living spaces are not shared. The _________ is the basic unit of analysis in many social, microeconomic and government models, and is important to economics and inheritance.

Exam Probability: **High**

10. *Answer choices:*

(see index for correct answer)

- a. surface-level diversity
- b. empathy
- c. hierarchical perspective
- d. corporate values

Guidance: level 1

:: Credit cards ::

The ________ Company, also known as Amex, is an American multinational financial services corporation headquartered in Three World Financial Center in New York City. The company was founded in 1850 and is one of the 30 components of the Dow Jones Industrial Average. The company is best known for its charge card, credit card, and traveler`s cheque businesses.

Exam Probability: **Low**

11. *Answer choices:*

(see index for correct answer)

- a. Ingenico
- b. Access
- c. Fuel card
- d. CardLab

Guidance: level 1

:: ::

In international relations, ________ is – from the perspective of governments – a voluntary transfer of resources from one country to another.

Exam Probability: **High**

12. *Answer choices:*

(see index for correct answer)

- a. personal values
- b. cultural
- c. empathy
- d. surface-level diversity

Guidance: level 1

:: ::

A __________ is a discussion or informational website published on the World Wide Web consisting of discrete, often informal diary-style text entries . Posts are typically displayed in reverse chronological order, so that the most recent post appears first, at the top of the web page. Until 2009, __________ s were usually the work of a single individual, occasionally of a small group, and often covered a single subject or topic. In the 2010s, "multi-author __________ s" emerged, featuring the writing of multiple authors and sometimes professionally edited. MABs from newspapers, other media outlets, universities, think tanks, advocacy groups, and similar institutions account for an increasing quantity of __________ traffic. The rise of Twitter and other "micro __________ ging" systems helps integrate MABs and single-author __________ s into the news media. __________ can also be used as a verb, meaning to maintain or add content to a __________ .

Exam Probability: **High**

13. *Answer choices:*

(see index for correct answer)

- a. Blog

- b. levels of analysis
- c. hierarchical perspective
- d. surface-level diversity

Guidance: level 1

:: Marketing terminology ::

_________ is used in marketing to describe the inability to assess the value gained from engaging in an activity using any tangible evidence. It is often used to describe services where there is no tangible product that the customer can purchase, that can be seen or touched.

Exam Probability: **High**

14. *Answer choices:*

(see index for correct answer)

- a. sponsored link
- b. Factory-to-consumer
- c. Intangibility
- d. Payback period

Guidance: level 1

:: ::

In law, a __________ is a coming together of parties to a dispute, to present information in a tribunal, a formal setting with the authority to adjudicate claims or disputes. One form of tribunal is a court. The tribunal, which may occur before a judge, jury, or other designated trier of fact, aims to achieve a resolution to their dispute.

Exam Probability: **Medium**

15. *Answer choices:*

(see index for correct answer)

- a. open system
- b. corporate values
- c. Trial
- d. empathy

Guidance: level 1

:: Organizational structure ::

An __________ defines how activities such as task allocation, coordination, and supervision are directed toward the achievement of organizational aims.

Exam Probability: **High**

16. *Answer choices:*

(see index for correct answer)

- a. Unorganisation
- b. Organization of the New York City Police Department
- c. The Starfish and the Spider
- d. Followership

Guidance: level 1

:: Business ::

In commerce, _________ is the product of an interaction between an organization and a customer over the duration of their relationship.This interaction is made up of three parts: the customer journey, the brand touchpoints the customer interacts with, and the environments the _________ s during their experience. A good _________ means that the individual`s experience during all points of contact matches the individual`s expectations. Gartner asserts the importance of managing the customer`s experience.

Exam Probability: **Medium**

17. *Answer choices:*

(see index for correct answer)

- a. Casengo
- b. Customer experience
- c. Policy capturing
- d. Corporate housing

Guidance: level 1

:: Consumer behaviour ::

Convenient procedures, products and services are those intended to increase ease in accessibility, save resources and decrease frustration. A modern _________ is a labor-saving device, service or substance which make a task easier or more efficient than a traditional method. _________ is a relative concept, and depends on context. For example, automobiles were once considered a _________, yet today are regarded as a normal part of life.

Exam Probability: **Low**

18. *Answer choices:*

(see index for correct answer)

- a. Itamar Simonson
- b. Conspicuous conservation
- c. Almost ideal demand system
- d. Gruen transfer

Guidance: level 1

:: ::

_________ or commercialisation is the process of introducing a new product or production method into commerce—making it available on the market. The term often connotes especially entry into the mass market , but it also includes a move from the laboratory into commerce. Many technologies begin in a research and development laboratory or in an inventor`s workshop and may not be practical for commercial use in their infancy . The "development" segment of the "research and development" spectrum requires time and money as systems are engineered with a view to making the product or method a paying commercial proposition. The product launch of a new product is the final stage of new product development - at this point advertising, sales promotion, and other marketing efforts encourage commercial adoption of the product or method. Beyond _________ can lie consumerization .

Exam Probability: **Medium**

19. *Answer choices:*

(see index for correct answer)

- a. Commercialization
- b. imperative
- c. hierarchical
- d. corporate values

Guidance: level 1

:: Evaluation methods ::

__________ is a scientific method of observation to gather non-numerical data. This type of research "refers to the meanings, concepts definitions, characteristics, metaphors, symbols, and description of things" and not to their "counts or measures." This research answers why and how a certain phenomenon may occur rather than how often. __________ approaches are employed across many academic disciplines, focusing particularly on the human elements of the social and natural sciences; in less academic contexts, areas of application include qualitative market research, business, service demonstrations by non-profits, and journalism.

Exam Probability: **High**

20. *Answer choices:*

(see index for correct answer)

- a. Design science
- b. Reference class forecasting
- c. Qualitative research
- d. Economic impact analysis

Guidance: level 1

:: ::

__________ is a concept of English common law and is a necessity for simple contracts but not for special contracts . The concept has been adopted by other common law jurisdictions, including the US.

Exam Probability: **Low**

21. *Answer choices:*

(see index for correct answer)

- a. Consideration
- b. co-culture
- c. information systems assessment
- d. personal values

Guidance: level 1

:: Industry ::

__________ describes various measures of the efficiency of production. Often , a __________ measure is expressed as the ratio of an aggregate output to a single input or an aggregate input used in a production process, i.e. output per unit of input. Most common example is the labour __________ measure, e.g., such as GDP per worker. There are many different definitions of __________ and the choice among them depends on the purpose of the __________ measurement and/or data availability. The key source of difference between various __________ measures is also usually related to how the outputs and the inputs are aggregated into scalars to obtain such a ratio-type measure of __________ .

Exam Probability: **Low**

22. *Answer choices:*

(see index for correct answer)

- a. Industrial region
- b. Fordism
- c. Industrial archaeology
- d. Straw plaiting

Guidance: level 1

:: ::

A _________ is any person who contracts to acquire an asset in return for some form of consideration.

Exam Probability: **High**

23. *Answer choices:*

(see index for correct answer)

- a. interpersonal communication
- b. surface-level diversity
- c. Buyer
- d. levels of analysis

Guidance: level 1

:: Health promotion ::

__________ , as defined by the World __________ Organization , is "a state of complete physical, mental and social well-being and not merely the absence of disease or infirmity." This definition has been subject to controversy, as it may have limited value for implementation. __________ may be defined as the ability to adapt and manage physical, mental and social challenges throughout life.

Exam Probability: **Medium**

24. *Answer choices:*

(see index for correct answer)

- a. LivingWorks
- b. National Care Standards
- c. Health
- d. The Gordie Foundation

Guidance: level 1

:: Summary statistics ::

__________ is the number of occurrences of a repeating event per unit of time. It is also referred to as temporal __________ , which emphasizes the contrast to spatial __________ and angular __________ . The period is the duration of time of one cycle in a repeating event, so the period is the reciprocal of the __________ . For example: if a newborn baby's heart beats at a __________ of 120 times a minute, its period—the time interval between beats—is half a second . __________ is an important parameter used in science and engineering to specify the rate of oscillatory and vibratory phenomena, such as mechanical vibrations, audio signals , radio waves, and light.

Exam Probability: **High**

25. *Answer choices:*

(see index for correct answer)

- a. Multiple of the median
- b. Quantile
- c. Frequency distribution
- d. Location parameter

Guidance: level 1

:: Data collection ::

A __________ is an utterance which typically functions as a request for information. __________ s can thus be understood as a kind of illocutionary act in the field of pragmatics or as special kinds of propositions in frameworks of formal semantics such as alternative semantics or inquisitive semantics. The information requested is expected to be provided in the form of an answer. __________ s are often conflated with interrogatives, which are the grammatical forms typically used to achieve them. Rhetorical __________ s, for example, are interrogative in form but may not be considered true __________ s as they are not expected to be answered. Conversely, non-interrogative grammatical structures may be considered __________ s as in the case of the imperative sentence "tell me your name".

Exam Probability: **Low**

26. *Answer choices:*

(see index for correct answer)

- a. European Social Survey
- b. Unstructured data
- c. Question
- d. Guardian

Guidance: level 1

:: Market research ::

_________ is the action of defining, gathering, analyzing, and distributing intelligence about products, customers, competitors, and any aspect of the environment needed to support executives and managers in strategic decision making for an organization.

Exam Probability: **Medium**

27. *Answer choices:*

(see index for correct answer)

- a. Cambashi
- b. Cluster sampling
- c. Market research and opinion polling in China
- d. National Analysts

Guidance: level 1

:: Marketing ::

_________ is the percentage of a market accounted for by a specific entity. In a survey of nearly 200 senior marketing managers, 67% responded that they found the revenue- "dollar _________ " metric very useful, while 61% found "unit _________ " very useful.

Exam Probability: **High**

28. *Answer choices:*

(see index for correct answer)

- a. Pricing objectives
- b. Dialogue marketing
- c. Call to action
- d. Need

Guidance: level 1

:: Evaluation methods ::

In natural and social sciences, and sometimes in other fields, __________ is the systematic empirical investigation of observable phenomena via statistical, mathematical, or computational techniques. The objective of __________ is to develop and employ mathematical models, theories, and hypotheses pertaining to phenomena. The process of measurement is central to __________ because it provides the fundamental connection between empirical observation and mathematical expression of quantitative relationships.

Exam Probability: **High**

29. *Answer choices:*

(see index for correct answer)

- a. Quantitative research
- b. Video ethnography
- c. Self-assessment
- d. Creative participation

Guidance: level 1

:: ::

Market segmentation is the activity of dividing a broad consumer or business market, normally consisting of existing and potential customers, into sub-groups of consumers based on some type of shared characteristics. In dividing or segmenting markets, researchers typically look for common characteristics such as shared needs, common interests, similar lifestyles or even similar demographic profiles. The overall aim of segmentation is to identify high yield segments – that is, those segments that are likely to be the most profitable or that have growth potential – so that these can be selected for special attention .

Exam Probability: **Medium**

30. *Answer choices:*

(see index for correct answer)

- a. co-culture
- b. Market segments
- c. functional perspective
- d. Character

Guidance: level 1

:: Brand management ::

In marketing, _________ is the analysis and planning on how a brand is perceived in the market. Developing a good relationship with the target market is essential for _________. Tangible elements of _________ include the product itself; its look, price, and packaging, etc. The intangible elements are the experiences that the consumers share with the brand, and also the relationships they have with the brand. A brand manager would oversee all aspects of the consumer`s brand association as well as relationships with members of the supply chain.

Exam Probability: **Medium**

31. *Answer choices:*

(see index for correct answer)

- a. Brand relationship
- b. DreamWorks Classics
- c. BrandActive
- d. Imation

Guidance: level 1

:: ::

An __________ is a contingent motivator. Traditional __________ s are extrinsic motivators which reward actions to yield a desired outcome. The effectiveness of traditional __________ s has changed as the needs of Western society have evolved. While the traditional __________ model is effective when there is a defined procedure and goal for a task, Western society started to require a higher volume of critical thinkers, so the traditional model became less effective. Institutions are now following a trend in implementing strategies that rely on intrinsic motivations rather than the extrinsic motivations that the traditional __________ s foster.

Exam Probability: **Medium**

32. *Answer choices:*

(see index for correct answer)

- a. Incentive
- b. empathy
- c. deep-level diversity
- d. surface-level diversity

Guidance: level 1

:: Data management ::

In computing, a _________ , also known as an enterprise _________ , is a system used for reporting and data analysis, and is considered a core component of business intelligence. DWs are central repositories of integrated data from one or more disparate sources. They store current and historical data in one single place that are used for creating analytical reports for workers throughout the enterprise.

Exam Probability: **Medium**

33. *Answer choices:*

(see index for correct answer)

- a. Inverted index
- b. Physical schema
- c. Data warehouse
- d. Reference data

Guidance: level 1

:: ::

Competition arises whenever at least two parties strive for a goal which cannot be shared: where one`s gain is the other`s loss .

Exam Probability: **High**

34. *Answer choices:*

(see index for correct answer)

- a. Competitor
- b. co-culture
- c. levels of analysis
- d. similarity-attraction theory

Guidance: level 1

:: Project management ::

__________ is the right to exercise power, which can be formalized by a state and exercised by way of judges, appointed executives of government, or the ecclesiastical or priestly appointed representatives of a God or other deities.

Exam Probability: **Medium**

35. *Answer choices:*

(see index for correct answer)

- a. Constructability
- b. Cash flow diagram
- c. Authority
- d. Financial plan

Guidance: level 1

:: Brand management ::

Marketing communications uses different marketing channels and tools in combination: Marketing communication channels focus on any way a business communicates a message to its desired market, or the market in general. A marketing communication tool can be anything from: advertising, personal selling, direct marketing, sponsorship, communication, and promotion to public relations.

Exam Probability: **Low**

36. *Answer choices:*

(see index for correct answer)

- a. Web 2.0
- b. Sustainability brand
- c. Integrated marketing
- d. Purple Cow: Transform Your Business by Being Remarkable

Guidance: level 1

:: Data ::

Data has two ways of being created or generated. The first is what is called `captured data`, and is found through purposeful investigation or analysis. The second is called `exhaust data`, and is gathered usually by machines or terminals as a secondary function. For example, cash registers, smartphones, and speedometers serve a main function but may collect data as a secondary task. Exhaustive data is usually too large or of little use to process and becomes `transient` or thrown away.

Exam Probability: **High**

37. *Answer choices:*

(see index for correct answer)

- a. S-LINK
- b. Primary data
- c. Synthetic data
- d. Empress Embedded Database

Guidance: level 1

:: Generally Accepted Accounting Principles ::

In accounting, _________ is the income that a business have from its normal business activities, usually from the sale of goods and services to customers. _________ is also referred to as sales or turnover.Some companies receive _________ from interest, royalties, or other fees. _________ may refer to business income in general, or it may refer to the amount, in a monetary unit, earned during a period of time, as in "Last year, Company X had _________ of $42 million". Profits or net income generally imply total _________ minus total expenses in a given period. In accounting, in the balance statement it is a subsection of the Equity section and _________ increases equity, it is often referred to as the "top line" due to its position on the income statement at the very top. This is to be contrasted with the "bottom line" which denotes net income .

Exam Probability: **High**

38. *Answer choices:*

(see index for correct answer)

- a. Revenue
- b. Generally Accepted Accounting Practice
- c. Operating statement
- d. French generally accepted accounting principles

Guidance: level 1

:: Cultural appropriation ::

__________ is a social and economic order that encourages the acquisition of goods and services in ever-increasing amounts. With the industrial revolution, but particularly in the 20th century, mass production led to an economic crisis: there was overproduction—the supply of goods would grow beyond consumer demand, and so manufacturers turned to planned obsolescence and advertising to manipulate consumer spending. In 1899, a book on __________ published by Thorstein Veblen, called The Theory of the Leisure Class, examined the widespread values and economic institutions emerging along with the widespread "leisure time" in the beginning of the 20th century. In it Veblen "views the activities and spending habits of this leisure class in terms of conspicuous and vicarious consumption and waste. Both are related to the display of status and not to functionality or usefulness."

Exam Probability: **High**

39. *Answer choices:*

(see index for correct answer)

- a. Portrayal of Native Americans in film
- b. Cleveland Indians
- c. Cool
- d. Consumerism

Guidance: level 1

:: Management ::

A _________ is a promise of value to be delivered, communicated, and acknowledged. It is also a belief from the customer about how value will be delivered, experienced and acquired.

Exam Probability: **Low**

40. *Answer choices:*

(see index for correct answer)

- a. Logistics support analysis
- b. Professional performances
- c. Value proposition
- d. DMSMS

Guidance: level 1

:: Commerce ::

_________ relates to "the exchange of goods and services, especially on a large scale". It includes legal, economic, political, social, cultural and technological systems that operate in a country or in international trade.

Exam Probability: **Low**

41. *Answer choices:*

(see index for correct answer)

- a. European Retail Round Table
- b. Commerce
- c. Drawback
- d. Kiosk

Guidance: level 1

:: ::

_________ is an abstract concept of management of complex systems according to a set of rules and trends. In systems theory, these types of rules exist in various fields of biology and society, but the term has slightly different meanings according to context. For example.

Exam Probability: **Low**

42. *Answer choices:*

(see index for correct answer)

- a. Regulation
- b. process perspective
- c. Character
- d. functional perspective

Guidance: level 1

:: Monopoly (economics) ::

The _________ of 1890 was a United States antitrust law that regulates competition among enterprises, which was passed by Congress under the presidency of Benjamin Harrison.

Exam Probability: **High**

43. *Answer choices:*

(see index for correct answer)

- a. Sherman Antitrust Act
- b. De facto monopoly
- c. Average cost pricing
- d. Statute of Monopolies

Guidance: level 1

:: Sales ::

_________ is a business discipline which is focused on the practical application of sales techniques and the management of a firm`s sales operations. It is an important business function as net sales through the sale of products and services and resulting profit drive most commercial business. These are also typically the goals and performance indicators of _________ .

Exam Probability: **Low**

44. *Answer choices:*

(see index for correct answer)

- a. Souvenir
- b. Closed-end leasing
- c. Sale and rent back
- d. Split payment

Guidance: level 1

:: Business models ::

A __________ , __________ company or daughter company is a company that is owned or controlled by another company, which is called the parent company, parent, or holding company. The __________ can be a company, corporation, or limited liability company. In some cases it is a government or state-owned enterprise. In some cases, particularly in the music and book publishing industries, subsidiaries are referred to as imprints.

Exam Probability: **Low**

45. *Answer choices:*

(see index for correct answer)

- a. 70/20/10 Model
- b. Dependent growth business model
- c. Organizational architecture
- d. Subsidiary

Guidance: level 1

:: Management ::

In business, a _________ is the attribute that allows an organization to outperform its competitors. A _________ may include access to natural resources, such as high-grade ores or a low-cost power source, highly skilled labor, geographic location, high entry barriers, and access to new technology.

Exam Probability: **High**

46. *Answer choices:*

(see index for correct answer)

- a. Supply chain network
- b. Opera management
- c. Competitive advantage
- d. Adhocracy

Guidance: level 1

:: Advertising ::

_________ is the behavioral and cognitive process of selectively concentrating on a discrete aspect of information, whether deemed subjective or objective, while ignoring other perceivable information. It is a state of arousal. It is the taking possession by the mind in clear and vivid form of one out of what seem several simultaneous objects or trains of thought. Focalization, the concentration of consciousness, is of its essence. _________ has also been described as the allocation of limited cognitive processing resources.

Exam Probability: **Medium**

47. *Answer choices:*

(see index for correct answer)

- a. Retargeter
- b. Change-ad
- c. Retail media
- d. Attention

Guidance: level 1

:: ::

Consumer behaviour is the study of individuals, groups, or organizations and all the activities associated with the purchase, use and disposal of goods and services, including the consumer`s emotional, mental and behavioural responses that precede or follow these activities. Consumer behaviour emerged in the 1940s and 50s as a distinct sub-discipline in the marketing area.

Exam Probability: **Low**

48. *Answer choices:*

(see index for correct answer)

- a. functional perspective
- b. Consumer behavior
- c. interpersonal communication
- d. Sarbanes-Oxley act of 2002

Guidance: level 1

:: ::

_________ consists of using generic or ad hoc methods in an orderly manner to find solutions to problems. Some of the problem-solving techniques developed and used in philosophy, artificial intelligence, computer science, engineering, mathematics, or medicine are related to mental problem-solving techniques studied in psychology.

Exam Probability: **High**

49. *Answer choices:*

(see index for correct answer)

- a. similarity-attraction theory
- b. process perspective

- c. hierarchical
- d. cultural

Guidance: level 1

:: Legal terms ::

A __________ is a person who is called upon to issue a response to a communication made by another. The term is used in legal contexts, in survey methodology, and in psychological conditioning.

Exam Probability: **Low**

50. *Answer choices:*

(see index for correct answer)

- a. Respondent
- b. Hung jury
- c. Force
- d. Duplicity

Guidance: level 1

:: Goods ::

In most contexts, the concept of _________ denotes the conduct that should be preferred when posed with a choice between possible actions. _________ is generally considered to be the opposite of evil, and is of interest in the study of morality, ethics, religion and philosophy. The specific meaning and etymology of the term and its associated translations among ancient and contemporary languages show substantial variation in its inflection and meaning depending on circumstances of place, history, religious, or philosophical context.

Exam Probability: **High**

51. *Answer choices:*

(see index for correct answer)

- a. Neutral good
- b. Private good
- c. Good
- d. Information good

Guidance: level 1

:: Marketing ::

_________ is the process of using surveys to evaluate consumer acceptance of a new product idea prior to the introduction of a product to the market. It is important not to confuse _________ with advertising testing, brand testing and packaging testing; as is sometimes done. _________ focuses on the basic product idea, without the embellishments and puffery inherent in advertising.

Exam Probability: **Medium**

52. *Answer choices:*

(see index for correct answer)

- a. Penetration pricing
- b. Gift suite
- c. Inbound marketing automation
- d. Concept testing

Guidance: level 1

:: Direct marketing ::

__________ is a method of direct marketing in which a salesperson solicits prospective customers to buy products or services, either over the phone or through a subsequent face to face or Web conferencing appointment scheduled during the call. __________ can also include recorded sales pitches programmed to be played over the phone via automatic dialing.

Exam Probability: **Low**

53. *Answer choices:*

(see index for correct answer)

- a. Telemarketing
- b. Drayton Bird

- c. Inktel
- d. Mailshot

Guidance: level 1

:: Product management ::

_________ or brand stretching is a marketing strategy in which a firm marketing a product with a well-developed image uses the same brand name in a different product category. The new product is called a spin-off. Organizations use this strategy to increase and leverage brand equity . An example of a _________ is Jello-gelatin creating Jello pudding pops. It increases awareness of the brand name and increases profitability from offerings in more than one product category.

Exam Probability: **Medium**

54. *Answer choices:*

(see index for correct answer)

- a. Product information
- b. Brand equity
- c. Consumer adoption of technological innovations
- d. Brand extension

Guidance: level 1

:: Television commercials ::

_________ is a phenomenon whereby something new and somehow valuable is formed. The created item may be intangible or a physical object .

Exam Probability: **Low**

55. *Answer choices:*

(see index for correct answer)

- a. Creativity
- b. Cake
- c. Knock-off Nigel
- d. HeadOn

Guidance: level 1

:: Marketing ::

_________ is a pricing strategy where the price of a product is initially set low to rapidly reach a wide fraction of the market and initiate word of mouth. The strategy works on the expectation that customers will switch to the new brand because of the lower price. _________ is most commonly associated with marketing objectives of enlarging market share and exploiting economies of scale or experience.

Exam Probability: **Low**

56. *Answer choices:*

(see index for correct answer)

- a. Penetration pricing
- b. The International Customer Service Institute
- c. DeusM
- d. Breakthrough Moments

Guidance: level 1

:: ::

Employment is a relationship between two parties, usually based on a contract where work is paid for, where one party, which may be a corporation, for profit, not-for-profit organization, co-operative or other entity is the employer and the other is the employee. Employees work in return for payment, which may be in the form of an hourly wage, by piecework or an annual salary, depending on the type of work an employee does or which sector she or he is working in. Employees in some fields or sectors may receive gratuities, bonus payment or stock options. In some types of employment, employees may receive benefits in addition to payment. Benefits can include health insurance, housing, disability insurance or use of a gym. Employment is typically governed by employment laws, regulations or legal contracts.

Exam Probability: **Low**

57. *Answer choices:*

(see index for correct answer)

- a. similarity-attraction theory
- b. empathy
- c. process perspective
- d. levels of analysis

Guidance: level 1

:: Workplace ::

_________ is asystematic determination of a subject`s merit, worth and significance, using criteria governed by a set of standards. It can assist an organization, program, design, project or any other intervention or initiative to assess any aim, realisable concept/proposal, or any alternative, to help in decision-making; or to ascertain the degree of achievement or value in regard to the aim and objectives and results of any such action that has been completed. The primary purpose of _________ , in addition to gaining insight into prior or existing initiatives, is to enable reflection and assist in the identification of future change.

Exam Probability: **Low**

58. *Answer choices:*

(see index for correct answer)

- a. Control freak
- b. Evaluation
- c. Discrimination based on hair texture
- d. Workplace romance

Guidance: level 1

:: Business ::

The seller, or the provider of the goods or services, completes a sale in response to an acquisition, appropriation, requisition or a direct interaction with the buyer at the point of sale. There is a passing of title of the item, and the settlement of a price, in which agreement is reached on a price for which transfer of ownership of the item will occur. The seller, not the purchaser typically executes the sale and it may be completed prior to the obligation of payment. In the case of indirect interaction, a person who sells goods or service on behalf of the owner is known as a _________ man or _________ woman or _________ person, but this often refers to someone selling goods in a store/shop, in which case other terms are also common, including _________ clerk, shop assistant, and retail clerk.

Exam Probability: **High**

59. *Answer choices:*

(see index for correct answer)

- a. Architecture of Interoperable Information Systems
- b. Sales
- c. Counter trade
- d. Les Vergers du Mekong

Guidance: level 1

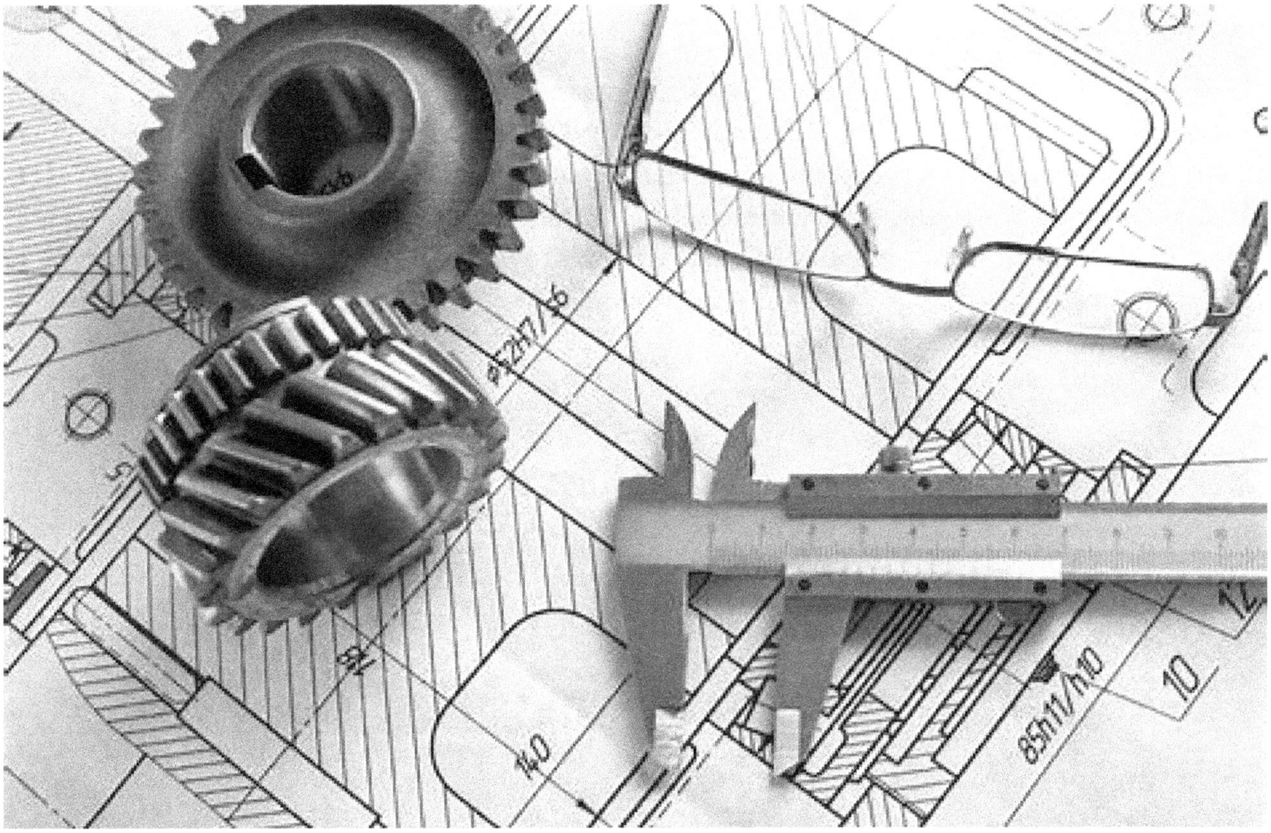

Manufacturing

Manufacturing is the production of merchandise for use or sale using labor and machines, tools, chemical and biological processing, or formulation. The term may refer to a range of human activity, from handicraft to high tech, but is most commonly applied to industrial design , in which raw materials are transformed into finished goods on a large scale. Such finished goods may be sold to other manufacturers for the production of other, more complex products, such as aircraft, household appliances, furniture, sports equipment or automobiles, or sold to wholesalers, who in turn sell them to retailers, who then sell them to end users and consumers.

:: Process management ::

_________ is a statistics package developed at the Pennsylvania State University by researchers Barbara F. Ryan, Thomas A. Ryan, Jr., and Brian L. Joiner in 1972. It began as a light version of OMNITAB 80, a statistical analysis program by NIST. Statistical analysis software such as _________ automates calculations and the creation of graphs, allowing the user to focus more on the analysis of data and the interpretation of results. It is compatible with other _________, Inc. software.

Exam Probability: **High**

1. *Answer choices:*

(see index for correct answer)

- a. business process re-engineering
- b. Integrated business planning
- c. Process lifecycle
- d. Business triage

Guidance: level 1

:: Production and manufacturing ::

_________ consists of organization-wide efforts to "install and make permanent climate where employees continuously improve their ability to provide on demand products and services that customers will find of particular value." "Total" emphasizes that departments in addition to production are obligated to improve their operations; "management" emphasizes that executives are obligated to actively manage quality through funding, training, staffing, and goal setting. While there is no widely agreed-upon approach, TQM efforts typically draw heavily on the previously developed tools and techniques of quality control. TQM enjoyed widespread attention during the late 1980s and early 1990s before being overshadowed by ISO 9000, Lean manufacturing, and Six Sigma.

Exam Probability: **Medium**

2. *Answer choices:*

(see index for correct answer)

- a. Report generator
- b. Total quality management
- c. Assembly line
- d. Cycle time variation

Guidance: level 1

:: ::

__________ is the quantity of three-dimensional space enclosed by a closed surface, for example, the space that a substance or shape occupies or contains. __________ is often quantified numerically using the SI derived unit, the cubic metre. The __________ of a container is generally understood to be the capacity of the container; i. e., the amount of fluid that the container could hold, rather than the amount of space the container itself displaces.Three dimensional mathematical shapes are also assigned __________ s. __________ s of some simple shapes, such as regular, straight-edged, and circular shapes can be easily calculated using arithmetic formulas. __________ s of complicated shapes can be calculated with integral calculus if a formula exists for the shape`s boundary. One-dimensional figures and two-dimensional shapes are assigned zero __________ in the three-dimensional space.

Exam Probability: **Low**

3. *Answer choices:*

(see index for correct answer)

- a. deep-level diversity
- b. hierarchical perspective
- c. surface-level diversity
- d. corporate values

Guidance: level 1

:: Outsourcing ::

__________ is an institutional procurement process that continuously improves and re-evaluates the purchasing activities of a company. In the services industry, __________ refers to a service solution, sometimes called a strategic partnership, which is specifically customized to meet the client's individual needs. In a production environment, it is often considered one component of supply chain management. Modern supply chain management professionals have placed emphasis on defining the distinct differences between __________ and procurement. Procurement operations support tactical day-to-day transactions such as issuing Purchase Orders to suppliers, whereas __________ represents to strategic planning, supplier development, contract negotiation, supply chain infrastructure, and outsourcing models.

Exam Probability: **Low**

4. *Answer choices:*

(see index for correct answer)

- a. Shared services center
- b. Pillsbury Winthrop Shaw Pittman
- c. Online outsourcing
- d. Strategic sourcing

Guidance: level 1

:: Decision theory ::

_________ is a method developed in Japan beginning in 1966 to help transform the voice of the customer into engineering characteristics for a product. Yoji Akao, the original developer, described QFD as a "method to transform qualitative user demands into quantitative parameters, to deploy the functions forming quality, and to deploy methods for achieving the design quality into subsystems and component parts, and ultimately to specific elements of the manufacturing process." The author combined his work in quality assurance and quality control points with function deployment used in value engineering.

Exam Probability: **Low**

5. *Answer choices:*

(see index for correct answer)

- a. Quality function deployment
- b. TOPSIS
- c. Decision-theoretic rough sets
- d. Movement pattern analysis

Guidance: level 1

:: Management accounting ::

" _________ s are the structural determinants of the cost of an activity, reflecting any linkages or interrelationships that affect it". Therefore we could assume that the _________ s determine the cost behavior within the activities, reflecting the links that these have with other activities and relationships that affect them.

Exam Probability: **High**

6. *Answer choices:*

(see index for correct answer)

- a. Relevant cost
- b. Variable cost
- c. Cost driver
- d. Cost accounting

Guidance: level 1

:: Business process ::

A _________ or business method is a collection of related, structured activities or tasks by people or equipment which in a specific sequence produce a service or product for a particular customer or customers. _________ es occur at all organizational levels and may or may not be visible to the customers. A _________ may often be visualized as a flowchart of a sequence of activities with interleaving decision points or as a process matrix of a sequence of activities with relevance rules based on data in the process. The benefits of using _________ es include improved customer satisfaction and improved agility for reacting to rapid market change. Process-oriented organizations break down the barriers of structural departments and try to avoid functional silos.

Exam Probability: **High**

7. *Answer choices:*

(see index for correct answer)

- a. Business process reengineering
- b. Process mapping
- c. Signavio
- d. Information technology outsourcing

Guidance: level 1

:: Alchemical processes ::

In chemistry, a _________ is a special type of homogeneous mixture composed of two or more substances. In such a mixture, a solute is a substance dissolved in another substance, known as a solvent. The mixing process of a _________ happens at a scale where the effects of chemical polarity are involved, resulting in interactions that are specific to solvation. The _________ assumes the phase of the solvent when the solvent is the larger fraction of the mixture, as is commonly the case. The concentration of a solute in a _________ is the mass of that solute expressed as a percentage of the mass of the whole _________ . The term aqueous _________ is when one of the solvents is water.

Exam Probability: **Medium**

8. *Answer choices:*

(see index for correct answer)

- a. Digestion
- b. Solution
- c. Sublimation apparatus

- d. Unity of opposites

Guidance: level 1

:: Management ::

A process is a unique combination of tools, materials, methods, and people engaged in producing a measurable output; for example a manufacturing line for machine parts. All processes have inherent statistical variability which can be evaluated by statistical methods.

Exam Probability: **High**

9. *Answer choices:*

(see index for correct answer)

- a. Completed Staff Work
- b. Production flow analysis
- c. Process capability
- d. Shamrock Organization

Guidance: level 1

:: Business process ::

__________ is the value to an enterprise which is derived from the techniques, procedures, and programs that implement and enhance the delivery of goods and services. __________ is one of the three components of structural capital, itself a component of intellectual capital. __________ can be seen as the value of processes to any entity, whether for profit or not-for profit, but is most commonly used in reference to for-profit entities.

Exam Probability: **Low**

10. *Answer choices:*

(see index for correct answer)

- a. Open door policy
- b. Process-centered design
- c. Captive service
- d. Business communication

Guidance: level 1

:: Building materials ::

__________ is an alloy of iron and carbon, and sometimes other elements. Because of its high tensile strength and low cost, it is a major component used in buildings, infrastructure, tools, ships, automobiles, machines, appliances, and weapons.

Exam Probability: **Low**

11. *Answer choices:*

(see index for correct answer)

- a. Asphalt roll roofing
- b. Mangalore tiles
- c. Fiber roll
- d. Cast earth

Guidance: level 1

:: Industrial engineering ::

The __________ is the design of any task that aims to describe or explain the variation of information under conditions that are hypothesized to reflect the variation. The term is generally associated with experiments in which the design introduces conditions that directly affect the variation, but may also refer to the design of quasi-experiments, in which natural conditions that influence the variation are selected for observation.

Exam Probability: **Medium**

12. *Answer choices:*

(see index for correct answer)

- a. Response surface methodology
- b. Bayesian experimental design
- c. H. Milton Stewart School of Industrial and Systems Engineering
- d. Work sampling

Guidance: level 1

:: Distribution, retailing, and wholesaling ::

_________ measures the performance of a system. Certain goals are defined and the _________ gives the percentage to which those goals should be achieved. Fill rate is different from _________ .

Exam Probability: **High**

13. *Answer choices:*

(see index for correct answer)

- a. Bullwhip effect
- b. Silenzio Music
- c. Sales variance
- d. Service level

Guidance: level 1

:: Quality management ::

_________ is a not-for-profit membership foundation in Brussels, established in 1989 to increase the competitiveness of the European economy. The initial impetus for forming _________ was a response to the work of W. Edwards Deming and the development of the concepts of Total Quality Management.

Exam Probability: **Low**

14. *Answer choices:*

(see index for correct answer)

- a. Quality management system
- b. Dana Ulery
- c. Regulatory translation
- d. EFQM

Guidance: level 1

:: Project management ::

In political science, an _________ is a means by which a petition signed by a certain minimum number of registered voters can force a government to choose to either enact a law or hold a public vote in parliament in what is called indirect _________, or under direct _________, the proposition is immediately put to a plebiscite or referendum, in what is called a Popular initiated Referendum or citizen-initiated referendum).

Exam Probability: **High**

15. *Answer choices:*

(see index for correct answer)

- a. Disciplined Agile Delivery
- b. Scope creep
- c. Deployment Plan
- d. Initiative

Guidance: level 1

:: Unit operations ::

__________ is a discipline of thermal engineering that concerns the generation, use, conversion, and exchange of thermal energy between physical systems. __________ is classified into various mechanisms, such as thermal conduction, thermal convection, thermal radiation, and transfer of energy by phase changes. Engineers also consider the transfer of mass of differing chemical species, either cold or hot, to achieve __________. While these mechanisms have distinct characteristics, they often occur simultaneously in the same system.

Exam Probability: **Medium**

16. *Answer choices:*

(see index for correct answer)

- a. Solvent impregnated resin
- b. Heat transfer

- c. Sedimentation coefficient
- d. Settling

Guidance: level 1

:: Lean manufacturing ::

_________ is a scheduling system for lean manufacturing and just-in-time manufacturing . Taiichi Ohno, an industrial engineer at Toyota, developed _________ to improve manufacturing efficiency. _________ is one method to achieve JIT. The system takes its name from the cards that track production within a factory. For many in the automotive sector, _________ is known as the "Toyota nameplate system" and as such the term is not used by some other automakers.

Exam Probability: **Medium**

17. *Answer choices:*

(see index for correct answer)

- a. Kanban board
- b. 5S
- c. Statistical thinking
- d. Kanban

Guidance: level 1

:: Materials ::

A _________ , also known as a feedstock, unprocessed material, or primary commodity, is a basic material that is used to produce goods, finished products, energy, or intermediate materials which are feedstock for future finished products. As feedstock, the term connotes these materials are bottleneck assets and are highly important with regard to producing other products. An example of this is crude oil, which is a _________ and a feedstock used in the production of industrial chemicals, fuels, plastics, and pharmaceutical goods; lumber is a _________ used to produce a variety of products including all types of furniture. The term " _________ " denotes materials in minimally processed or unprocessed in states; e.g., raw latex, crude oil, cotton, coal, raw biomass, iron ore, air, logs, or water i.e. "...any product of agriculture, forestry, fishing and any other mineral that is in its natural form or which has undergone the transformation required to prepare it for internationally marketing in substantial volumes."

Exam Probability: **High**

18. *Answer choices:*

(see index for correct answer)

- a. Tensometer
- b. Raw material
- c. Samuel Peal
- d. Printing and writing paper

Guidance: level 1

:: Production and manufacturing ::

_________ is a theory of management that analyzes and synthesizes workflows. Its main objective is improving economic efficiency, especially labor productivity. It was one of the earliest attempts to apply science to the engineering of processes and to management. _________ is sometimes known as Taylorism after its founder, Frederick Winslow Taylor.

Exam Probability: **High**

19. *Answer choices:*

(see index for correct answer)

- a. Pegging report
- b. Assembly line
- c. Program evaluation and review technique
- d. Scientific management

Guidance: level 1

:: Industries ::

The _________ comprises the companies that produce industrial chemicals. Central to the modern world economy, it converts raw materials into more than 70,000 different products. The plastics industry contains some overlap, as most chemical companies produce plastic as well as other chemicals.

Exam Probability: **Medium**

20. *Answer choices:*

(see index for correct answer)

- a. Sport industry
- b. Software industry
- c. Bicycle industry
- d. Chemical industry

Guidance: level 1

:: Costs ::

In process improvement efforts, _________ or cost of quality is a means to quantify the total cost of quality-related efforts and deficiencies. It was first described by Armand V. Feigenbaum in a 1956 Harvard Business Review article.

Exam Probability: **High**

21. *Answer choices:*

(see index for correct answer)

- a. Average variable cost
- b. Further processing cost
- c. Total cost
- d. Quality costs

Guidance: level 1

:: ::

Some scenarios associate "this kind of planning" with learning "life skills".Schedules are necessary, or at least useful, in situations where individuals need to know what time they must be at a specific location to receive a specific service, and where people need to accomplish a set of goals within a set time period.

Exam Probability: **Medium**

22. *Answer choices:*

(see index for correct answer)

- a. personal values
- b. corporate values
- c. Scheduling
- d. deep-level diversity

Guidance: level 1

:: ::

In production, research, retail, and accounting, a _________ is the value of money that has been used up to produce something or deliver a service, and hence is not available for use anymore. In business, the _________ may be one of acquisition, in which case the amount of money expended to acquire it is counted as _________. In this case, money is the input that is gone in order to acquire the thing. This acquisition _________ may be the sum of the _________ of production as incurred by the original producer, and further _________s of transaction as incurred by the acquirer over and above the price paid to the producer. Usually, the price also includes a mark-up for profit over the _________ of production.

Exam Probability: **Medium**

23. *Answer choices:*

(see index for correct answer)

- a. surface-level diversity
- b. Sarbanes-Oxley act of 2002
- c. functional perspective
- d. Cost

Guidance: level 1

:: Industrial processes ::

_________ is a technique involving the condensation of vapors and the return of this condensate to the system from which it originated. It is used in industrial and laboratory distillations. It is also used in chemistry to supply energy to reactions over a long period of time.

Exam Probability: **High**

24. *Answer choices:*

(see index for correct answer)

- a. Metallizing
- b. Electrolysis
- c. Textile bleaching
- d. Mineral processing

Guidance: level 1

:: Production and manufacturing ::

_________ is the production under license of technology developed elsewhere. It is an especially prominent commercial practice in developing nations, which often approach _________ as a starting point for indigenous industrial development.

Exam Probability: **Low**

25. *Answer choices:*

(see index for correct answer)

- a. Six Sigma
- b. Rolled throughput yield
- c. Time to market

- d. Digital materialization

Guidance: level 1

:: Management ::

__________ is a term used in business and Information Technology to describe the in-depth process of capturing customer's expectations, preferences and aversions. Specifically, the __________ is a market research technique that produces a detailed set of customer wants and needs, organized into a hierarchical structure, and then prioritized in terms of relative importance and satisfaction with current alternatives. __________ studies typically consist of both qualitative and quantitative research steps. They are generally conducted at the start of any new product, process, or service design initiative in order to better understand the customer's wants and needs, and as the key input for new product definition, Quality Function Deployment , and the setting of detailed design specifications.

Exam Probability: **High**

26. *Answer choices:*

(see index for correct answer)

- a. Corporate recovery
- b. Community of practice
- c. Voice of the customer
- d. SimulTrain

Guidance: level 1

:: Lean manufacturing ::

__________ is a Japanese term that means "mistake-proofing" or "inadvertent error prevention". A __________ is any mechanism in any process that helps an equipment operator avoid mistakes . Its purpose is to eliminate product defects by preventing, correcting, or drawing attention to human errors as they occur. The concept was formalised, and the term adopted, by Shigeo Shingo as part of the Toyota Production System. It was originally described as baka-yoke, but as this means "fool-proofing" the name was changed to the milder __________ .

Exam Probability: **Low**

27. *Answer choices:*

(see index for correct answer)

- a. Poka-yoke
- b. Failure mode and effects analysis
- c. Value stream mapping
- d. Lean construction

Guidance: level 1

:: Quality awards ::

The __________ recognizes U.S. organizations in the business, health care, education, and nonprofit sectors for performance excellence. The Baldrige Award is the only formal recognition of the performance excellence of both public and private U.S. organizations given by the President of the United States. It is administered by the Baldrige Performance Excellence Program, which is based at and managed by the National Institute of Standards and Technology , an agency of the U.S. Department of Commerce.

Exam Probability: **High**

28. *Answer choices:*

(see index for correct answer)

- a. The Deming Cup
- b. Canada Awards for Excellence
- c. Rajiv Gandhi National Quality Award
- d. Malcolm Baldrige National Quality Award

Guidance: level 1

:: Metal heat treatments ::

__________ is a group of industrial and metalworking processes used to alter the physical, and sometimes chemical, properties of a material. The most common application is metallurgical. Heat treatments are also used in the manufacture of many other materials, such as glass. Heat treatment involves the use of heating or chilling, normally to extreme temperatures, to achieve a desired result such as hardening or softening of a material. Heat treatment techniques include annealing, case hardening, precipitation strengthening, tempering, carburizing, normalizing and quenching. It is noteworthy that while the term heat treatment applies only to processes where the heating and cooling are done for the specific purpose of altering properties intentionally, heating and cooling often occur incidentally during other manufacturing processes such as hot forming or welding.

Exam Probability: **Low**

29. *Answer choices:*

(see index for correct answer)

- a. Carburizing
- b. Martempering
- c. Low hydrogen annealing
- d. Tempering

Guidance: level 1

:: Product development ::

In business and engineering, _________ covers the complete process of bringing a new product to market. A central aspect of NPD is product design, along with various business considerations. _________ is described broadly as the transformation of a market opportunity into a product available for sale. The product can be tangible or intangible , though sometimes services and other processes are distinguished from "products." NPD requires an understanding of customer needs and wants, the competitive environment, and the nature of the market.Cost, time and quality are the main variables that drive customer needs. Aiming at these three variables, innovative companies develop continuous practices and strategies to better satisfy customer requirements and to increase their own market share by a regular development of new products. There are many uncertainties and challenges which companies must face throughout the process. The use of best practices and the elimination of barriers to communication are the main concerns for the management of the NPD .

Exam Probability: **Medium**

30. *Answer choices:*

(see index for correct answer)

- a. Engineering design management
- b. Design specification
- c. Virtual prototyping
- d. New product development

Guidance: level 1

:: Quality management ::

In quality management system, a _________ is a document developed by management to express the directive of the top management with respect to quality. _________ management is a strategic item.

Exam Probability: **Low**

31. *Answer choices:*

(see index for correct answer)

- a. TL 9000
- b. ISO 9000
- c. Quality circle
- d. Quality policy

Guidance: level 1

:: E-commerce ::

_________ is the activity of buying or selling of products on online services or over the Internet. Electronic commerce draws on technologies such as mobile commerce, electronic funds transfer, supply chain management, Internet marketing, online transaction processing, electronic data interchange , inventory management systems, and automated data collection systems.

Exam Probability: **Low**

32. *Answer choices:*

(see index for correct answer)

- a. Global Product Classification
- b. E-commerce
- c. SwapSimple
- d. CA/Browser Forum

Guidance: level 1

:: Information systems ::

_________ is the process of creating, sharing, using and managing the knowledge and information of an organisation. It refers to a multidisciplinary approach to achieving organisational objectives by making the best use of knowledge.

Exam Probability: **Low**

33. *Answer choices:*

(see index for correct answer)

- a. Digital marketing system
- b. Laws of information systems
- c. Knowledge management
- d. Proactive information delivery

Guidance: level 1

:: Chemical processes ::

_________ is the understanding and application of the fundamental principles and laws of nature that allow us to transform raw material and energy into products that are useful to society, at an industrial level. By taking advantage of the driving forces of nature such as pressure, temperature and concentration gradients, as well as the law of conservation of mass, process engineers can develop methods to synthesize and purify large quantities of desired chemical products. _________ focuses on the design, operation, control, optimization and intensification of chemical, physical, and biological processes. _________ encompasses a vast range of industries, such as agriculture, automotive, biotechnical, chemical, food, material development, mining, nuclear, petrochemical, pharmaceutical, and software development. The application of systematic computer-based methods to _________ is "process systems engineering".

Exam Probability: **Low**

34. *Answer choices:*

(see index for correct answer)

- a. FFC Cambridge process
- b. Calcium looping
- c. Process engineering
- d. Staged reforming

Guidance: level 1

:: Industrial processes ::

A _________ is a device used for high-temperature heating. The name derives from Latin word fornax, which means oven. The heat energy to fuel a _________ may be supplied directly by fuel combustion, by electricity such as the electric arc _________ , or through induction heating in induction _________ s.

Exam Probability: **Low**

35. *Answer choices:*

(see index for correct answer)

- a. Glass-ceramic-to-metal seals
- b. Comminution
- c. Sintering
- d. Transfer hydrogenation

Guidance: level 1

:: Gas technologies ::

A __________ is a device used to transfer heat between two or more fluids. __________ s are used in both cooling and heating processes. The fluids may be separated by a solid wall to prevent mixing or they may be in direct contact. They are widely used in space heating, refrigeration, air conditioning, power stations, chemical plants, petrochemical plants, petroleum refineries, natural-gas processing, and sewage treatment. The classic example of a __________ is found in an internal combustion engine in which a circulating fluid known as engine coolant flows through radiator coils and air flows past the coils, which cools the coolant and heats the incoming air. Another example is the heat sink, which is a passive __________ that transfers the heat generated by an electronic or a mechanical device to a fluid medium, often air or a liquid coolant.

Exam Probability: **Low**

36. *Answer choices:*

(see index for correct answer)

- a. Gas mantle
- b. Cascade storage system
- c. Gas meter prover
- d. Heat exchanger

Guidance: level 1

:: Business ::

The seller, or the provider of the goods or services, completes a sale in response to an acquisition, appropriation, requisition or a direct interaction with the buyer at the point of sale. There is a passing of title of the item, and the settlement of a price, in which agreement is reached on a price for which transfer of ownership of the item will occur. The seller, not the purchaser typically executes the sale and it may be completed prior to the obligation of payment. In the case of indirect interaction, a person who sells goods or service on behalf of the owner is known as a _________ man or _________ woman or _________ person, but this often refers to someone selling goods in a store/shop, in which case other terms are also common, including _________ clerk, shop assistant, and retail clerk.

Exam Probability: **Low**

37. *Answer choices:*

(see index for correct answer)

- a. Free trade
- b. GoCardless
- c. Serviced office broker
- d. Organizational life cycle

Guidance: level 1

:: ::

An __________ is, most an organized examination or formal evaluation exercise. In engineering activities __________ involves the measurements, tests, and gauges applied to certain characteristics in regard to an object or activity. The results are usually compared to specified requirements and standards for determining whether the item or activity is in line with these targets, often with a Standard __________ Procedure in place to ensure consistent checking. __________ s are usually non-destructive.

Exam Probability: **Low**

38. *Answer choices:*

(see index for correct answer)

- a. surface-level diversity
- b. imperative
- c. Inspection
- d. process perspective

Guidance: level 1

:: Promotion and marketing communications ::

The __________ of American Manufacturers, now ThomasNet, is an online platform for supplier discovery and product sourcing in the US and Canada. It was once known as the "big green books" and "Thomas Registry", and was a multi-volume directory of industrial product information covering 650,000 distributors, manufacturers and service companies within 67,000-plus industrial categories that is now published on ThomasNet.

Exam Probability: **High**

39. *Answer choices:*

(see index for correct answer)

- a. Next Jump
- b. Radio advertisement
- c. National Consumer Panel
- d. Satellite media tour

Guidance: level 1

:: Management ::

__________ is a process by which entities review the quality of all factors involved in production. ISO 9000 defines __________ as "A part of quality management focused on fulfilling quality requirements".

Exam Probability: **High**

40. *Answer choices:*

(see index for correct answer)

- a. Information excellence
- b. Evidence-based management
- c. Quality control
- d. Stakeholder

Guidance: level 1

:: Management ::

_________ is a method of quality control which employs statistical methods to monitor and control a process. This helps to ensure that the process operates efficiently, producing more specification-conforming products with less waste . SPC can be applied to any process where the "conforming product" output can be measured. Key tools used in SPC include run charts, control charts, a focus on continuous improvement, and the design of experiments. An example of a process where SPC is applied is manufacturing lines.

Exam Probability: **Medium**

41. *Answer choices:*

(see index for correct answer)

- a. Preventive action
- b. Corticon
- c. Statistical process control
- d. Management cockpit

Guidance: level 1

:: Quality ::

__________ is a concept first outlined by quality expert Joseph M. Juran in publications, most notably Juran on __________ . Designing for quality and innovation is one of the three universal processes of the Juran Trilogy, in which Juran describes what is required to achieve breakthroughs in new products, services, and processes. Juran believed that quality could be planned, and that most quality crises and problems relate to the way in which quality was planned.

Exam Probability: **Low**

42. *Answer choices:*

(see index for correct answer)

- a. American Society for Quality
- b. Root cause
- c. Quality by Design
- d. Secure Stations Scheme

Guidance: level 1

:: Project management ::

A __________ is one of a series of numbered markers placed along a road or boundary at intervals of one mile or occasionally, parts of a mile. They are typically located at the side of the road or in a median or central reservation. They are alternatively known as mile markers, mileposts or mile posts . Mileage is the distance along the road from a fixed commencement point. Commonly the term " __________ " may also refer to markers placed at other distances, such as every kilometre.

Exam Probability: **Medium**

43. *Answer choices:*

(see index for correct answer)

- a. Milestone
- b. Project Initiation Documentation
- c. Level of Effort
- d. Project charter

Guidance: level 1

:: Project management ::

In economics, _________ is the assignment of available resources to various uses. In the context of an entire economy, resources can be allocated by various means, such as markets or central planning.

Exam Probability: **Low**

44. *Answer choices:*

(see index for correct answer)

- a. Resource allocation
- b. Theory X
- c. Terms of reference
- d. Float

Guidance: level 1

:: Data management ::

__________ is an object-oriented program and library developed by CERN. It was originally designed for particle physics data analysis and contains several features specific to this field, but it is also used in other applications such as astronomy and data mining. The latest release is 6.16.00, as of 2018-11-14.

Exam Probability: **Medium**

45. *Answer choices:*

(see index for correct answer)

- a. ROOT
- b. Storage area network
- c. Single Source of Truth
- d. Serializability

Guidance: level 1

:: Water ::

__________ is a transparent, tasteless, odorless, and nearly colorless chemical substance, which is the main constituent of Earth's streams, lakes, and oceans, and the fluids of most living organisms. It is vital for all known forms of life, even though it provides no calories or organic nutrients. Its chemical formula is H2O, meaning that each of its molecules contains one oxygen and two hydrogen atoms, connected by covalent bonds. __________ is the name of the liquid state of H2O at standard ambient temperature and pressure. It forms precipitation in the form of rain and aerosols in the form of fog. Clouds are formed from suspended droplets of __________ and ice, its solid state. When finely divided, crystalline ice may precipitate in the form of snow. The gaseous state of __________ is steam or __________ vapor. __________ moves continually through the __________ cycle of evaporation, transpiration, condensation, precipitation, and runoff, usually reaching the sea.

Exam Probability: **High**

46. *Answer choices:*

(see index for correct answer)

- a. Hydraulic ram
- b. Water
- c. Brine rejection
- d. Groundwater recharge

Guidance: level 1

:: Management ::

In inventory management, _________ is the order quantity that minimizes the total holding costs and ordering costs. It is one of the oldest classical production scheduling models. The model was developed by Ford W. Harris in 1913, but R. H. Wilson, a consultant who applied it extensively, and K. Andler are given credit for their in-depth analysis.

Exam Probability: **High**

47. *Answer choices:*

(see index for correct answer)

- a. The Toyota Way
- b. Change advisory board
- c. Real property administrator
- d. Organizational conflict

Guidance: level 1

:: Production and manufacturing ::

An _________ is a manufacturing process in which parts are added as the semi-finished assembly moves from workstation to workstation where the parts are added in sequence until the final assembly is produced. By mechanically moving the parts to the assembly work and moving the semi-finished assembly from work station to work station, a finished product can be assembled faster and with less labor than by having workers carry parts to a stationary piece for assembly.

Exam Probability: **Medium**

48. *Answer choices:*

(see index for correct answer)

- a. Nesting
- b. International Automotive Task Force
- c. Dynamic Manufacturing Network
- d. Assembly line

Guidance: level 1

:: Production economics ::

_________ is the creation of a whole that is greater than the simple sum of its parts. The term _________ comes from the Attic Greek word sea synergia from synergos, , meaning "working together".

Exam Probability: **Low**

49. *Answer choices:*

(see index for correct answer)

- a. Sectoral output
- b. Choice of techniques
- c. short run
- d. Synergy

Guidance: level 1

:: Risk analysis ::

Supply-chain risk management is "the implementation of strategies to manage both everyday and exceptional risks along the supply chain based on continuous risk assessment with the objective of reducing vulnerability and ensuring continuity".

Exam Probability: **High**

50. *Answer choices:*

(see index for correct answer)

- a. Supply chain risk management
- b. Litigation risk analysis
- c. Wilderness Risk Management Conference
- d. Singleton

Guidance: level 1

:: Distribution, retailing, and wholesaling ::

The __________ is a distribution channel phenomenon in which forecasts yield supply chain inefficiencies. It refers to increasing swings in inventory in response to shifts in customer demand as one moves further up the supply chain. The concept first appeared in Jay Forrester`s Industrial Dynamics and thus it is also known as the Forrester effect. The __________ was named for the way the amplitude of a whip increases down its length. The further from the originating signal, the greater the distortion of the wave pattern. In a similar manner, forecast accuracy decreases as one moves upstream along the supply chain. For example, many consumer goods have fairly consistent consumption at retail but this signal becomes more chaotic and unpredictable as the focus moves away from consumer purchasing behavior.

Exam Probability: **High**

51. *Answer choices:*

(see index for correct answer)

- a. Wholesale list
- b. Bridgewater House, Manchester
- c. Bullwhip effect
- d. Independent News

Guidance: level 1

:: Quality ::

A __________ is an initiating cause of either a condition or a causal chain that leads to an outcome or effect of interest. The term denotes the earliest, most basic, `deepest`, cause for a given behavior; most often a fault. The idea is that you can only see an error by its manifest signs. Those signs can be widespread, multitudinous, and convoluted, whereas the __________ leading to them often is a lot simpler.

Exam Probability: **Low**

52. *Answer choices:*

(see index for correct answer)

- a. Robustification
- b. The Partnership for Excellence
- c. Japanese quality
- d. Root cause

Guidance: level 1

:: Marketing techniques ::

A __________ is an award to be given to a person, a group of people like a sports team, or organization to recognise and reward actions or achievements. Official __________ s often involve monetary rewards as well as the fame that comes with them. Some __________ s are also associated with extravagant awarding ceremonies, such as the Academy Awards.

Exam Probability: **Medium**

53. *Answer choices:*

(see index for correct answer)

- a. Cereal box prize
- b. Product placement
- c. Celebrity branding
- d. Vendor lock-in

Guidance: level 1

:: Quality assurance ::

Organizations that issue credentials or certify third parties against official standards are themselves formally accredited by _________ bodies ; hence they are sometimes known as "accredited certification bodies". The _________ process ensures that their certification practices are acceptable, typically meaning that they are competent to test and certify third parties, behave ethically and employ suitable quality assurance.

Exam Probability: **High**

54. *Answer choices:*

(see index for correct answer)

- a. Accreditation
- b. PCOLA-SOQ
- c. State Acceptance of Production
- d. Static testing

Guidance: level 1

:: Management ::

_________ is an iterative four-step management method used in business for the control and continuous improvement of processes and products. It is also known as the Deming circle/cycle/wheel, the Shewhart cycle, the control circle/cycle, or plan–do–study–act . Another version of this _________ cycle is O _________ . The added "O" stands for observation or as some versions say: "Observe the current condition." This emphasis on observation and current condition has currency with the literature on lean manufacturing and the Toyota Production System. The _________ cycle, with Ishikawa's changes, can be traced back to S. Mizuno of the Tokyo Institute of Technology in 1959.

Exam Probability: **High**

55. *Answer choices:*

(see index for correct answer)

- a. Force-field analysis
- b. Concept of the Corporation
- c. Industrial market segmentation
- d. PDCA

Guidance: level 1

:: ::

_________ is the process of finding an estimate, or approximation, which is a value that is usable for some purpose even if input data may be incomplete, uncertain, or unstable. The value is nonetheless usable because it is derived from the best information available. Typically, _________ involves "using the value of a statistic derived from a sample to estimate the value of a corresponding population parameter". The sample provides information that can be projected, through various formal or informal processes, to determine a range most likely to describe the missing information. An estimate that turns out to be incorrect will be an overestimate if the estimate exceeded the actual result, and an underestimate if the estimate fell short of the actual result.

Exam Probability: **Medium**

56. *Answer choices:*

(see index for correct answer)

- a. co-culture
- b. Sarbanes-Oxley act of 2002
- c. empathy
- d. Estimation

Guidance: level 1

:: Management accounting ::

_________ are costs that are not directly accountable to a cost object . _________ may be either fixed or variable. _________ include administration, personnel and security costs. These are those costs which are not directly related to production. Some _________ may be overhead. But some overhead costs can be directly attributed to a project and are direct costs.

Exam Probability: **Low**

57. *Answer choices:*

(see index for correct answer)

- a. Indirect costs
- b. Certified Management Accountants of Canada
- c. Factory overhead
- d. Spend management

Guidance: level 1

:: Retailing ::

_________ is the process of selling consumer goods or services to customers through multiple channels of distribution to earn a profit. _________ ers satisfy demand identified through a supply chain. The term " _________ er" is typically applied where a service provider fills the small orders of a large number of individuals, who are end-users, rather than large orders of a small number of wholesale, corporate or government clientele. Shopping generally refers to the act of buying products. Sometimes this is done to obtain final goods, including necessities such as food and clothing; sometimes it takes place as a recreational activity. Recreational shopping often involves window shopping and browsing: it does not always result in a purchase.

Exam Probability: **Medium**

58. *Answer choices:*

(see index for correct answer)

- a. Tourist trap
- b. Street date
- c. Bastyr Dispensary
- d. Retail

Guidance: level 1

:: ::

A _________ or till is a mechanical or electronic device for registering and calculating transactions at a point of sale. It is usually attached to a drawer for storing cash and other valuables. A modern _________ is usually attached to a printer that can print out receipts for record-keeping purposes.

Exam Probability: **High**

59. *Answer choices:*

(see index for correct answer)

- a. empathy
- b. Character
- c. hierarchical
- d. open system

Guidance: level 1

Commerce

Commerce relates to "the exchange of goods and services, especially on a large scale." It includes legal, economic, political, social, cultural and technological systems that operate in any country or internationally.

:: E-commerce ::

__________ is a United States-based payment gateway service provider allowing merchants to accept credit card and electronic check payments through their website and over an Internet Protocol connection. Founded in 1996, __________ is now a subsidiary of Visa Inc. Its service permits customers to enter credit card and shipping information directly onto a web page, in contrast to some alternatives that require the customer to sign up for a payment service before performing a transaction.

Exam Probability: **Medium**

1. *Answer choices:*

(see index for correct answer)

- a. E-commerce in Southeast Asia
- b. Dark store
- c. Infomediary
- d. Authorize.Net

Guidance: level 1

:: Supply chain management ::

_________ is a variable pricing strategy, based on understanding, anticipating and influencing consumer behavior in order to maximize revenue or profits from a fixed, time-limited resource . As a specific, inventory-focused branch of revenue management, _________ involves strategic control of inventory to sell the right product to the right customer at the right time for the right price. This process can result in price discrimination, in which customers consuming identical goods or services are charged different prices. _________ is a large revenue generator for several major industries; Robert Crandall, former Chairman and CEO of American Airlines, gave _________ its name and has called it "the single most important technical development in transportation management since we entered deregulation."

Exam Probability: **Low**

2. *Answer choices:*

(see index for correct answer)

- a. RevPAR
- b. Distribution software
- c. Service management
- d. Yield management

Guidance: level 1

:: Economics terminology ::

__________ is the total receipts a seller can obtain from selling goods or services to buyers. It can be written as P × Q, which is the price of the goods multiplied by the quantity of the sold goods.

Exam Probability: **High**

3. *Answer choices:*

(see index for correct answer)

- a. Bond issue
- b. End user
- c. Capital stock
- d. Total revenue

Guidance: level 1

:: Generally Accepted Accounting Principles ::

In accounting, _________ is the income that a business have from its normal business activities, usually from the sale of goods and services to customers. _________ is also referred to as sales or turnover.Some companies receive _________ from interest, royalties, or other fees. _________ may refer to business income in general, or it may refer to the amount, in a monetary unit, earned during a period of time, as in "Last year, Company X had _________ of $42 million". Profits or net income generally imply total _________ minus total expenses in a given period. In accounting, in the balance statement it is a subsection of the Equity section and _________ increases equity, it is often referred to as the "top line" due to its position on the income statement at the very top. This is to be contrasted with the "bottom line" which denotes net income .

Exam Probability: **Medium**

4. *Answer choices:*

(see index for correct answer)

- a. Liability
- b. Expense
- c. Revenue
- d. Generally Accepted Accounting Practice

Guidance: level 1

:: Decision theory ::

A _________ is a deliberate system of principles to guide decisions and achieve rational outcomes. A _________ is a statement of intent, and is implemented as a procedure or protocol. Policies are generally adopted by a governance body within an organization. Policies can assist in both subjective and objective decision making. Policies to assist in subjective decision making usually assist senior management with decisions that must be based on the relative merits of a number of factors, and as a result are often hard to test objectively, e.g. work-life balance _________ . In contrast policies to assist in objective decision making are usually operational in nature and can be objectively tested, e.g. password _________ .

Exam Probability: **Low**

5. *Answer choices:*

(see index for correct answer)

- a. Option grid
- b. Movement pattern analysis
- c. Pignistic probability
- d. Nash equilibrium

Guidance: level 1

:: Dot-com bubble ::

Yahoo! _________ was a web hosting service. It was founded in November 1994 by David Bohnett and John Rezner, and was called Beverly Hills Internet for a very short time before being named _________ .

Exam Probability: **Low**

6. *Answer choices:*

(see index for correct answer)

- a. Webvan
- b. Lycos
- c. E-Dreams
- d. CyberRebate

Guidance: level 1

:: Income ::

_________ is a ratio between the net profit and cost of investment resulting from an investment of some resources. A high ROI means the investment`s gains favorably to its cost. As a performance measure, ROI is used to evaluate the efficiency of an investment or to compare the efficiencies of several different investments. In purely economic terms, it is one way of relating profits to capital invested. _________ is a performance measure used by businesses to identify the efficiency of an investment or number of different investments.

Exam Probability: **Low**

7. *Answer choices:*

(see index for correct answer)

- a. Return on investment
- b. Meetup fee
- c. Revenue management
- d. Real income

Guidance: level 1

:: ::

In marketing jargon, product lining is offering several related products for sale individually. Unlike product bundling, where several products are combined into one group, which is then offered for sale as a units, product lining involves offering the products for sale separately. A line can comprise related products of various sizes, types, colors, qualities, or prices. Line depth refers to the number of subcategories a category has. Line consistency refers to how closely related the products that make up the line are. Line vulnerability refers to the percentage of sales or profits that are derived from only a few products in the line.

Exam Probability: **Low**

8. *Answer choices:*

(see index for correct answer)

- a. hierarchical perspective
- b. Product mix
- c. co-culture
- d. process perspective

Guidance: level 1

:: ::

__________ is the production of products for use or sale using labour and machines, tools, chemical and biological processing, or formulation. The term may refer to a range of human activity, from handicraft to high tech, but is most commonly applied to industrial design, in which raw materials are transformed into finished goods on a large scale. Such finished goods may be sold to other manufacturers for the production of other, more complex products, such as aircraft, household appliances, furniture, sports equipment or automobiles, or sold to wholesalers, who in turn sell them to retailers, who then sell them to end users and consumers.

Exam Probability: **High**

9. *Answer choices:*

(see index for correct answer)

- a. information systems assessment
- b. Sarbanes-Oxley act of 2002
- c. interpersonal communication
- d. open system

Guidance: level 1

:: ::

_________ is the social science that studies the production, distribution, and consumption of goods and services.

Exam Probability: **Medium**

10. *Answer choices:*

(see index for correct answer)

- a. cultural
- b. Economics
- c. deep-level diversity
- d. empathy

Guidance: level 1

:: E-commerce ::

_________ is a type of performance-based marketing in which a business rewards one or more affiliates for each visitor or customer brought by the affiliate's own marketing efforts.

Exam Probability: **Medium**

11. *Answer choices:*

(see index for correct answer)

- a. Online food ordering
- b. Affiliate marketing
- c. MonkeySports
- d. Buyhatke

Guidance: level 1

:: E-commerce ::

The phrase _________ was originally coined in 1997 by Kevin Duffey at the launch of the Global _________ Forum, to mean "the delivery of electronic commerce capabilities directly into the consumer's hand, anywhere, via wireless technology." Many choose to think of _________ as meaning "a retail outlet in your customer's pocket."

Exam Probability: **Low**

12. *Answer choices:*

(see index for correct answer)

- a. Cooling-off period
- b. Onbuy
- c. USAePay
- d. ITransact

Guidance: level 1

:: ::

An _________ is a systematic and independent examination of books, accounts, statutory records, documents and vouchers of an organization to ascertain how far the financial statements as well as non-financial disclosures present a true and fair view of the concern. It also attempts to ensure that the books of accounts are properly maintained by the concern as required by law. _________ ing has become such a ubiquitous phenomenon in the corporate and the public sector that academics started identifying an " _________ Society". The _________ or perceives and recognises the propositions before them for examination, obtains evidence, evaluates the same and formulates an opinion on the basis of his judgement which is communicated through their _________ ing report.

Exam Probability: **High**

13. *Answer choices:*

(see index for correct answer)

- a. hierarchical perspective
- b. Audit
- c. Sarbanes-Oxley act of 2002
- d. process perspective

Guidance: level 1

:: Packaging ::

In work place, _________ or job _________ means good ranking with the hypothesized conception of requirements of a role. There are two types of job _________ s: contextual and task. Task _________ is related to cognitive ability while contextual _________ is dependent upon personality. Task _________ are behavioral roles that are recognized in job descriptions and by remuneration systems, they are directly related to organizational _________ , whereas, contextual _________ are value based and additional behavioral roles that are not recognized in job descriptions and covered by compensation; they are extra roles that are indirectly related to organizational _________ . Citizenship _________ like contextual _________ means a set of individual activity/contribution that supports the organizational culture.

Exam Probability: **High**

14. *Answer choices:*

(see index for correct answer)

- a. Performance
- b. Intermediate bulk container
- c. Envelope
- d. Skin pack

Guidance: level 1

:: Theories ::

A _________ union is a type of multinational political union where negotiated power is delegated to an authority by governments of member states.

Exam Probability: **Low**

15. *Answer choices:*

(see index for correct answer)

- a. Supranational
- b. incrementalism

Guidance: level 1

:: Information technology ::

__________ is the use of computers to store, retrieve, transmit, and manipulate data, or information, often in the context of a business or other enterprise. IT is considered to be a subset of information and communications technology . An __________ system is generally an information system, a communications system or, more specifically speaking, a computer system – including all hardware, software and peripheral equipment – operated by a limited group of users.

Exam Probability: **Medium**

16. *Answer choices:*

(see index for correct answer)

- a. ISO/IEC JTC 1/SC 23
- b. ISO/IEC JTC 1/SC 25
- c. Zimperium

- d. Legal aspects of computing

Guidance: level 1

:: ::

_________ is the practice of deliberately managing the spread of information between an individual or an organization and the public. _________ may include an organization or individual gaining exposure to their audiences using topics of public interest and news items that do not require direct payment. This differentiates it from advertising as a form of marketing communications. _________ is the idea of creating coverage for clients for free, rather than marketing or advertising. But now, advertising is also a part of greater PR Activities.An example of good _________ would be generating an article featuring a client, rather than paying for the client to be advertised next to the article. The aim of _________ is to inform the public, prospective customers, investors, partners, employees, and other stakeholders and ultimately persuade them to maintain a positive or favorable view about the organization, its leadership, products, or political decisions. _________ professionals typically work for PR and marketing firms, businesses and companies, government, and public officials as PIOs and nongovernmental organizations, and nonprofit organizations. Jobs central to _________ include account coordinator, account executive, account supervisor, and media relations manager.

Exam Probability: **Medium**

17. *Answer choices:*

(see index for correct answer)

- a. co-culture

- b. Public relations
- c. Sarbanes-Oxley act of 2002
- d. open system

Guidance: level 1

:: ::

Employment is a relationship between two parties, usually based on a contract where work is paid for, where one party, which may be a corporation, for profit, not-for-profit organization, co-operative or other entity is the employer and the other is the employee. Employees work in return for payment, which may be in the form of an hourly wage, by piecework or an annual salary, depending on the type of work an employee does or which sector she or he is working in. Employees in some fields or sectors may receive gratuities, bonus payment or stock options. In some types of employment, employees may receive benefits in addition to payment. Benefits can include health insurance, housing, disability insurance or use of a gym. Employment is typically governed by employment laws, regulations or legal contracts.

Exam Probability: **Medium**

18. *Answer choices:*

(see index for correct answer)

- a. functional perspective
- b. empathy
- c. imperative
- d. cultural

Guidance: level 1

:: Marketing ::

_________ or stock is the goods and materials that a business holds for the ultimate goal of resale .

Exam Probability: **Medium**

19. *Answer choices:*

(see index for correct answer)

- a. Franchising
- b. Mass customization
- c. Marketing communications
- d. Inventory

Guidance: level 1

:: Mereology ::

_________ , in the abstract, is what belongs to or with something, whether as an attribute or as a component of said thing. In the context of this article, it is one or more components , whether physical or incorporeal, of a person`s estate; or so belonging to, as in being owned by, a person or jointly a group of people or a legal entity like a corporation or even a society. Depending on the nature of the _________ , an owner of _________ has the right to consume, alter, share, redefine, rent, mortgage, pawn, sell, exchange, transfer, give away or destroy it, or to exclude others from doing these things, as well as to perhaps abandon it; whereas regardless of the nature of the _________ , the owner thereof has the right to properly use it , or at the very least exclusively keep it.

Exam Probability: **High**

20. *Answer choices:*

(see index for correct answer)

- a. Property
- b. Mereology
- c. Simple
- d. Meronomy

Guidance: level 1

:: E-commerce ::

__________ is a method of e-commerce where shoppers` friends become involved in the shopping experience. __________ attempts to use technology to mimic the social interactions found in physical malls and stores. With the rise of mobile devices, __________ is now extending beyond the online world and into the offline world of shopping.

Exam Probability: **Low**

21. *Answer choices:*

(see index for correct answer)

- a. GS1 US
- b. Point of sale
- c. Social shopping
- d. Coinye

Guidance: level 1

:: Business law ::

A __________ is a business entity created by two or more parties, generally characterized by shared ownership, shared returns and risks, and shared governance. Companies typically pursue __________ s for one of four reasons: to access a new market, particularly emerging markets; to gain scale efficiencies by combining assets and operations; to share risk for major investments or projects; or to access skills and capabilities.

Exam Probability: **Low**

22. *Answer choices:*

(see index for correct answer)

- a. United States labor law
- b. Trusted Computing
- c. Joint venture
- d. Economic torts

Guidance: level 1

:: Materials ::

A _________ , also known as a feedstock, unprocessed material, or primary commodity, is a basic material that is used to produce goods, finished products, energy, or intermediate materials which are feedstock for future finished products. As feedstock, the term connotes these materials are bottleneck assets and are highly important with regard to producing other products. An example of this is crude oil, which is a _________ and a feedstock used in the production of industrial chemicals, fuels, plastics, and pharmaceutical goods; lumber is a _________ used to produce a variety of products including all types of furniture. The term " _________ " denotes materials in minimally processed or unprocessed in states; e.g., raw latex, crude oil, cotton, coal, raw biomass, iron ore, air, logs, or water i.e. "...any product of agriculture, forestry, fishing and any other mineral that is in its natural form or which has undergone the transformation required to prepare it for internationally marketing in substantial volumes."

Exam Probability: **Low**

23. *Answer choices:*

(see index for correct answer)

- a. Putty
- b. Agricultural lime
- c. Superhard material
- d. Raw material

Guidance: level 1

:: Free market ::

In economics, a _________ is a system in which the prices for goods and services are determined by the open market and by consumers. In a _________, the laws and forces of supply and demand are free from any intervention by a government or other authority and from all forms of economic privilege, monopolies and artificial scarcities. Proponents of the concept of _________ contrast it with a regulated market in which a government intervenes in supply and demand through various methods, such as tariffs, used to restrict trade and to protect the local economy. In an idealized free-market economy, prices for goods and services are set freely by the forces of supply and demand and are allowed to reach their point of equilibrium without intervention by government policy.

Exam Probability: **Low**

24. *Answer choices:*

(see index for correct answer)

- a. Free market

- b. Regulated market

Guidance: level 1

:: ::

_________ is both a research area and a practical skill encompassing the ability of an individual or organization to "lead" or guide other individuals, teams, or entire organizations. Specialist literature debates various viewpoints, contrasting Eastern and Western approaches to _________ , and also United States versus European approaches. U.S. academic environments define _________ as "a process of social influence in which a person can enlist the aid and support of others in the accomplishment of a common task".

Exam Probability: **High**

25. *Answer choices:*

(see index for correct answer)

- a. open system
- b. hierarchical
- c. surface-level diversity
- d. similarity-attraction theory

Guidance: level 1

:: Commerce ::

A __________ is an employee within a company, business or other organization who is responsible at some level for buying or approving the acquisition of goods and services needed by the company. Responsible for buying the best quality products, goods and services for their company at the most competitive prices, __________ s work in a wide range of sectors for many different organizations. The position responsibilities may be the same as that of a buyer or purchasing agent, or may include wider supervisory or managerial responsibilities. A __________ may oversee the acquisition of materials needed for production, general supplies for offices and facilities, equipment, or construction contracts. A __________ often supervises purchasing agents and buyers, but in small companies the __________ may also be the purchasing agent or buyer. The __________ position may also carry the title "Procurement Manager" or in the public sector, "Procurement Officer". He or she can come from both an Engineering or Economics background.

Exam Probability: **Medium**

26. *Answer choices:*

(see index for correct answer)

- a. Video rental shop
- b. Purchasing manager
- c. Treasure voyages
- d. Council of the Americas

Guidance: level 1

:: ::

__________ is the administration of an organization, whether it is a business, a not-for-profit organization, or government body. __________ includes the activities of setting the strategy of an organization and coordinating the efforts of its employees to accomplish its objectives through the application of available resources, such as financial, natural, technological, and human resources. The term " __________ " may also refer to those people who manage an organization.

Exam Probability: **Low**

27. *Answer choices:*

(see index for correct answer)

- a. personal values
- b. Management
- c. hierarchical perspective
- d. corporate values

Guidance: level 1

:: ::

_________ is "property consisting of land and the buildings on it, along with its natural resources such as crops, minerals or water; immovable property of this nature; an interest vested in this an item of real property, buildings or housing in general. Also: the business of _________ ; the profession of buying, selling, or renting land, buildings, or housing." It is a legal term used in jurisdictions whose legal system is derived from English common law, such as India, England, Wales, Northern Ireland, United States, Canada, Pakistan, Australia, and New Zealand.

Exam Probability: **Low**

28. *Answer choices:*

(see index for correct answer)

- a. Sarbanes-Oxley act of 2002
- b. hierarchical
- c. Real estate
- d. co-culture

Guidance: level 1

:: ::

_________ is the study and management of exchange relationships. _________ is the business process of creating relationships with and satisfying customers. With its focus on the customer, _________ is one of the premier components of business management.

Exam Probability: **High**

29. *Answer choices:*

(see index for correct answer)

- a. Sarbanes-Oxley act of 2002
- b. co-culture
- c. Marketing
- d. Character

Guidance: level 1

:: Business law ::

A _________ is a contractual arrangement calling for the lessee to pay the lessor for use of an asset. Property, buildings and vehicles are common assets that are _________ d. Industrial or business equipment is also _________ d.

Exam Probability: **Low**

30. *Answer choices:*

(see index for correct answer)

- a. TRIPS Agreement
- b. Lease
- c. Extraordinary resolution
- d. OHADA

Guidance: level 1

:: Payment systems ::

A _________ is any system used to settle financial transactions through the transfer of monetary value. This includes the institutions, instruments, people, rules, procedures, standards, and technologies that make it exchange possible. A common type of _________ is called an operational network that links bank accounts and provides for monetary exchange using bank deposits. Some _________ s also include credit mechanisms, which are essentially a different aspect of payment.

Exam Probability: **High**

31. *Answer choices:*

(see index for correct answer)

- a. Payment system
- b. Visa Buxx
- c. CNG Processing A/S
- d. ACI Worldwide

Guidance: level 1

:: Supply chain management ::

__________ is the removal of intermediaries in economics from a supply chain, or cutting out the middlemen in connection with a transaction or a series of transactions. Instead of going through traditional distribution channels, which had some type of intermediary , companies may now deal with customers directly, for example via the Internet. Hence, the use of factory direct and direct from the factory to mean the same thing.

Exam Probability: **High**

32. *Answer choices:*

(see index for correct answer)

- a. Supply chain diversification
- b. Disintermediation
- c. Supply Chain Management Review
- d. Supply-chain operations reference

Guidance: level 1

:: Dot-com bubble ::

__________ is an internet portal launched in 1995 that provides a variety of content including news and weather, a metasearch engine, a web-based email, instant messaging, stock quotes, and a customizable user homepage. It is currently operated by IAC Applications of IAC, and __________ Networks. In the U.S., the main __________ site has long been a personal start page called My __________ . __________ also operates an e-mail service, although it is no longer open for new customers.

Exam Probability: **Medium**

33. *Answer choices:*

(see index for correct answer)

- a. Excite
- b. Urbanfetch
- c. The Industry Standard
- d. Paid to surf

Guidance: level 1

:: ::

_________ is the extraction of valuable minerals or other geological materials from the earth, usually from an ore body, lode, vein, seam, reef or placer deposit. These deposits form a mineralized package that is of economic interest to the miner.

Exam Probability: **Low**

34. *Answer choices:*

(see index for correct answer)

- a. cultural
- b. deep-level diversity
- c. hierarchical

- d. Mining

Guidance: level 1

:: Warrants issued in Hong Kong Stock Exchange ::

_________ is a chemical element with symbol Ag and atomic number 47. A soft, white, lustrous transition metal, it exhibits the highest electrical conductivity, thermal conductivity, and reflectivity of any metal. The metal is found in the Earth`s crust in the pure, free elemental form , as an alloy with gold and other metals, and in minerals such as argentite and chlorargyrite. Most _________ is produced as a byproduct of copper, gold, lead, and zinc refining.

Exam Probability: **Low**

35. *Answer choices:*

(see index for correct answer)

- a. CITIC Securities
- b. Industrial and Commercial Bank of China
- c. Emperor International Holdings Limited
- d. Silver

Guidance: level 1

:: ::

A _________ is a person who trades in commodities produced by other people. Historically, a _________ is anyone who is involved in business or trade. _________ s have operated for as long as industry, commerce, and trade have existed. During the 16th-century, in Europe, two different terms for _________ s emerged: One term, meerseniers, described local traders such as bakers, grocers, etc.; while a new term, koopman (Dutch: koopman, described _________ s who operated on a global stage, importing and exporting goods over vast distances, and offering added-value services such as credit and finance.

Exam Probability: **Medium**

36. *Answer choices:*

(see index for correct answer)

- a. interpersonal communication
- b. functional perspective
- c. Merchant
- d. information systems assessment

Guidance: level 1

:: Market research ::

_________ is an organized effort to gather information about target markets or customers. It is a very important component of business strategy. The term is commonly interchanged with marketing research; however, expert practitioners may wish to draw a distinction, in that marketing research is concerned specifically about marketing processes, while _________ is concerned specifically with markets.

Exam Probability: **Medium**

37. *Answer choices:*

(see index for correct answer)

- a. Market research
- b. Industry analyst
- c. Advertising Research Foundation
- d. ISO 20252

Guidance: level 1

:: ::

_________ s and acquisitions are transactions in which the ownership of companies, other business organizations, or their operating units are transferred or consolidated with other entities. As an aspect of strategic management, M&A can allow enterprises to grow or downsize, and change the nature of their business or competitive position.

Exam Probability: **Low**

38. *Answer choices:*

(see index for correct answer)

- a. Sarbanes-Oxley act of 2002
- b. Merger

- c. open system
- d. cultural

Guidance: level 1

:: Stock market ::

_________ is freedom from, or resilience against, potential harm caused by others. Beneficiaries of _________ may be of persons and social groups, objects and institutions, ecosystems or any other entity or phenomenon vulnerable to unwanted change by its environment.

Exam Probability: **Medium**

39. *Answer choices:*

(see index for correct answer)

- a. China Concepts Stock
- b. Secondary shares
- c. End of day
- d. Sell side

Guidance: level 1

:: ::

A _________ manages, commands, directs, or regulates the behavior of other devices or systems using control loops. It can range from a single home heating controller using a thermostat controlling a domestic boiler to large Industrial _________ s which are used for controlling processes or machines.

Exam Probability: **High**

40. *Answer choices:*

(see index for correct answer)

- a. interpersonal communication
- b. surface-level diversity
- c. open system
- d. Control system

Guidance: level 1

:: Evaluation ::

_________ is a way of preventing mistakes and defects in manufactured products and avoiding problems when delivering products or services to customers; which ISO 9000 defines as "part of quality management focused on providing confidence that quality requirements will be fulfilled". This defect prevention in _________ differs subtly from defect detection and rejection in quality control and has been referred to as a shift left since it focuses on quality earlier in the process .

Exam Probability: **High**

41. *Answer choices:*

(see index for correct answer)

- a. Joint Committee on Standards for Educational Evaluation
- b. Knowledge survey
- c. Program evaluation
- d. Evaluation Assurance Level

Guidance: level 1

:: Payments ::

A _________ or government incentive is a form of financial aid or support extended to an economic sector generally with the aim of promoting economic and social policy. Although commonly extended from government, the term _________ can relate to any type of support – for example from NGOs or as implicit subsidies. Subsidies come in various forms including: direct and indirect .

Exam Probability: **Medium**

42. *Answer choices:*

(see index for correct answer)

- a. Payment
- b. KlickEx
- c. VersaPay
- d. County payments

Guidance: level 1

:: Confidence tricks ::

_________ is the fraudulent attempt to obtain sensitive information such as usernames, passwords and credit card details by disguising oneself as a trustworthy entity in an electronic communication. Typically carried out by email spoofing or instant messaging, it often directs users to enter personal information at a fake website which matches the look and feel of the legitimate site.

Exam Probability: **Medium**

43. *Answer choices:*

(see index for correct answer)

- a. First International Bank of Grenada
- b. Ponzi scheme
- c. Welsh Thrasher faith scam
- d. Hongcheng Magic Liquid

Guidance: level 1

:: Statutory law ::

_________ or statute law is written law set down by a body of legislature or by a singular legislator . This is as opposed to oral or customary law; or regulatory law promulgated by the executive or common law of the judiciary. Statutes may originate with national, state legislatures or local municipalities.

Exam Probability: **Medium**

44. *Answer choices:*

(see index for correct answer)

- a. Statute of repose
- b. ratification
- c. incorporation by reference
- d. statute law

Guidance: level 1

:: ::

A _________ consists of one people who live in the same dwelling and share meals. It may also consist of a single family or another group of people. A dwelling is considered to contain multiple _________ s if meals or living spaces are not shared. The _________ is the basic unit of analysis in many social, microeconomic and government models, and is important to economics and inheritance.

Exam Probability: **Medium**

45. *Answer choices:*

(see index for correct answer)

- a. information systems assessment
- b. surface-level diversity
- c. cultural
- d. levels of analysis

Guidance: level 1

:: Marketing ::

The _________ is a foundation model for businesses. The _________ has been defined as the "set of marketing tools that the firm uses to pursue its marketing objectives in the target market". Thus the _________ refers to four broad levels of marketing decision, namely: product, price, place, and promotion. Marketing practice has been occurring for millennia, but marketing theory emerged in the early twentieth century. The contemporary _________ , or the 4 Ps, which has become the dominant framework for marketing management decisions, was first published in 1960. In services marketing, an extended _________ is used, typically comprising 7 Ps, made up of the original 4 Ps extended by process, people, and physical evidence. Occasionally service marketers will refer to 8 Ps, comprising these 7 Ps plus performance.

Exam Probability: **High**

46. *Answer choices:*

(see index for correct answer)

- a. John Neeson
- b. The Cellar
- c. Grand cru
- d. Marketing mix

Guidance: level 1

:: Industry ::

__________ describes various measures of the efficiency of production. Often, a __________ measure is expressed as the ratio of an aggregate output to a single input or an aggregate input used in a production process, i.e. output per unit of input. Most common example is the labour __________ measure, e.g., such as GDP per worker. There are many different definitions of __________ and the choice among them depends on the purpose of the __________ measurement and/or data availability. The key source of difference between various __________ measures is also usually related to how the outputs and the inputs are aggregated into scalars to obtain such a ratio-type measure of __________.

Exam Probability: **Medium**

47. *Answer choices:*

(see index for correct answer)

- a. Straw plaiting
- b. Sisyphism
- c. Consciousness Industry
- d. Productivity

Guidance: level 1

:: Consortia ::

A __________ is an association of two or more individuals, companies, organizations or governments with the objective of participating in a common activity or pooling their resources for achieving a common goal.

Exam Probability: **Medium**

48. *Answer choices:*

(see index for correct answer)

- a. Consortium
- b. ACEnet
- c. OHS Consortium
- d. Linguistic Data Consortium

Guidance: level 1

:: Management ::

A __________ is an idea of the future or desired result that a person or a group of people envisions, plans and commits to achieve. People endeavor to reach __________ s within a finite time by setting deadlines.

Exam Probability: **High**

49. *Answer choices:*

(see index for correct answer)

- a. Process capability
- b. Business-oriented architecture
- c. Change advisory board
- d. Goal

Guidance: level 1

:: ::

__________ Holdings, Inc. is an American company operating a worldwide online payments system that supports online money transfers and serves as an electronic alternative to traditional paper methods like checks and money orders. The company operates as a payment processor for online vendors, auction sites, and many other commercial users, for which it charges a fee in exchange for benefits such as one-click transactions and password memory. __________ `s payment system, also called __________ , is considered a type of payment rail.

Exam Probability: **Low**

50. *Answer choices:*

(see index for correct answer)

- a. empathy

- b. functional perspective
- c. surface-level diversity
- d. Sarbanes-Oxley act of 2002

Guidance: level 1

:: Management occupations ::

_________ ship is the process of designing, launching and running a new business, which is often initially a small business. The people who create these businesses are called _________ s.

Exam Probability: **Medium**

51. *Answer choices:*

(see index for correct answer)

- a. Chief gaming officer
- b. Business magnate
- c. Legislator
- d. Entrepreneur

Guidance: level 1

:: E-commerce ::

__________ Inc. was an electronic money corporation founded by David Chaum in 1989. __________ transactions were unique in that they were anonymous due to a number of cryptographic protocols developed by its founder. __________ declared bankruptcy in 1998, and subsequently sold its assets to eCash Technologies, another digital currency company, which was acquired by InfoSpace on Feb. 19, 2002.

Exam Probability: **Low**

52. *Answer choices:*

(see index for correct answer)

- a. Online insurance
- b. Coinye
- c. DigiCash
- d. Switchwise

Guidance: level 1

:: Commerce ::

An __________ is a bank that offers card association branded payment cards directly to consumers. The name is derived from the practice of issuing payment to the acquiring bank on behalf of its customer .

Exam Probability: **Medium**

53. *Answer choices:*

(see index for correct answer)

- a. Factory
- b. PIN pad
- c. Electronic article surveillance
- d. Issuing bank

Guidance: level 1

:: ::

The Walt _______ Company, commonly known as Walt _______ or simply _______ , is an American diversified multinational mass media and entertainment conglomerate headquartered at the Walt _______ Studios in Burbank, California.

Exam Probability: **Low**

54. *Answer choices:*

(see index for correct answer)

- a. information systems assessment
- b. process perspective
- c. personal values
- d. corporate values

Guidance: level 1

:: ::

__________ or standardisation is the process of implementing and developing technical standards based on the consensus of different parties that include firms, users, interest groups, standards organizations and governments. __________ can help maximize compatibility, interoperability, safety, repeatability, or quality. It can also facilitate commoditization of formerly custom processes. In social sciences, including economics, the idea of __________ is close to the solution for a coordination problem, a situation in which all parties can realize mutual gains, but only by making mutually consistent decisions. This view includes the case of "spontaneous __________ processes", to produce de facto standards.

Exam Probability: **Low**

55. *Answer choices:*

(see index for correct answer)

- a. cultural
- b. hierarchical perspective
- c. Standardization
- d. interpersonal communication

Guidance: level 1

:: Market structure and pricing ::

__________ has historically emerged in two separate types of discussions in economics, that of Adam Smith on the one hand, and that of Karl Marx on the other hand. Adam Smith in his writing on economics stressed the importance of laissez-faire principles outlining the operation of the market in the absence of dominant political mechanisms of control, while Karl Marx discussed the working of the market in the presence of a controlled economy sometimes referred to as a command economy in the literature. Both types of __________ have been in historical evidence throughout the twentieth century and twenty-first century.

Exam Probability: **High**

56. *Answer choices:*

(see index for correct answer)

- a. Open source
- b. Liberalization
- c. industry concentration
- d. Open-source economics

Guidance: level 1

:: ::

In logic and philosophy, an _________ is a series of statements , called the premises or premisses , intended to determine the degree of truth of another statement, the conclusion. The logical form of an _________ in a natural language can be represented in a symbolic formal language, and independently of natural language formally defined " _________ s" can be made in math and computer science.

Exam Probability: **Low**

57. *Answer choices:*

(see index for correct answer)

- a. information systems assessment
- b. Argument
- c. process perspective
- d. empathy

Guidance: level 1

:: Trading posts of the Hanseatic League ::

__________ is a city and unitary authority area in North __________ shire, England, with a population of 208,200 as of 2017. Located at the confluence of the Rivers Ouse and Foss, it is the county town of the historic county of __________ shire and was the home of the House of __________ throughout its existence. The city is known for its famous historical landmarks such as __________ Minster and the city walls, as well as a variety of cultural and sporting activities, which makes it a popular tourist destination in England. The local authority is the City of __________ Council, a single tier governing body responsible for providing all local services and facilities throughout the city. The City of __________ local government district includes rural areas beyond the old city boundaries.

Exam Probability: **Low**

58. *Answer choices:*

(see index for correct answer)

- a. Pskov Republic
- b. Polotsk
- c. Antwerp
- d. York

Guidance: level 1

:: ::

__________ is getting a diploma or academic degree or the ceremony that is sometimes associated with it, in which students become graduates. The date of __________ is often called __________ day. The __________ ceremony itself is also called commencement, convocation or invocation.

Exam Probability: **Low**

59. *Answer choices:*

(see index for correct answer)

- a. personal values
- b. Graduation
- c. Character
- d. hierarchical perspective

Guidance: level 1

Business ethics

Business ethics (also known as corporate ethics) is a form of applied ethics or professional ethics, that examines ethical principles and moral or ethical problems that can arise in a business environment. It applies to all aspects of business conduct and is relevant to the conduct of individuals and entire organizations. These ethics originate from individuals, organizational statements or from the legal system. These norms, values, ethical, and unethical practices are what is used to guide business. They help those businesses maintain a better connection with their stakeholders.

:: Patent law ::

A _________ is generally any statement intended to specify or delimit the scope of rights and obligations that may be exercised and enforced by parties in a legally recognized relationship. In contrast to other terms for legally operative language, the term _________ usually implies situations that involve some level of uncertainty, waiver, or risk.

Exam Probability: **High**

1. *Answer choices:*

(see index for correct answer)

- a. Design around
- b. Essential patent
- c. Disclaimer
- d. Opposition proceeding

Guidance: level 1

:: Professional ethics ::

In the mental health field, a _________ is a situation where multiple roles exist between a therapist, or other mental health practitioner, and a client. _________ s are also referred to as multiple relationships, and these two terms are used interchangeably in the research literature. The American Psychological Association Ethical Principles of Psychologists and Code of Conduct is a resource that outlines ethical standards and principles to which practitioners are expected to adhere. Standard 3.05 of the APA ethics code outlines the definition of multiple relationships. Dual or multiple relationships occur when.

Exam Probability: **Medium**

2. *Answer choices:*

(see index for correct answer)

- a. Continuous professional development
- b. Dual relationship
- c. professional conduct

Guidance: level 1

:: ::

_________ ism is a form of government characterized by strong central power and limited political freedoms. Individual freedoms are subordinate to the state and there is no constitutional accountability and rule of law under an _________ regime. _________ regimes can be autocratic with power concentrated in one person or it can be more spread out between multiple officials and government institutions. Juan Linz`s influential 1964 description of _________ ism characterized _________ political systems by four qualities.

Exam Probability: **Low**

3. *Answer choices:*

(see index for correct answer)

- a. Character

- b. Authoritarian
- c. deep-level diversity
- d. open system

Guidance: level 1

:: ::

__________ in the United States is a federal and state program that helps with medical costs for some people with limited income and resources. __________ also offers benefits not normally covered by Medicare, including nursing home care and personal care services. The Health Insurance Association of America describes __________ as "a government insurance program for persons of all ages whose income and resources are insufficient to pay for health care." __________ is the largest source of funding for medical and health-related services for people with low income in the United States, providing free health insurance to 74 million low-income and disabled people as of 2017. It is a means-tested program that is jointly funded by the state and federal governments and managed by the states, with each state currently having broad leeway to determine who is eligible for its implementation of the program. States are not required to participate in the program, although all have since 1982. __________ recipients must be U.S. citizens or qualified non-citizens, and may include low-income adults, their children, and people with certain disabilities. Poverty alone does not necessarily qualify someone for __________ .

Exam Probability: **Low**

4. *Answer choices:*

(see index for correct answer)

- a. Medicaid
- b. co-culture
- c. imperative
- d. open system

Guidance: level 1

:: Real estate ::

_________ s serve several societal needs – primarily as shelter from weather, security, living space, privacy, to store belongings, and to comfortably live and work. A _________ as a shelter represents a physical division of the human habitat and the outside .

Exam Probability: **Medium**

5. *Answer choices:*

(see index for correct answer)

- a. Cadastre
- b. Pocket listing
- c. 3D floor plan
- d. Building

Guidance: level 1

:: ::

The _________ of 1973 serves as the enacting legislation to carry out the provisions outlined in The Convention on International Trade in Endangered Species of Wild Fauna and Flora . Designed to protect critically imperiled species from extinction as a "consequence of economic growth and development untempered by adequate concern and conservation", the ESA was signed into law by President Richard Nixon on December 28, 1973. The law requires federal agencies to consult with the Fish and Wildlife Service &/or the NOAA Fisheries Service to ensure their actions are not likely to jeopardize the continued existence of any listed species or result in the destruction or adverse modification of designated critical habitat of such species. The U.S. Supreme Court found that "the plain intent of Congress in enacting" the ESA "was to halt and reverse the trend toward species extinction, whatever the cost." The Act is administered by two federal agencies, the United States Fish and Wildlife Service and the National Marine Fisheries Service .

Exam Probability: **High**

6. *Answer choices:*

(see index for correct answer)

- a. similarity-attraction theory
- b. hierarchical perspective
- c. Endangered Species Act
- d. Character

Guidance: level 1

:: Business ::

__________ , or built-in obsolescence, in industrial design and economics is a policy of planning or designing a product with an artificially limited useful life, so that it becomes obsolete after a certain period of time. The rationale behind this strategy is to generate long-term sales volume by reducing the time between repeat purchases .

Exam Probability: **Low**

7. *Answer choices:*

(see index for correct answer)

- a. Winklevoss Capital Management
- b. Business history
- c. Resource slack
- d. Legal governance, risk management, and compliance

Guidance: level 1

:: Toxicology ::

__________ or lead-based paint is paint containing lead. As pigment, lead chromate , Lead oxide, , and lead carbonate are the most common forms. Lead is added to paint to accelerate drying, increase durability, maintain a fresh appearance, and resist moisture that causes corrosion. It is one of the main health and environmental hazards associated with paint. In some countries, lead continues to be added to paint intended for domestic use, whereas countries such as the U.S. and the UK have regulations prohibiting this, although __________ may still be found in older properties painted prior to the introduction of such regulations. Although lead has been banned from household paints in the United States since 1978, paint used in road markings may still contain it. Alternatives such as water-based, lead-free traffic paint are readily available, and many states and federal agencies have changed their purchasing contracts to buy these instead.

Exam Probability: **Medium**

8. *Answer choices:*

(see index for correct answer)

- a. Epidemic dropsy
- b. Medical toxicology
- c. Lead paint
- d. Cholinergic crisis

Guidance: level 1

:: Criminal law ::

__________ is the body of law that relates to crime. It proscribes conduct perceived as threatening, harmful, or otherwise endangering to the property, health, safety, and moral welfare of people inclusive of one`s self. Most __________ is established by statute, which is to say that the laws are enacted by a legislature. __________ includes the punishment and rehabilitation of people who violate such laws. __________ varies according to jurisdiction, and differs from civil law, where emphasis is more on dispute resolution and victim compensation, rather than on punishment or rehabilitation. Criminal procedure is a formalized official activity that authenticates the fact of commission of a crime and authorizes punitive or rehabilitative treatment of the offender.

Exam Probability: **High**

9. *Answer choices:*

(see index for correct answer)

- a. Self-incrimination
- b. Criminal law
- c. Mala in se
- d. Mala prohibita

Guidance: level 1

:: Environmental economics ::

__________ is the process of people maintaining change in a balanced environment, in which the exploitation of resources, the direction of investments, the orientation of technological development and institutional change are all in harmony and enhance both current and future potential to meet human needs and aspirations. For many in the field, __________ is defined through the following interconnected domains or pillars: environment, economic and social, which according to Fritjof Capra is based on the principles of Systems Thinking. Sub-domains of sustainable development have been considered also: cultural, technological and political. While sustainable development may be the organizing principle for __________ for some, for others, the two terms are paradoxical . Sustainable development is the development that meets the needs of the present without compromising the ability of future generations to meet their own needs. Brundtland Report for the World Commission on Environment and Development introduced the term of sustainable development.

Exam Probability: **Medium**

10. *Answer choices:*

(see index for correct answer)

- a. Gas depletion
- b. Journal of Environmental Economics and Management
- c. Environmental impact assessment
- d. Sustainability

Guidance: level 1

:: Cognitive biases ::

In personality psychology, _________ is the degree to which people believe that they have control over the outcome of events in their lives, as opposed to external forces beyond their control. Understanding of the concept was developed by Julian B. Rotter in 1954, and has since become an aspect of personality studies. A person`s "locus" is conceptualized as internal or external .

Exam Probability: **Medium**

11. *Answer choices:*

(see index for correct answer)

- a. Availability heuristic
- b. Locus of control
- c. Normalcy bias
- d. Precision bias

Guidance: level 1

:: Organizational structure ::

An _________ defines how activities such as task allocation, coordination, and supervision are directed toward the achievement of organizational aims.

Exam Probability: **High**

12. *Answer choices:*

(see index for correct answer)

- a. Unorganisation
- b. Organizational structure
- c. Organization of the New York City Police Department
- d. The Starfish and the Spider

Guidance: level 1

:: ::

A _________ is the ability to carry out a task with determined results often within a given amount of time, energy, or both. _________ s can often be divided into domain-general and domain-specific _________ s. For example, in the domain of work, some general _________ s would include time management, teamwork and leadership, self-motivation and others, whereas domain-specific _________ s would be used only for a certain job. _________ usually requires certain environmental stimuli and situations to assess the level of _________ being shown and used.

Exam Probability: **Medium**

13. *Answer choices:*

(see index for correct answer)

- a. Sarbanes-Oxley act of 2002
- b. levels of analysis
- c. co-culture

- d. Skill

Guidance: level 1

:: Ethical banking ::

A _________ or community development finance institution - abbreviated in both cases to CDFI - is a financial institution that provides credit and financial services to underserved markets and populations, primarily in the USA but also in the UK. A CDFI may be a community development bank, a community development credit union , a community development loan fund , a community development venture capital fund , a microenterprise development loan fund, or a community development corporation.

Exam Probability: **Low**

14. *Answer choices:*

(see index for correct answer)

- a. Triodos Bank
- b. Reliance Bank
- c. Charity Bank
- d. Community development financial institution

Guidance: level 1

:: Renewable energy ::

A _________ is a fuel that is produced through contemporary biological processes, such as agriculture and anaerobic digestion, rather than a fuel produced by geological processes such as those involved in the formation of fossil fuels, such as coal and petroleum, from prehistoric biological matter. If the source biomatter can regrow quickly, the resulting fuel is said to be a form of renewable energy.

Exam Probability: **High**

15. *Answer choices:*

(see index for correct answer)

- a. Biofuel
- b. Hi-VAWT
- c. Carbon neutrality
- d. Electric aircraft

Guidance: level 1

:: Corporate crime ::

_________ LLP, based in Chicago, was an American holding company. Formerly one of the "Big Five" accounting firms , the firm had provided auditing, tax, and consulting services to large corporations. By 2001, it had become one of the world's largest multinational companies.

Exam Probability: **High**

16. *Answer choices:*

(see index for correct answer)

- a. General Development Corporation
- b. Ovson Egg
- c. Anti-corporate
- d. Arthur Andersen

Guidance: level 1

:: Nepotism ::

_________ is the granting of favour to relatives in various fields, including business, politics, entertainment, sports, religion and other activities. The term originated with the assignment of nephews to important positions by Catholic popes and bishops. Trading parliamentary employment for favors is a modern-day example of _________ . Criticism of _________ , however, can be found in ancient Indian texts such as the Kural literature.

Exam Probability: **Medium**

17. *Answer choices:*

(see index for correct answer)

- a. Cardinal-nephew
- b. Ethnic nepotism
- c. Nepotism
- d. Crachach

Guidance: level 1

:: Socialism ::

_________ is a label used to define the first currents of modern socialist thought as exemplified by the work of Henri de Saint-Simon, Charles Fourier, Étienne Cabet and Robert Owen.

Exam Probability: **Low**

18. *Answer choices:*

(see index for correct answer)

- a. Revolutionary socialism
- b. Wage labour
- c. Socialist International
- d. Socialist law

Guidance: level 1

:: Types of marketing ::

__________ is an advertisement strategy in which a company uses surprise and/or unconventional interactions in order to promote a product or service. It is a type of publicity. The term was popularized by Jay Conrad Levinson`s 1984 book __________ .

Exam Probability: **High**

19. *Answer choices:*

(see index for correct answer)

- a. Guerrilla Marketing
- b. Vertical integration
- c. Close Range Marketing
- d. Share of voice

Guidance: level 1

:: Human resource management ::

__________ is the ethics of an organization, and it is how an organization responds to an internal or external stimulus. __________ is interdependent with the organizational culture. Although it is akin to both organizational behavior and industrial and organizational psychology as well as business ethics on the micro and macro levels, __________ is neither OB or I/O psychology, nor is it solely business ethics . __________ express the values of an organization to its employees and/or other entities irrespective of governmental and/or regulatory laws.

Exam Probability: **Medium**

20. *Answer choices:*

(see index for correct answer)

- a. Organizational ethics
- b. On-ramping
- c. Behavioral Competencies
- d. Emotional labor

Guidance: level 1

:: Natural gas ::

_________ is a naturally occurring hydrocarbon gas mixture consisting primarily of methane, but commonly including varying amounts of other higher alkanes, and sometimes a small percentage of carbon dioxide, nitrogen, hydrogen sulfide, or helium. It is formed when layers of decomposing plant and animal matter are exposed to intense heat and pressure under the surface of the Earth over millions of years. The energy that the plants originally obtained from the sun is stored in the form of chemical bonds in the gas.

Exam Probability: **Medium**

21. *Answer choices:*

(see index for correct answer)

- a. Natural gasoline

- b. Twister Supersonic Separator
- c. Natural gas
- d. True vapor pressure

Guidance: level 1

:: Business ethics ::

The _________ are the names of two corporate codes of conduct, developed by the African-American preacher Rev. Leon Sullivan, promoting corporate social responsibility.

Exam Probability: **Medium**

22. *Answer choices:*

(see index for correct answer)

- a. Being Globally Responsible Conference
- b. Sullivan principles
- c. Business and Professional Ethics Journal
- d. Society of Corporate Compliance and Ethics

Guidance: level 1

:: Auditing ::

__________ refers to the independence of the internal auditor or of the external auditor from parties that may have a financial interest in the business being audited. Independence requires integrity and an objective approach to the audit process. The concept requires the auditor to carry out his or her work freely and in an objective manner.

Exam Probability: **Low**

23. *Answer choices:*

(see index for correct answer)

- a. Auditor independence
- b. Control environment
- c. Chartered Institute of Internal Auditors
- d. International Register of Certificated Auditors

Guidance: level 1

:: Renewable energy ::

__________ is the conversion of energy from sunlight into electricity, either directly using photovoltaics , indirectly using concentrated __________ , or a combination. Concentrated __________ systems use lenses or mirrors and tracking systems to focus a large area of sunlight into a small beam. Photovoltaic cells convert light into an electric current using the photovoltaic effect.

Exam Probability: **Low**

24. *Answer choices:*

(see index for correct answer)

- a. Wind power
- b. Solar water heating
- c. Solar thermal energy
- d. Solar power

Guidance: level 1

:: Corporate scandals ::

_________ was a bank based in the Caribbean, which operated from 1986 to 2009 when it went into receivership. It was an affiliate of the Stanford Financial Group and failed when the its parent was seized by United States authorities in early 2009 as part of the investigation into Allen Stanford.

Exam Probability: **Medium**

25. *Answer choices:*

(see index for correct answer)

- a. Saradha Group financial scandal
- b. Harken Energy scandal
- c. Noricum scandal
- d. Stanford International Bank

Guidance: level 1

:: ::

The _________ was a severe worldwide economic depression that took place mostly during the 1930s, beginning in the United States. The timing of the _________ varied across nations; in most countries it started in 1929 and lasted until the late-1930s. It was the longest, deepest, and most widespread depression of the 20th century. In the 21st century, the _________ is commonly used as an example of how intensely the world`s economy can decline.

Exam Probability: **Medium**

26. *Answer choices:*

(see index for correct answer)

- a. Sarbanes-Oxley act of 2002
- b. co-culture
- c. deep-level diversity
- d. Character

Guidance: level 1

:: ::

_________ is a naturally occurring, yellowish-black liquid found in geological formations beneath the Earth`s surface. It is commonly refined into various types of fuels. Components of _________ are separated using a technique called fractional distillation, i.e. separation of a liquid mixture into fractions differing in boiling point by means of distillation, typically using a fractionating column.

Exam Probability: **Low**

27. *Answer choices:*

(see index for correct answer)

- a. open system
- b. surface-level diversity
- c. empathy
- d. Petroleum

Guidance: level 1

:: Dutch inventions ::

The Fairtrade certification initiative was created to form a new method for economic trade. This method takes an ethical standpoint, and considers the producers first.

Exam Probability: **High**

28. *Answer choices:*

(see index for correct answer)

- a. Fairtrade
- b. Dijkstra's algorithm

Guidance: level 1

:: Decentralization ::

_________ or sub _________ mainly refers to the unrestricted growth in many urban areas of housing, commercial development, and roads over large expanses of land, with little concern for urban planning. In addition to describing a particular form of urbanization, the term also relates to the social and environmental consequences associated with this development. In Continental Europe the term "peri-urbanisation" is often used to denote similar dynamics and phenomena, although the term _________ is currently being used by the European Environment Agency. There is widespread disagreement about what constitutes sprawl and how to quantify it. For example, some commentators measure sprawl only with the average number of residential units per acre in a given area. But others associate it with decentralization , discontinuity , segregation of uses, and so forth.

Exam Probability: **Low**

29. *Answer choices:*

(see index for correct answer)

- a. National Question
- b. Urban sprawl

- c. Water supply and sanitation in Indonesia
- d. Hacker ethic

Guidance: level 1

:: Auditing ::

_________ is a general term that can reflect various types of evaluations intended to identify environmental compliance and management system implementation gaps, along with related corrective actions. In this way they perform an analogous function to financial audits. There are generally two different types of _________ s: compliance audits and management systems audits. Compliance audits tend to be the primary type in the US or within US-based multinationals.

Exam Probability: **High**

30. *Answer choices:*

(see index for correct answer)

- a. ISACA
- b. Auditing and Assurance Standards Board
- c. Environmental audit
- d. Certified Quality Auditor

Guidance: level 1

:: Pyramid and Ponzi schemes ::

_________ was an Italian swindler and con artist in the U.S. and Canada. His aliases include Charles Ponci, Carlo, and Charles P. Bianchi. Born and raised in Italy, he became known in the early 1920s as a swindler in North America for his money-making scheme. He promised clients a 50% profit within 45 days or 100% profit within 90 days, by buying discounted postal reply coupons in other countries and redeeming them at face value in the United States as a form of arbitrage. In reality, Ponzi was paying earlier investors using the investments of later investors. While this type of fraudulent investment scheme was not originally invented by Ponzi, it became so identified with him that it now is referred to as a "Ponzi scheme". His scheme ran for over a year before it collapsed, costing his "investors" $20 million.

Exam Probability: **High**

31. *Answer choices:*

(see index for correct answer)

- a. Charles Ponzi
- b. Matrix scheme
- c. Solomon Dwek
- d. Stock Generation

Guidance: level 1

:: ::

Cannabis, also known as _________ among other names, is a psychoactive drug from the Cannabis plant used for medical or recreational purposes. The main psychoactive part of cannabis is tetrahydrocannabinol , one of 483 known compounds in the plant, including at least 65 other cannabinoids. Cannabis can be used by smoking, vaporizing, within food, or as an extract.

Exam Probability: **Low**

32. *Answer choices:*

(see index for correct answer)

- a. deep-level diversity
- b. Character
- c. corporate values
- d. Marijuana

Guidance: level 1

:: ::

The _________ is an 1848 political pamphlet by the German philosophers Karl Marx and Friedrich Engels. Commissioned by the Communist League and originally published in London just as the Revolutions of 1848 began to erupt, the Manifesto was later recognised as one of the world`s most influential political documents. It presents an analytical approach to the class struggle and the conflicts of capitalism and the capitalist mode of production, rather than a prediction of communism`s potential future forms.

Exam Probability: **High**

33. *Answer choices:*

(see index for correct answer)

- a. corporate values
- b. open system
- c. Character
- d. process perspective

Guidance: level 1

:: Minimum wage ::

The _________ are working people whose incomes fall below a given poverty line due to lack of work hours and/or low wages.Largely because they are earning such low wages, the _________ face numerous obstacles that make it difficult for many of them to find and keep a job, save up money, and maintain a sense of self-worth.

Exam Probability: **Low**

34. *Answer choices:*

(see index for correct answer)

- a. Guaranteed minimum income
- b. National Anti-Sweating League

- c. Minimum Wage Fairness Act
- d. Working poor

Guidance: level 1

:: Management ::

The term __________ refers to measures designed to increase the degree of autonomy and self-determination in people and in communities in order to enable them to represent their interests in a responsible and self-determined way, acting on their own authority. It is the process of becoming stronger and more confident, especially in controlling one`s life and claiming one`s rights. __________ as action refers both to the process of self- __________ and to professional support of people, which enables them to overcome their sense of powerlessness and lack of influence, and to recognize and use their resources. To do work with power.

Exam Probability: **Medium**

35. *Answer choices:*

(see index for correct answer)

- a. Statistical process control
- b. Infrastructure asset management
- c. Nonconformity
- d. Total security management

Guidance: level 1

:: Financial regulatory authorities of the United States ::

The __________ is an agency of the United States government responsible for consumer protection in the financial sector. CFPB`s jurisdiction includes banks, credit unions, securities firms, payday lenders, mortgage-servicing operations, foreclosure relief services, debt collectors and other financial companies operating in the United States.

Exam Probability: **High**

36. *Answer choices:*

(see index for correct answer)

- a. Office of the Comptroller of the Currency
- b. Consumer Financial Protection Bureau
- c. Federal Reserve Board
- d. Municipal Securities Rulemaking Board

Guidance: level 1

:: ::

_________ is the practice of deliberately managing the spread of information between an individual or an organization and the public. _________ may include an organization or individual gaining exposure to their audiences using topics of public interest and news items that do not require direct payment. This differentiates it from advertising as a form of marketing communications. _________ is the idea of creating coverage for clients for free, rather than marketing or advertising. But now, advertising is also a part of greater PR Activities.An example of good _________ would be generating an article featuring a client, rather than paying for the client to be advertised next to the article. The aim of _________ is to inform the public, prospective customers, investors, partners, employees, and other stakeholders and ultimately persuade them to maintain a positive or favorable view about the organization, its leadership, products, or political decisions. _________ professionals typically work for PR and marketing firms, businesses and companies, government, and public officials as PIOs and nongovernmental organizations, and nonprofit organizations. Jobs central to _________ include account coordinator, account executive, account supervisor, and media relations manager.

Exam Probability: **High**

37. *Answer choices:*

(see index for correct answer)

- a. process perspective
- b. surface-level diversity
- c. cultural
- d. Public relations

Guidance: level 1

:: Carbon finance ::

The __________ is an international treaty which extends the 1992 United Nations Framework Convention on Climate Change that commits state parties to reduce greenhouse gas emissions, based on the scientific consensus that global warming is occurring and it is extremely likely that human-made CO2 emissions have predominantly caused it. The __________ was adopted in Kyoto, Japan on 11 December 1997 and entered into force on 16 February 2005. There are currently 192 parties to the Protocol.

Exam Probability: **Medium**

38. *Answer choices:*

(see index for correct answer)

- a. CEB VER
- b. Carbon Clear
- c. Kyoto Protocol
- d. Voluntary Carbon Standard

Guidance: level 1

:: Industry ::

_________ is the manner in which a given entity has decided to address issues of energy development including energy production, distribution and consumption. The attributes of _________ may include legislation, international treaties, incentives to investment, guidelines for energy conservation, taxation and other public policy techniques. Energy is a core component of modern economies. A functioning economy requires not only labor and capital but also energy, for manufacturing processes, transportation, communication, agriculture, and more.

Exam Probability: **Medium**

39. *Answer choices:*

(see index for correct answer)

- a. Group technology
- b. Industrial district
- c. Energy policy
- d. Productivity

Guidance: level 1

:: Business law ::

A _________ is an arrangement where parties, known as partners, agree to cooperate to advance their mutual interests. The partners in a _________ may be individuals, businesses, interest-based organizations, schools, governments or combinations. Organizations may partner to increase the likelihood of each achieving their mission and to amplify their reach. A _________ may result in issuing and holding equity or may be only governed by a contract.

Exam Probability: **High**

40. *Answer choices:*

(see index for correct answer)

- a. Ordinary resolution
- b. TRIPS Agreement
- c. Partnership
- d. Bulk transfer

Guidance: level 1

:: Anti-Revisionism ::

__________ , officially the German Democratic Republic , was a country that existed from 1949 to 1990, when the eastern portion of Germany was part of the Eastern Bloc during the Cold War. It described itself as a socialist "workers` and peasants` state", and the territory was administered and occupied by Soviet forces at the end of World War II — the Soviet Occupation Zone of the Potsdam Agreement, bounded on the east by the Oder–Neisse line. The Soviet zone surrounded West Berlin but did not include it; as a result, West Berlin remained outside the jurisdiction of the GDR.

Exam Probability: **Medium**

41. *Answer choices:*

(see index for correct answer)

- a. Party of Labour of Albania
- b. Anti-Revisionism
- c. East Germany
- d. New Communist Movement

Guidance: level 1

:: Supply chain management terms ::

In business and finance, _________ is a system of organizations, people, activities, information, and resources involved inmoving a product or service from supplier to customer. _________ activities involve the transformation of natural resources, raw materials, and components into a finished product that is delivered to the end customer. In sophisticated _________ systems, used products may re-enter the _________ at any point where residual value is recyclable. _________ s link value chains.

Exam Probability: **High**

42. *Answer choices:*

(see index for correct answer)

- a. Consumables
- b. Supply Chain
- c. Most valuable customers
- d. Overstock

Guidance: level 1

:: Progressive Era in the United States ::

The Clayton Antitrust Act of 1914 , was a part of United States antitrust law with the goal of adding further substance to the U.S. antitrust law regime; the _________ sought to prevent anticompetitive practices in their incipiency. That regime started with the Sherman Antitrust Act of 1890, the first Federal law outlawing practices considered harmful to consumers . The _________ specified particular prohibited conduct, the three-level enforcement scheme, the exemptions, and the remedial measures.

Exam Probability: **Low**

43. *Answer choices:*

(see index for correct answer)

- a. Clayton Act
- b. Clayton Antitrust Act
- c. pragmatism

Guidance: level 1

:: Statutory law ::

__________ or statute law is written law set down by a body of legislature or by a singular legislator . This is as opposed to oral or customary law; or regulatory law promulgated by the executive or common law of the judiciary. Statutes may originate with national, state legislatures or local municipalities.

Exam Probability: **High**

44. *Answer choices:*

(see index for correct answer)

- a. Statutory law
- b. ratification
- c. Statute of repose
- d. incorporation by reference

Guidance: level 1

:: Leadership ::

__________ is a theory of leadership where a leader works with teams to identify needed change, creating a vision to guide the change through inspiration, and executing the change in tandem with committed members of a group; it is an integral part of the Full Range Leadership Model. __________ serves to enhance the motivation, morale, and job performance of followers through a variety of mechanisms; these include connecting the follower`s sense of identity and self to a project and to the collective identity of the organization; being a role model for followers in order to inspire them and to raise their interest in the project; challenging followers to take greater ownership for their work, and understanding the strengths and weaknesses of followers, allowing the leader to align followers with tasks that enhance their performance.

Exam Probability: **High**

45. *Answer choices:*

(see index for correct answer)

- a. The Leadership Council
- b. Sex differences in leadership
- c. Tribal Leadership
- d. Transformational leadership

Guidance: level 1

:: Business ethics ::

__________ is a type of international private business self-regulation. While once it was possible to describe CSR as an internal organisational policy or a corporate ethic strategy, that time has passed as various international laws have been developed and various organisations have used their authority to push it beyond individual or even industry-wide initiatives. While it has been considered a form of corporate self-regulation for some time, over the last decade or so it has moved considerably from voluntary decisions at the level of individual organisations, to mandatory schemes at regional, national and even transnational levels.

Exam Probability: **Medium**

46. *Answer choices:*

(see index for correct answer)

- a. FRISK Software International
- b. Corporate behaviour
- c. Corporate sustainable profitability
- d. Corporate social responsibility

Guidance: level 1

:: ::

__________ generally refers to a focus on the needs or desires of one`s self. A number of philosophical, psychological, and economic theories examine the role of __________ in motivating human action.

Exam Probability: **High**

47. *Answer choices:*

(see index for correct answer)

- a. Self-interest
- b. hierarchical
- c. Character
- d. Sarbanes-Oxley act of 2002

Guidance: level 1

:: ::

_________ , O.S.A. was a German professor of theology, composer, priest, monk, and a seminal figure in the Protestant Reformation.

Exam Probability: **High**

48. *Answer choices:*

(see index for correct answer)

- a. corporate values
- b. empathy
- c. Martin Luther
- d. deep-level diversity

Guidance: level 1

:: Minimum wage ::

A _________ is the lowest remuneration that employers can legally pay their workers—the price floor below which workers may not sell their labor. Most countries had introduced _________ legislation by the end of the 20th century.

Exam Probability: **High**

49. *Answer choices:*

(see index for correct answer)

- a. Minimum wage
- b. Minimum Wage Fairness Act
- c. Minimum wage in Taiwan
- d. Working poor

Guidance: level 1

:: ::

A _________ is a problem offering two possibilities, neither of which is unambiguously acceptable or preferable. The possibilities are termed the horns of the _________ , a clichéd usage, but distinguishing the _________ from other kinds of predicament as a matter of usage.

Exam Probability: **High**

50. *Answer choices:*

(see index for correct answer)

- a. functional perspective
- b. Dilemma
- c. empathy
- d. hierarchical perspective

Guidance: level 1

:: ::

_________ is a non-governmental environmental organization with offices in over 39 countries and an international coordinating body in Amsterdam, the Netherlands. _________ was founded in 1971 by Irving Stowe, and Dorothy Stowe, Canadian and US ex-pat environmental activists. _________ states its goal is to "ensure the ability of the Earth to nurture life in all its diversity" and focuses its campaigning on worldwide issues such as climate change, deforestation, overfishing, commercial whaling, genetic engineering, and anti-nuclear issues. It uses direct action, lobbying, research, and ecotage to achieve its goals. The global organization does not accept funding from governments, corporations, or political parties, relying on three million individual supporters and foundation grants. _________ has a general consultative status with the United Nations Economic and Social Council and is a founding member of the INGO Accountability Charter, an international non-governmental organization that intends to foster accountability and transparency of non-governmental organizations.

Exam Probability: **High**

51. *Answer choices:*

(see index for correct answer)

- a. Sarbanes-Oxley act of 2002
- b. Greenpeace
- c. hierarchical perspective
- d. functional perspective

Guidance: level 1

:: ::

A _________ is a set of rules, often written, with regards to clothing. _________ s are created out of social perceptions and norms, and vary based on purpose, circumstances and occasions. Different societies and cultures are likely to have different _________ s.

Exam Probability: **Medium**

52. *Answer choices:*

(see index for correct answer)

- a. co-culture
- b. deep-level diversity
- c. corporate values
- d. imperative

Guidance: level 1

:: Corporate governance ::

_________ refers to the practice of members of a corporate board of directors serving on the boards of multiple corporations. A person that sits on multiple boards is known as a multiple director. Two firms have a direct interlock if a director or executive of one firm is also a director of the other, and an indirect interlock if a director of each sits on the board of a third firm. This practice, although widespread and lawful, raises questions about the quality and independence of board decisions.

Exam Probability: **Low**

53. *Answer choices:*

(see index for correct answer)

- a. Interlocking directorate
- b. Chief learning officer
- c. The Samuel and Ronnie Heyman Center on Corporate Governance
- d. Chief privacy officer

Guidance: level 1

:: Law ::

__________ is a body of law which defines the role, powers, and structure of different entities within a state, namely, the executive, the parliament or legislature, and the judiciary; as well as the basic rights of citizens and, in federal countries such as the United States and Canada, the relationship between the central government and state, provincial, or territorial governments.

Exam Probability: **Medium**

54. *Answer choices:*

(see index for correct answer)

- a. Constitutional law
- b. Comparative law

Guidance: level 1

:: Business ethics ::

_________ is an area of applied ethics which deals with the moral principles behind the operation and regulation of marketing. Some areas of _________ overlap with media ethics.

Exam Probability: **Medium**

55. *Answer choices:*

(see index for correct answer)

- a. United Nations Global Compact
- b. Sexual harassment
- c. Enron Code of Ethics
- d. Journal of Business Ethics Education

Guidance: level 1

:: Monopoly (economics) ::

A __________ is a form of intellectual property that gives its owner the legal right to exclude others from making, using, selling, and importing an invention for a limited period of years, in exchange for publishing an enabling public disclosure of the invention. In most countries __________ rights fall under civil law and the __________ holder needs to sue someone infringing the __________ in order to enforce his or her rights. In some industries __________ s are an essential form of competitive advantage; in others they are irrelevant.

Exam Probability: **Medium**

56. *Answer choices:*

(see index for correct answer)

- a. Economies of scope
- b. Government monopoly
- c. Patent
- d. Copyright law of the European Union

Guidance: level 1

:: United Kingdom labour law ::

The __________ was a series of programs, public work projects, financial reforms, and regulations enacted by President Franklin D. Roosevelt in the United States between 1933 and 1936. It responded to needs for relief, reform, and recovery from the Great Depression. Major federal programs included the Civilian Conservation Corps , the Civil Works Administration , the Farm Security Administration , the National Industrial Recovery Act of 1933 and the Social Security Administration . They provided support for farmers, the unemployed, youth and the elderly. The __________ included new constraints and safeguards on the banking industry and efforts to re-inflate the economy after prices had fallen sharply. __________ programs included both laws passed by Congress as well as presidential executive orders during the first term of the presidency of Franklin D. Roosevelt.

Exam Probability: **Low**

57. *Answer choices:*

(see index for correct answer)

- a. Collective Redundancies Directive
- b. Transnational Works Council Directive
- c. New Deal
- d. Employment Agency Standards Inspectorate

Guidance: level 1

:: Electronic waste ::

_________ or e-waste describes discarded electrical or electronic devices. Used electronics which are destined for refurbishment, reuse, resale, salvage, recycling through material recovery, or disposal are also considered e-waste. Informal processing of e-waste in developing countries can lead to adverse human health effects and environmental pollution.

Exam Probability: **Low**

58. *Answer choices:*

(see index for correct answer)

- a. Solving the E-waste Problem
- b. ReGlobe
- c. Techreturns
- d. World Reuse, Repair and Recycling Association

Guidance: level 1

:: Corporate scandals ::

Exxon Mobil Corporation, doing business as _________ , is an American multinational oil and gas corporation headquartered in Irving, Texas. It is the largest direct descendant of John D. Rockefeller`s Standard Oil Company, and was formed on November 30, 1999 by the merger of Exxon and Mobil . _________ `s primary brands are Exxon, Mobil, Esso, and _________ Chemical.

Exam Probability: **High**

59. *Answer choices:*

(see index for correct answer)

- a. Crazy Eddie
- b. Aluminium price-fixing conspiracy
- c. Trustor affair
- d. Harken Energy scandal

Guidance: level 1

Accounting

Accounting or accountancy is the measurement, processing, and communication of financial information about economic entities such as businesses and corporations. The modern field was established by the Italian mathematician Luca Pacioli in 1494. Accounting, which has been called the "language of business", measures the results of an organization's economic activities and conveys this information to a variety of users, including investors, creditors, management, and regulators.

:: ::

__________ , also known as internet banking, is an electronic payment system that enables customers of a bank or other financial institution to conduct a range of financial transactions through the financial institution`s website. The __________ system will typically connect to or be part of the core banking system operated by a bank and is in contrast to branch banking which was the traditional way customers accessed banking services.

Exam Probability: **High**

1. *Answer choices:*

(see index for correct answer)

- a. hierarchical perspective
- b. surface-level diversity
- c. Online banking
- d. personal values

Guidance: level 1

:: Generally Accepted Accounting Principles ::

In business and accounting, _________ is an entity`s income minus cost of goods sold, expenses and taxes for an accounting period. It is computed as the residual of all revenues and gains over all expenses and losses for the period, and has also been defined as the net increase in shareholders` equity that results from a company`s operations. In the context of the presentation of financial statements, the IFRS Foundation defines _________ as synonymous with profit and loss. The difference between revenue and the cost of making a product or providing a service, before deducting overheads, payroll, taxation, and interest payments. This is different from operating income .

Exam Probability: **Low**

2. *Answer choices:*

(see index for correct answer)

- a. Management accounting principles
- b. deferred revenue
- c. Access to finance
- d. Net income

Guidance: level 1

:: Auditing ::

A __________, also called "Internal __________", is a term of financial audit, internal audit and Enterprise Risk Management. It means the overall attitude, awareness and actions of directors and management regarding the internal control system and its importance to the entity. They express it in management style, corporate culture, values, philosophy and operating style, the organisational structure, and human resources policies and procedures.

Exam Probability: **High**

3. *Answer choices:*

(see index for correct answer)

- a. Communication audit
- b. Circulation Verification Council
- c. Walk-through test
- d. RSM International

Guidance: level 1

:: Tax reform ::

__________ is the process of changing the way taxes are collected or managed by the government and is usually undertaken to improve tax administration or to provide economic or social benefits. __________ can include reducing the level of taxation of all people by the government, making the tax system more progressive or less progressive, or simplifying the tax system and making the system more understandable or more accountable.

Exam Probability: **High**

4. *Answer choices:*

(see index for correct answer)

- a. Tax reform
- b. Goods and Services Tax
- c. John Sherwin Crosby
- d. Enterprise Value Tax

Guidance: level 1

:: Project management ::

__________ is the widespread practice of collecting information and attempting to spot a pattern. In some fields of study, the term " __________ " has more formally defined meanings.

Exam Probability: **High**

5. *Answer choices:*

(see index for correct answer)

- a. Outcomes theory
- b. Advanced Integrated Practice
- c. Defense Acquisition Workforce Improvement Act
- d. Trend analysis

Guidance: level 1

:: United States federal income tax ::

Under United States tax law, the _________ is a dollar amount that non-itemizers may subtract from their income before income tax is applied. Taxpayers may choose either itemized deductions or the _________ , but usually choose whichever results in the lesser amount of tax payable. The _________ is available to US citizens and aliens who are resident for tax purposes and who are individuals, married persons, and heads of household. The _________ is based on filing status and typically increases each year. It is not available to nonresident aliens residing in the United States . Additional amounts are available for persons who are blind and/or are at least 65 years of age.

Exam Probability: **Medium**

6. *Answer choices:*

(see index for correct answer)

- a. Standard deduction
- b. Personal Casualty Gains
- c. Filing status
- d. Stepped-up basis

Guidance: level 1

:: Finance ::

__________ is a notional asset or liability to reflect corporate income taxation on a basis that is the same or more similar to recognition of profits than the taxation treatment. __________ liabilities can arise as a result of corporate taxation treatment of capital expenditure being more rapid than the accounting depreciation treatment. __________ assets can arise due to net loss carry-overs, which are only recorded as asset if it is deemed more likely than not that the asset will be used in future fiscal periods. Different countries may also allow or require discounting of the assets or particularly liabilities. There are often disclosure requirements for potential liabilities and assets that are not actually recognised as an asset or liability.

Exam Probability: **Low**

7. *Answer choices:*

(see index for correct answer)

- a. Soft dollar
- b. OnDeck
- c. XBRLS
- d. Deferred tax

Guidance: level 1

:: Basic financial concepts ::

In finance, maturity or __________ refers to the final payment date of a loan or other financial instrument, at which point the principal is due to be paid.

Exam Probability: **Low**

8. *Answer choices:*

(see index for correct answer)

- a. Maturity date
- b. Future-oriented
- c. Present value of benefits
- d. Forward guidance

Guidance: level 1

:: Accounting software ::

_________ is a freely available and global framework for exchanging business information. _________ allows the expression of semantic meaning commonly required in business reporting. The language is XML-based and uses the XML syntax and related XML technologies such as XML Schema, XLink, XPath, and Namespaces. One use of _________ is to define and exchange financial information, such as a financial statement. The _________ Specification is developed and published by _________ International, Inc. .

Exam Probability: **Low**

9. *Answer choices:*

(see index for correct answer)

- a. Money

- b. XBRL
- c. FinanceWorks
- d. Passport Software

Guidance: level 1

:: Management accounting ::

_________ is the process of recording, classifying, analyzing, summarizing, and allocating costs associated with a process,after that developing various courses of action to control the costs. Its goal is to advise the management on how to optimize business practices and processes based on cost efficiency and capability. _________ provides the detailed cost information that management needs to control current operations and plan for the future.

Exam Probability: **Medium**

10. *Answer choices:*

(see index for correct answer)

- a. Constraints accounting
- b. Management accounting in supply chains
- c. Cost accounting
- d. Factory overhead

Guidance: level 1

:: Management accounting ::

_________ is a professional business study of Accounts and management in which we learn importance of accounts in our management system.

Exam Probability: **Medium**

11. *Answer choices:*

(see index for correct answer)

- a. Financial statement analysis
- b. Owner earnings
- c. RCA open-source application
- d. Accounting management

Guidance: level 1

:: Accounting ::

_________ is a process of providing relief to shared service organization`s cost centers that provide a product or service. In turn, the associated expense is assigned to internal clients` cost centers that consume the products and services. For example, the CIO may provide all IT services within the company and assign the costs back to the business units that consume each offering.

Exam Probability: **High**

12. *Answer choices:*

(see index for correct answer)

- a. Cost allocation
- b. Earnings surprise
- c. INPACT International
- d. Part exchange

Guidance: level 1

:: Management accounting ::

_________ , or dollar contribution per unit, is the selling price per unit minus the variable cost per unit. "Contribution" represents the portion of sales revenue that is not consumed by variable costs and so contributes to the coverage of fixed costs. This concept is one of the key building blocks of break-even analysis.

Exam Probability: **Medium**

13. *Answer choices:*

(see index for correct answer)

- a. Holding cost
- b. Backflush accounting
- c. Variable Costing
- d. Contribution margin

Guidance: level 1

:: Financial ratios ::

_________ or interest coverage ratio is a measure of a company's ability to honor its debt payments. It may be calculated as either EBIT or EBITDA divided by the total interest payable.

Exam Probability: **High**

14. *Answer choices:*

(see index for correct answer)

- a. Days payable outstanding
- b. Bias ratio
- c. Net interest spread
- d. Envy ratio

Guidance: level 1

:: Costs ::

The _________ is computed by dividing the total cost of goods available for sale by the total units available for sale. This gives a weighted-average unit cost that is applied to the units in the ending inventory.

Exam Probability: **Medium**

15. *Answer choices:*

(see index for correct answer)

- a. Khozraschyot
- b. Customer Cost
- c. Cost of poor quality
- d. Explicit cost

Guidance: level 1

:: Retail financial services ::

A __________ is a prepaid stored-value money card, usually issued by a retailer or bank, to be used as an alternative to cash for purchases within a particular store or related businesses. __________ s are also given out by employers or organizations as rewards or gifts. They may also be distributed by retailers and marketers as part of a promotion strategy, to entice the recipient to come in or return to the store, and at times such cards are called cash cards. __________ s are generally redeemable only for purchases at the relevant retail premises and cannot be cashed out, and in some situations may be subject to an expiry date or fees. American Express, MasterCard, and Visa offer generic __________ s which need not be redeemed at particular stores, and which are widely used for cashback marketing strategies. A feature of these cards is that they are generally anonymous and are disposed of when the stored value on a card is exhausted.

Exam Probability: **High**

16. *Answer choices:*

(see index for correct answer)

- a. Metropolitan Educational Enterprises
- b. Borro
- c. VantageScore
- d. Gift card

Guidance: level 1

:: Real estate valuation ::

_________ or OMV is the price at which an asset would trade in a competitive auction setting. _________ is often used interchangeably with open _________, fair value or fair _________, although these terms have distinct definitions in different standards, and may or may not differ in some circumstances.

Exam Probability: **Medium**

17. *Answer choices:*

(see index for correct answer)

- a. cap rate
- b. Market value
- c. Appraisal Standards Board
- d. Uniform Standards of Professional Appraisal Practice

Guidance: level 1

:: Income ::

__________ is a ratio between the net profit and cost of investment resulting from an investment of some resources. A high ROI means the investment`s gains favorably to its cost. As a performance measure, ROI is used to evaluate the efficiency of an investment or to compare the efficiencies of several different investments. In purely economic terms, it is one way of relating profits to capital invested. __________ is a performance measure used by businesses to identify the efficiency of an investment or number of different investments.

Exam Probability: **High**

18. *Answer choices:*

(see index for correct answer)

- a. Income Per User
- b. Passive income
- c. Return on investment
- d. Real income

Guidance: level 1

:: Types of accounting ::

Various __________ systems are used by various public sector entities. In the United States, for instance, there are two levels of government which follow different accounting standards set forth by independent, private sector boards. At the federal level, the Federal Accounting Standards Advisory Board sets forth the accounting standards to follow. Similarly, there is the __________ Standards Board for state and local level government.

Exam Probability: **Low**

19. *Answer choices:*

(see index for correct answer)

- a. Sustainability accounting
- b. Personal environmental impact accounting
- c. Governmental accounting

Guidance: level 1

:: Corporate governance ::

The _________ is the officer of a company that has primary responsibility for managing the company`s finances, including financial planning, management of financial risks, record-keeping, and financial reporting. In some sectors, the CFO is also responsible for analysis of data. Some CFOs have the title CFOO for chief financial and operating officer. In the United Kingdom, the typical term for a CFO is finance director . The CFO typically reports to the chief executive officer and the board of directors and may additionally have a seat on the board.The CFO supervises the finance unit and is the chief financial spokesperson for the organization. The CFO directly assists the chief operating officer on all strategic and tactical matters relating to budget management, cost–benefit analysis, forecasting needs, and securing of new funding.

Exam Probability: **High**

20. *Answer choices:*

(see index for correct answer)

- a. Chief financial officer
- b. Independent director
- c. Hawkama
- d. Chief analytics officer

Guidance: level 1

:: ::

Accounts _________ is a legally enforceable claim for payment held by a business for goods supplied and/or services rendered that customers/clients have ordered but not paid for. These are generally in the form of invoices raised by a business and delivered to the customer for payment within an agreed time frame. Accounts _________ is shown in a balance sheet as an asset. It is one of a series of accounting transactions dealing with the billing of a customer for goods and services that the customer has ordered. These may be distinguished from notes _________ , which are debts created through formal legal instruments called promissory notes.

Exam Probability: **High**

21. *Answer choices:*

(see index for correct answer)

- a. Character
- b. open system
- c. process perspective
- d. Receivable

Guidance: level 1

:: Generally Accepted Accounting Principles ::

A _________ , in accrual accounting, is any account where the asset or liability is not realized until a future date , e.g. annuities, charges, taxes, income, etc. The deferred item may be carried, dependent on type of _________ , as either an asset or liability. See also accrual.

Exam Probability: **High**

22. *Answer choices:*

(see index for correct answer)

- a. Generally accepted accounting principles
- b. Deferral
- c. Earnings before interest, taxes and depreciation
- d. Insurance asset management

Guidance: level 1

:: Management accounting ::

An __________ allows a company to provide a monetary value for items that make up their inventory. Inventories are usually the largest current asset of a business, and proper measurement of them is necessary to assure accurate financial statements. If inventory is not properly measured, expenses and revenues cannot be properly matched and a company could make poor business decisions.

Exam Probability: **High**

23. *Answer choices:*

(see index for correct answer)

- a. Resource consumption accounting
- b. Inventory valuation

- c. Operating profit margin
- d. Chartered Institute of Management Accountants

Guidance: level 1

:: Information systems ::

An accounting as an information system is a system of collecting, storing and processing financial and accounting data that are used by decision makers. An __________ is generally a computer-based method for tracking accounting activity in conjunction with information technology resources. The resulting financial reports can be used internally by management or externally by other interested parties including investors, creditors and tax authorities. __________ s are designed to support all accounting functions and activities including auditing, financial accounting & reporting, managerial/ management accounting and tax. The most widely adopted accounting information systems are auditing and financial reporting modules.

Exam Probability: **High**

24. *Answer choices:*

(see index for correct answer)

- a. Virtual USA
- b. Earthquake Early Warning
- c. Urban and Regional Information Systems Association
- d. Accounting information system

Guidance: level 1

:: Legal terms ::

An _________ is an action which is inaccurate or incorrect. In some usages, an _________ is synonymous with a mistake. In statistics, " _________ " refers to the difference between the value which has been computed and the correct value. An _________ could result in failure or in a deviation from the intended performance or behaviour.

Exam Probability: **High**

25. *Answer choices:*

(see index for correct answer)

- a. Error
- b. Constructive notice
- c. Arguido
- d. Partial verdict

Guidance: level 1

:: Taxation ::

_________ refers to instances where a taxpayer can delay paying taxes to some future period. In theory, the net taxes paid should be the same. Taxes can sometimes be deferred indefinitely, or may be taxed at a lower rate in the future, particularly for deferral of income taxes.

Exam Probability: **High**

26. *Answer choices:*

(see index for correct answer)

- a. Benefit principle
- b. Tax deferral
- c. Value capture
- d. Payment in lieu of taxes

Guidance: level 1

:: Taxation in the United States ::

The Modified Accelerated Cost Recovery System is the current tax depreciation system in the United States. Under this system, the capitalized cost of tangible property is recovered over a specified life by annual deductions for depreciation. The lives are specified broadly in the Internal Revenue Code. The Internal Revenue Service publishes detailed tables of lives by classes of assets. The deduction for depreciation is computed under one of two methods at the election of the taxpayer, with limitations. See IRS Publication 946 for a 120-page guide to _________ .

Exam Probability: **Medium**

27. *Answer choices:*

(see index for correct answer)

- a. Bypass trust
- b. MACRS
- c. School Infrastructure Local Option
- d. Medical savings account

Guidance: level 1

:: Inventory ::

Costs are associated with particular goods using one of the several formulas, including specific identification, first-in first-out , or average cost. Costs include all costs of purchase, costs of conversion and other costs that are incurred in bringing the inventories to their present location and condition. Costs of goods made by the businesses include material, labor, and allocated overhead. The costs of those goods which are not yet sold are deferred as costs of inventory until the inventory is sold or written down in value.

Exam Probability: **High**

28. *Answer choices:*

(see index for correct answer)

- a. Decomposition
- b. Stock-taking
- c. Cost of goods sold
- d. Lower of cost or market

Guidance: level 1

:: Generally Accepted Accounting Principles ::

The first published description of the process is found in Luca Pacioli`s 1494 work Summa de arithmetica, in the section titled Particularis de Computis et Scripturis. Although he did not use the term, he essentially prescribed a technique similar to a post-closing _________ .

Exam Probability: **High**

29. *Answer choices:*

(see index for correct answer)

- a. Trial balance
- b. AICPA Statements of Position
- c. Net profit
- d. Treasury stock

Guidance: level 1

:: Supply chain management terms ::

In business and finance, _________ is a system of organizations, people, activities, information, and resources involved inmoving a product or service from supplier to customer. _________ activities involve the transformation of natural resources, raw materials, and components into a finished product that is delivered to the end customer. In sophisticated _________ systems, used products may re-enter the _________ at any point where residual value is recyclable. _________s link value chains.

Exam Probability: **Medium**

30. *Answer choices:*

(see index for correct answer)

- a. Cool Chain Quality Indicator
- b. Consumables
- c. Supply chain
- d. Final assembly schedule

Guidance: level 1

:: Financial accounting ::

_________ in accounting is the process of treating investments in associate companies. Equity accounting is usually applied where an investor entity holds 20–50% of the voting stock of the associate company. The investor records such investments as an asset on its balance sheet. The investor`s proportional share of the associate company`s net income increases the investment , and proportional payments of dividends decrease it. In the investor's income statement, the proportional share of the investor's net income or net loss is reported as a single-line item.

Exam Probability: **Low**

31. *Answer choices:*

(see index for correct answer)

- a. Equity method
- b. Carry
- c. Advance payment
- d. Asset swap

Guidance: level 1

:: Money ::

In economics, _________ is money in the physical form of currency, such as banknotes and coins. In bookkeeping and finance, _________ is current assets comprising currency or currency equivalents that can be accessed immediately or near-immediately . _________ is seen either as a reserve for payments, in case of a structural or incidental negative _________ flow or as a way to avoid a downturn on financial markets.

Exam Probability: **Low**

32. *Answer choices:*

(see index for correct answer)

- a. Cash
- b. Automated cash handling
- c. Love of money
- d. Spondulix

Guidance: level 1

:: Accounting terminology ::

_________ is an accounting system for recording resources whose use has been limited by the donor, grant authority, governing agency, or other individuals or organisations or by law. It emphasizes accountability rather than profitability, and is used by Nonprofit organizations and by governments. In this method, a fund consists of a self-balancing set of accounts and each are reported as either unrestricted, temporarily restricted or permanently restricted based on the provider-imposed restrictions.

Exam Probability: **Low**

33. *Answer choices:*

(see index for correct answer)

- a. Internal auditing

- b. Mark-to-market
- c. Fund accounting
- d. Accounts payable

Guidance: level 1

:: Generally Accepted Accounting Principles ::

In accounting, _________ is the income that a business have from its normal business activities, usually from the sale of goods and services to customers. _________ is also referred to as sales or turnover.Some companies receive _________ from interest, royalties, or other fees. _________ may refer to business income in general, or it may refer to the amount, in a monetary unit, earned during a period of time, as in "Last year, Company X had _________ of $42 million". Profits or net income generally imply total _________ minus total expenses in a given period. In accounting, in the balance statement it is a subsection of the Equity section and _________ increases equity, it is often referred to as the "top line" due to its position on the income statement at the very top. This is to be contrasted with the "bottom line" which denotes net income .

Exam Probability: **High**

34. *Answer choices:*

(see index for correct answer)

- a. Normal balance
- b. Construction in progress
- c. Deferred income

- d. Engagement letter

Guidance: level 1

:: Cash flow ::

In corporate finance, __________ or __________ to firm is a way of looking at a business`s cash flow to see what is available for distribution among all the securities holders of a corporate entity. This may be useful to parties such as equity holders, debt holders, preferred stock holders, and convertible security holders when they want to see how much cash can be extracted from a company without causing issues to its operations.

Exam Probability: **Medium**

35. *Answer choices:*

(see index for correct answer)

- a. Factoring
- b. Invoice discounting
- c. Free cash flow
- d. First Chicago Method

Guidance: level 1

:: Asset ::

__________ s, also known as tangible assets or property, plant and equipment , is a term used in accounting for assets and property that cannot easily be converted into cash. This can be compared with current assets such as cash or bank accounts, described as liquid assets. In most cases, only tangible assets are referred to as fixed. IAS 16 defines __________ s as assets whose future economic benefit is probable to flow into the entity, whose cost can be measured reliably. __________ s belong to one of 2 types:"Freehold Assets" – assets which are purchased with legal right of ownership and used,and "Leasehold Assets" – assets used by owner without legal right for a particular period of time.

Exam Probability: **High**

36. *Answer choices:*

(see index for correct answer)

- a. Current asset
- b. Fixed asset

Guidance: level 1

:: Corporate crime ::

__________ LLP, based in Chicago, was an American holding company. Formerly one of the "Big Five" accounting firms , the firm had provided auditing, tax, and consulting services to large corporations. By 2001, it had become one of the world`s largest multinational companies.

Exam Probability: **High**

37. *Answer choices:*

(see index for correct answer)

- a. Equity Funding
- b. Arthur Andersen
- c. General Development Corporation
- d. Arthur Andersen LLP v. United States

Guidance: level 1

:: Generally Accepted Accounting Principles ::

The _________ principle is a cornerstone of accrual accounting together with the matching principle. They both determine the accounting period in which revenues and expenses are recognized. According to the principle, revenues are recognized when they are realized or realizable, and are earned , no matter when cash is received. In cash accounting – in contrast – revenues are recognized when cash is received no matter when goods or services are sold.

Exam Probability: **Low**

38. *Answer choices:*

(see index for correct answer)

- a. Income statement
- b. Trial balance
- c. Revenue recognition
- d. Gross income

Guidance: level 1

:: Accounting journals and ledgers ::

The subledger, or _________, provides details behind entries in the general ledger used in accounting. The subledger shows detail for part of the accounting records such as property and equipment, prepaid expenses, etc. The detail would include such items as date the item was purchased or expense incurred, a description of the item, the original balance, and the net book value. The total of the subledger would match the line item amount on the general ledger. This corresponding line item in the general ledger is referred to as the controlling account. The _________ balance is compared with its controlling account balance as part of the process of preparing a trial balance.

Exam Probability: **Low**

39. *Answer choices:*

(see index for correct answer)

- a. General journal
- b. Sales journal
- c. Check register
- d. Subsidiary ledger

Guidance: level 1

:: Financial statements ::

In financial accounting, a _________ or statement of financial position or statement of financial condition is a summary of the financial balances of an individual or organization, whether it be a sole proprietorship, a business partnership, a corporation, private limited company or other organization such as Government or not-for-profit entity. Assets, liabilities and ownership equity are listed as of a specific date, such as the end of its financial year. A _________ is often described as a "snapshot of a company's financial condition". Of the four basic financial statements, the _________ is the only statement which applies to a single point in time of a business' calendar year.

Exam Probability: **Medium**

40. *Answer choices:*

(see index for correct answer)

- a. Statement on Auditing Standards No. 55
- b. Quarterly finance report
- c. Emphasis of matter
- d. quarterly report

Guidance: level 1

:: Financial ratios ::

A __________ or accounting ratio is a relative magnitude of two selected numerical values taken from an enterprise`s financial statements. Often used in accounting, there are many standard ratios used to try to evaluate the overall financial condition of a corporation or other organization. __________ s may be used by managers within a firm, by current and potential shareholders of a firm, and by a firm`s creditors. Financial analysts use __________ s to compare the strengths and weaknesses in various companies. If shares in a company are traded in a financial market, the market price of the shares is used in certain __________ s.

Exam Probability: **Medium**

41. *Answer choices:*

(see index for correct answer)

- a. Financial ratio
- b. Net interest spread
- c. Return on equity
- d. Loan-to-value ratio

Guidance: level 1

:: Management accounting ::

__________ s are costs that change as the quantity of the good or service that a business produces changes. __________ s are the sum of marginal costs over all units produced. They can also be considered normal costs. Fixed costs and __________ s make up the two components of total cost. Direct costs are costs that can easily be associated with a particular cost object. However, not all __________ s are direct costs. For example, variable manufacturing overhead costs are __________ s that are indirect costs, not direct costs. __________ s are sometimes called unit-level costs as they vary with the number of units produced.

Exam Probability: **High**

42. *Answer choices:*

(see index for correct answer)

- a. Certified Management Accountant
- b. Variable cost
- c. Responsibility center
- d. Management accounting

Guidance: level 1

:: Labor terms ::

__________ , often called DI or disability income insurance, or income protection, is a form of insurance that insures the beneficiary`s earned income against the risk that a disability creates a barrier for a worker to complete the core functions of their work. For example, the worker may suffer from an inability to maintain composure in the case of psychological disorders or an injury, illness or condition that causes physical impairment or incapacity to work. It encompasses paid sick leave, short-term disability benefits , and long-term disability benefits . Statistics show that in the US a disabling accident occurs, on average, once every second. In fact, nearly 18.5% of Americans are currently living with a disability, and 1 out of every 4 persons in the US workforce will suffer a disabling injury before retirement.

Exam Probability: **Low**

43. *Answer choices:*

(see index for correct answer)

- a. Indexation of contracts
- b. Disability insurance
- c. All other occupational illnesses
- d. Displaced workers

Guidance: level 1

:: Accounting in the United States ::

The __________ is located in Norwalk, Connecticut, United States. It was organized in 1972 as a non-stock, Delaware Corporation. It is an independent organization in the private sector, operating with the goal of ensuring objectivity and integrity in financial reporting standards.

Exam Probability: **Low**

44. *Answer choices:*

(see index for correct answer)

- a. Certified Public Accountant
- b. Financial Accounting Foundation
- c. Revolving fund
- d. Joseph Eve, Certified Public Accountants

Guidance: level 1

:: Accounting in the United States ::

The __________ was formed by the American Institute of Certified Public Accountants in 1972, and developed the Objective of Financial Statements. The committee`s goal was to create financial statements that helped external users make decisions about the economics of companies. In 1978, the Financial Accounting Standards Board , whose purpose is to develop generally accepted accounting principles, adopted the key objectives established by the __________ .

Exam Probability: **High**

45. *Answer choices:*

(see index for correct answer)

- a. Federal Accounting Standards Advisory Board
- b. Institute of Internal Auditors
- c. Legal liability of certified public accountants
- d. Trueblood Committee

Guidance: level 1

:: United States Generally Accepted Accounting Principles ::

In the United States, a _________ is one of the five governmental fund types established by GAAP. It is classified as a restricted true endowment fund for governments and non-profit organizations. Put simply, a _________ may be used to generate and disburse money to those entitled to receive payments by qualification or agreement, as in the case of Alaska citizens or residents that satisfy the rules for payment from their _________ from State oil revenues. It was first introduced through GASB Statement 34. The name of the fund comes from the purpose of the fund: a sum of equity used to permanently generate payments to maintain some financial obligation. Also, a fund can only be classified as a _________ if the money is used to report the status of a restricted financial resource. The resource is restricted in the sense that only earnings from the resource are used and not the principal. For example, a fund can be classified as a _________ if it is being used to pay for accounting services for a perpetual endowment of a government-run cemetery or financial endowments towards a government-run library.

Exam Probability: **High**

46. *Answer choices:*

(see index for correct answer)

- a. Cost segregation study
- b. Single Audit
- c. Permanent fund
- d. GASB 45

Guidance: level 1

:: Accounting in the United States ::

Founded in 1887, the __________ is the national professional organization of Certified Public Accountants in the United States, with more than 418,000 members in 143 countries in business and industry, public practice, government, education, student affiliates and international associates. It sets ethical standards for the profession and U.S. auditing standards for audits of private companies, non-profit organizations, federal, state and local governments. It also develops and grades the Uniform CPA Examination. The AICPA maintains offices in New York City; Washington, DC; Durham, NC; and Ewing, NJ. The AICPA celebrated the 125th anniversary of its founding in 2012.

Exam Probability: **Medium**

47. *Answer choices:*

(see index for correct answer)

- a. Governmental Accounting Standards Board
- b. Uniform Certified Public Accountant Examination

- c. American Institute of Certified Public Accountants
- d. Other comprehensive income

Guidance: level 1

:: Accounting systems ::

In accounting, the _________ is an account in the general ledger for which a corresponding subsidiary ledger has been created. The subsidiary ledger allows for tracking transactions within the _________ in more detail. Individual transactions are posted both to the _________ and the corresponding subsidiary ledger, and the totals for both are compared when preparing a trial balance to ensure accuracy.

Exam Probability: **Low**

48. *Answer choices:*

(see index for correct answer)

- a. Open-book accounting
- b. Single-entry bookkeeping
- c. Substance over form
- d. Confidence accounting

Guidance: level 1

:: ::

An _________ is a contingent motivator. Traditional _________ s are extrinsic motivators which reward actions to yield a desired outcome. The effectiveness of traditional _________ s has changed as the needs of Western society have evolved. While the traditional _________ model is effective when there is a defined procedure and goal for a task, Western society started to require a higher volume of critical thinkers, so the traditional model became less effective. Institutions are now following a trend in implementing strategies that rely on intrinsic motivations rather than the extrinsic motivations that the traditional _________ s foster.

Exam Probability: **Medium**

49. *Answer choices:*

(see index for correct answer)

- a. Character
- b. surface-level diversity
- c. open system
- d. information systems assessment

Guidance: level 1

:: Financial ratios ::

_________ is a financial ratio that indicates the percentage of a company`s assets that are provided via debt. It is the ratio of total debt and total assets .

Exam Probability: **Medium**

50. *Answer choices:*

(see index for correct answer)

- a. Debt ratio
- b. Deleveraging
- c. stock turnover
- d. Debt-to-capital ratio

Guidance: level 1

:: Generally Accepted Accounting Principles ::

__________ is, in accrual accounting, money received for goods or services which have not yet been delivered. According to the revenue recognition principle, it is recorded as a liability until delivery is made, at which time it is converted into revenue.

Exam Probability: **High**

51. *Answer choices:*

(see index for correct answer)

- a. Standard Business Reporting
- b. Deferred income
- c. Chinese accounting standards

- d. Deprival value

Guidance: level 1

:: Generally Accepted Accounting Principles ::

In accrual accounting, the revenue recognition principle states that expenses should be recorded during the period in which they are incurred, regardless of when the transfer of cash occurs. Conversely, cash basis accounting calls for the recognition of an expense when the cash is paid, regardless of when the expense was actually incurred.

Exam Probability: **High**

52. *Answer choices:*

(see index for correct answer)

- a. Operating income before depreciation and amortization
- b. net realisable value
- c. Petty cash
- d. Fin 48

Guidance: level 1

:: Project management ::

In economics, _________ is the assignment of available resources to various uses. In the context of an entire economy, resources can be allocated by various means, such as markets or central planning.

Exam Probability: **Low**

53. *Answer choices:*

(see index for correct answer)

- a. Project
- b. Resource allocation
- c. Authority
- d. Enterprise project management

Guidance: level 1

:: Real estate ::

An _________ is to, interest in, or legal liability on real property that does not prohibit passing title to the property but that may diminish its value. _________ s can be classified in several ways. They may be financial or non-financial . Alternatively, they may be divided into those that affect title or those that affect the use or physical condition of the encumbered property . _________ s include security interests, liens, servitudes , leases, restrictions, encroachments, and air and subsurface rights. Also, those considered as potentially making the title defeasible are _________ s, for example, charging orders, building orders and structure alteration. _________ : charge upon or claim against land arising out of private grant or a contract.

Exam Probability: **Medium**

54. *Answer choices:*

(see index for correct answer)

- a. Garden real estate
- b. Emphyteutic lease
- c. Real-estate lock box
- d. Originating application

Guidance: level 1

:: Capital gains taxes ::

A _________ refers to profit that results from a sale of a capital asset, such as stock, bond or real estate, where the sale price exceeds the purchase price. The gain is the difference between a higher selling price and a lower purchase price. Conversely, a capital loss arises if the proceeds from the sale of a capital asset are less than the purchase price.

Exam Probability: **High**

55. *Answer choices:*

(see index for correct answer)

- a. Capital gain
- b. Capital gains tax

- c. Capital cost tax factor

Guidance: level 1

:: Business models ::

A _________ , _________ company or daughter company is a company that is owned or controlled by another company, which is called the parent company, parent, or holding company. The _________ can be a company, corporation, or limited liability company. In some cases it is a government or state-owned enterprise. In some cases, particularly in the music and book publishing industries, subsidiaries are referred to as imprints.

Exam Probability: **Medium**

56. *Answer choices:*

(see index for correct answer)

- a. Co-operative Wholesale Society
- b. InnovationXchange
- c. Subsidiary
- d. Artel

Guidance: level 1

:: ::

_________ science is the application of science to criminal and civil laws, mainly—on the criminal side—during criminal investigation, as governed by the legal standards of admissible evidence and criminal procedure.

Exam Probability: **Medium**

57. *Answer choices:*

(see index for correct answer)

- a. levels of analysis
- b. Forensic
- c. interpersonal communication
- d. process perspective

Guidance: level 1

:: Business models ::

A _________ is a company that owns enough voting stock in another firm to control management and operation by influencing or electing its board of directors. The company is deemed a subsidiary of the _________ .

Exam Probability: **Medium**

58. *Answer choices:*

(see index for correct answer)

- a. Component business model
- b. Pay to play
- c. Trade printing
- d. Parent company

Guidance: level 1

:: Accounting terminology ::

A _________ contains all the accounts for recording transactions relating to a company's assets, liabilities, owners' equity, revenue, and expenses. In modern accounting software or ERP, the _________ works as a central repository for accounting data transferred from all subledgers or modules like accounts payable, accounts receivable, cash management, fixed assets, purchasing and projects. The _________ is the backbone of any accounting system which holds financial and non-financial data for an organization. The collection of all accounts is known as the _________ . Each account is known as a ledger account. In a manual or non-computerized system this may be a large book.The statement of financial position and the statement of income and comprehensive income are both derived from the _________ . Each account in the _________ consists of one or more pages. The _________ is where posting to the accounts occurs. Posting is the process of recording amounts as credites , and amounts as debits , in the pages of the _________ . Additional columns to the right hold a running activity total .

Exam Probability: **High**

59. *Answer choices:*

(see index for correct answer)

- a. Share premium
- b. Cash flow management
- c. General ledger
- d. Capital appreciation

Guidance: level 1

INDEX: Correct Answers

Foundations of Business

1. a: Employment

2. : Limited liability

3. c: Economic Development

4. c: Stock market

5. b: Life

6. d: Need

7. : Business model

8. d: Supply chain

9. : Number

10. d: Foreign direct investment

11. d: Property rights

12. a: Franchising

13. : SWOT analysis

14. : Entrepreneurship

15. c: Property

16. b: Six Sigma

17. d: Chart

18. : Corporation

19. c: Exercise

20. b: Arbitration

21. d: Cultural

22. b: Patent

23. c: Career

24. a: Quality control

25. b: Budget

26. c: Customs

27. d: Strategic alliance

28. a: Preference

29. d: Income statement

30. b: Arthur Andersen

31. a: Information systems

32. d: Credit card

33. c: Sales

34. : Best practice

35. d: Target market

36. a: Board of directors

37. b: Size

38. : Specification

39. b: Feedback

40. b: Brand

41. b: Quality management

42. a: Organizational culture

43. c: Outsourcing

44. b: Import

45. a: Recession

46. a: Incentive

47. c: Partnership

48. d: Reputation

49. a: Management system

50. b: Technology

51. a: Publicity

52. b: Competition

53. : Copyright

54. a: Social security

55. d: Project

56. c: Negotiation

57. c: Alliance

58. b: ITeM

59. : Authority

Management

1. : Vertical integration

2. : General manager

3. a: Pension

4. d: Coaching

5. c: Environmental protection

6. a: Resource

7. d: Social loafing

8. c: Individualism

9. c: World Trade Organization

10. c: Job enrichment

11. c: Patent

12. d: Income

13. b: Return on investment

14. a: Virtual team

15. c: Chief executive officer

16. b: Goal setting

17. b: Myers-Briggs type

18. a: Reinforcement

19. a: Integrity

20. b: Organizational structure

21. b: Customer

22. a: Cost leadership

23. c: Training and development

24. c: Sexual harassment

25. d: Brainstorming

26. : Arbitration

27. d: Process control

28. b: Consultant

29. c: Accounting

30. d: Governance

31. d: Dilemma

32. b: Affirmative action

33. c: American Express

34. c: Enron

35. : Sharing

36. b: Raw material

37. a: Compromise

38. : Quality circle

39. : Corporate governance

40. d: Proactive

41. c: Questionnaire

42. b: Expert

43. a: Market research

44. d: Interaction

45. b: Gantt chart

46. : Labor relations

47. a: Project manager

48. d: Workforce

49. a: Feedback

50. d: Choice

51. : Committee

52. d: Review

53. d: Management process

54. d: Organizational learning

55. d: Information

56. b: Risk management

57. d: Benchmarking

58. : Lead

59. c: Product design

Business law

1. : Market value

2. : Argument

3. d: Impossibility

4. a: Opening statement

5. a: Sexual harassment

6. : Charter

7. a: Personal property

8. c: Trespass

9. c: Labor relations

10. : Federal question

11. d: Public policy

12. d: Substantive law

13. b: Testimony

14. c: Auction

15. d: Sherman Act

16. d: Wage

17. c: Treaty

18. d: Creditor

19. : Pregnancy discrimination

20. d: Independent contractor

21. b: Liquidated damages

22. b: Garnishment

23. b: Writ

24. c: Limited partnership

25. d: Deed

26. c: Personnel

27. b: Rescind

28. b: Presumption

29. b: Negligence

30. a: Assumption of risk

31. b: Offeree

32. a: Commerce

33. c: Accounting

34. b: Bailee

35. b: Lease

36. a: Brand

37. a: White-collar crime

38. d: Accord and satisfaction

39. d: Substantial performance

40. : Tangible

41. b: Promissory note

42. a: Bill of lading

43. a: Precedent

44. b: Criminal law

45. b: Warranty

46. c: Subsidiary

47. a: Insider trading

48. a: Specific performance

49. b: Restraint of trade

50. c: Directed verdict

51. b: Offeror

52. : Bankruptcy

53. b: Mortgage

54. c: Certiorari

55. a: Employment discrimination

56. : Hearing

57. a: Cooperative

58. a: Warehouse

59. a: Money laundering

Finance

1. a: Copyright

2. a: Net profit

3. c: Cost allocation

4. : Coupon

5. : Future value

6. d: Contract

7. d: Presentation

8. : Expense

9. a: Time value of money

10. b: Saving

11. d: Advertising

12. d: Interest rate risk

13. d: Amortization

14. c: Rate risk

15. c: Perpetual inventory

16. a: Cost driver

17. b: Merchandising

18. : Taxation

19. : Credit risk

20. c: Internal control

21. d: General journal

22. b: Need

23. a: Debtor

24. d: Property

25. b: Payroll

26. a: Monetary policy

27. a: Board of directors

28. b: Debenture

29. a: Consideration

30. d: Going concern

31. a: Payment

32. : Face

33. : Accrued interest

34. b: Historical cost

35. a: Operating Income

36. d: Free cash flow

37. : Limited liability

38. c: Revenue

39. d: Source document

40. : Stock split

41. c: Accrual

42. d: Cost

43. b: Current asset

44. b: Dividend

45. d: Yield curve

46. d: Interest

47. d: Inventory turnover

48. : Arbitrage

49. a: Specific identification

50. c: Insurance

51. : S corporation

52. a: Worksheet

53. d: Pension fund

54. a: Credit card

55. d: Deferral

56. c: Cash equivalent

57. c: Financial ratio

58. d: Hedge

59. c: Internal rate of return

Human resource management

1. d: Nearshoring

2. c: Employee stock

3. a: Conformity

4. d: Kelly Services

5. d: Featherbedding

6. a: Impasse

7. : 360-degree feedback

8. b: Xerox Corporation

9. d: Balanced scorecard

10. : Organizational chart

11. d: Job enrichment

12. : Vertical integration

13. a: Content validity

14. c: Adaptive

15. c: Innovation

16. a: Performance management

17. c: Meritor Savings Bank v. Vinson

18. : Salary

19. b: Delayering

20. b: Living wage

21. b: Control group

22. : Faragher v. City of Boca Raton

23. a: Cost

24. c: Hazard analysis

25. b: Hazard

26. a: Recruitment

27. c: Functional job analysis

28. : Sick leave

29. b: Employee stock ownership plan

30. d: Expert power

31. d: Trade union

32. : Business model

33. d: Performance measurement

34. c: Unemployment insurance

35. b: Job evaluation

36. b: Rating scale

37. b: Theory Z

38. : Restricted stock

39. : Wage

40. a: Selection ratio

41. : Sexual harassment

42. c: E-learning

43. : Schedule

44. : Social contract

45. d: Training

46. c: Exit interview

47. a: Job performance

48. b: Ingratiation

49. d: Management by objectives

50. b: Local union

51. d: Progressive discipline

52. b: Needs analysis

53. c: Price Waterhouse v. Hopkins

54. b: Sweatshop

55. d: Health Reimbursement Account

56. : Global sourcing

57. a: Arbitration

58. a: Census

59. b: Analysis

Information systems

1. : Business process

2. : Google Maps

3. a: Data governance

4. c: Local Area Network

5. c: Top-level domain

6. d: Software as a service

7. a: Computer security

8. : Business-to-business

9. b: Intranet

10. d: Phishing

11. d: Global Positioning System

12. b: Consumer-to-business

13. a: Digital rights management

14. b: Virtual reality

15. a: Privacy policy

16. d: Census

17. d: Information technology

18. c: Social shopping

19. b: Data integration

20. b: Byte

21. a: Web analytics

22. c: Management information system

23. a: Cookie

24. : System

25. b: Total cost of ownership

26. d: Competitive advantage

27. d: Common Criteria

28. b: Privacy

29. a: Consumer-to-consumer

30. b: Analytics

31. a: Code

32. a: Business rule

33. d: Open source

34. : Online transaction processing

35. c: Security management

36. a: Semantic Web

37. a: Magnetic tape

38. : BitTorrent

39. : System software

40. : Folksonomy

41. a: Data field

42. : Second Life

43. c: Collision

44. a: Data center

45. : Data

46. b: Business process reengineering

47. d: Zynga

48. b: Transaction processing

49. a: Decision-making

50. a: Payment card

51. c: Enterprise search

52. b: American Express

53. a: Domain name

54. d: Government-to-government

55. c: Structured query language

56. b: Data file

57. d: Information governance

58. : Automation

59. d: Throughput

Marketing

1. : Trade association

2. c: Brand awareness

3. c: Selling

4. a: Persuasion

5. : Retailing

6. d: Green marketing

7. c: Inventory

8. a: Loyalty

9. c: Customer retention

10. : Household

11. : American Express

12. : Aid

13. a: Blog

14. c: Intangibility

15. c: Trial

16. : Organizational structure

17. b: Customer experience

18. : Convenience

19. a: Commercialization

20. c: Qualitative research

21. a: Consideration

22. : Productivity

23. c: Buyer

24. c: Health

25. : Frequency

26. c: Question

27. : Competitive intelligence

28. : Market share

29. a: Quantitative research

30. b: Market segments

31. : Brand management

32. a: Incentive

33. c: Data warehouse

34. a: Competitor

35. c: Authority

36. c: Integrated marketing

37. b: Primary data

38. a: Revenue

39. d: Consumerism

40. c: Value proposition

41. b: Commerce

42. a: Regulation

43. a: Sherman Antitrust Act

44. : Sales management

45. d: Subsidiary

46. c: Competitive advantage

47. d: Attention

48. b: Consumer behavior

49. : Problem Solving

50. a: Respondent

51. c: Good

52. d: Concept testing

53. a: Telemarketing

54. d: Brand extension

55. a: Creativity

56. a: Penetration pricing

57. : Personnel

58. b: Evaluation

59. b: Sales

Manufacturing

1. : Minitab

2. b: Total quality management

3. : Volume

4. d: Strategic sourcing

5. a: Quality function deployment

6. c: Cost driver

7. : Business process

8. b: Solution

9. c: Process capability

10. : Process capital

11. : Steel

12. : Design of experiments

13. d: Service level

14. d: EFQM

15. d: Initiative

16. b: Heat transfer

17. d: Kanban

18. b: Raw material

19. d: Scientific management

20. d: Chemical industry

21. d: Quality costs

22. c: Scheduling

23. d: Cost

24. : Reflux

25. : Licensed production

26. c: Voice of the customer

27. a: Poka-yoke

28. d: Malcolm Baldrige National Quality Award

29. : Heat treating

30. d: New product development

31. d: Quality policy

32. b: E-commerce

33. c: Knowledge management

34. c: Process engineering

35. : Furnace

36. d: Heat exchanger

37. : Sales

38. c: Inspection

39. : Thomas Register

40. c: Quality control

41. c: Statistical process control

42. c: Quality by Design

43. a: Milestone

44. a: Resource allocation

45. a: ROOT

46. b: Water

47. : Economic order quantity

48. d: Assembly line

49. d: Synergy

50. a: Supply chain risk management

51. c: Bullwhip effect

52. d: Root cause

53. : Prize

54. a: Accreditation

55. d: PDCA

56. d: Estimation

57. a: Indirect costs

58. d: Retail

59. : Cash register

Commerce

1. d: Authorize.Net

2. d: Yield management

3. d: Total revenue

4. c: Revenue

5. : Policy

6. : GeoCities

7. a: Return on investment

8. b: Product mix

9. : Manufacturing

10. b: Economics

11. b: Affiliate marketing

12. : Mobile commerce

13. b: Audit

14. a: Performance

15. a: Supranational

16. : Information technology

17. b: Public relations

18. : Personnel

19. d: Inventory

20. a: Property

21. c: Social shopping

22. c: Joint venture

23. d: Raw material

24. a: Free market

25. : Leadership

26. b: Purchasing manager

27. b: Management

28. c: Real estate

29. c: Marketing

30. b: Lease

31. a: Payment system

32. b: Disintermediation

33. a: Excite

34. d: Mining

35. d: Silver

36. c: Merchant

37. a: Market research

38. b: Merger

39. : Security

40. d: Control system

41. : Quality assurance

42. : Subsidy

43. : Phishing

44. : Statutory law

45. : Household

46. d: Marketing mix

47. d: Productivity

48. a: Consortium

49. d: Goal

50. : PayPal

51. d: Entrepreneur

52. c: DigiCash

53. d: Issuing bank

54. : Disney

55. c: Standardization

56. : Market structure

57. b: Argument

58. d: York

59. b: Graduation

Business ethics

1. c: Disclaimer

2. b: Dual relationship

3. b: Authoritarian

4. a: Medicaid

5. d: Building

6. c: Endangered Species Act

7. : Planned obsolescence

8. c: Lead paint

9. b: Criminal law

10. d: Sustainability

11. b: Locus of control

12. b: Organizational structure

13. d: Skill

14. d: Community development financial institution

15. a: Biofuel

16. d: Arthur Andersen

17. c: Nepotism

18. : Utopian socialism

19. a: Guerrilla Marketing

20. a: Organizational ethics

21. c: Natural gas

22. b: Sullivan principles

23. a: Auditor independence

24. d: Solar power

25. d: Stanford International Bank

26. : Great Depression

27. d: Petroleum

28. c: Fair Trade Certified

29. b: Urban sprawl

30. c: Environmental audit

31. a: Charles Ponzi

32. d: Marijuana

33. : Communist Manifesto

34. d: Working poor

35. : Empowerment

36. b: Consumer Financial Protection Bureau

37. d: Public relations

38. c: Kyoto Protocol

39. c: Energy policy

40. c: Partnership

41. c: East Germany

42. b: Supply Chain

43. a: Clayton Act

44. a: Statutory law

45. d: Transformational leadership

46. d: Corporate social responsibility

47. a: Self-interest

48. c: Martin Luther

49. a: Minimum wage

50. b: Dilemma

51. b: Greenpeace

52. : Dress code

53. a: Interlocking directorate

54. a: Constitutional law

55. : Marketing ethics

56. c: Patent

57. c: New Deal

58. : Electronic waste

59. : ExxonMobil

Accounting

1. c: Online banking

2. d: Net income

3. : Control environment

4. a: Tax reform

5. d: Trend analysis

6. a: Standard deduction

7. d: Deferred tax

8. a: Maturity date

9. b: XBRL

10. c: Cost accounting

11. d: Accounting management

12. a: Cost allocation

13. d: Contribution margin

14. : Times interest earned

15. : Average cost

16. d: Gift card

17. b: Market value

18. c: Return on investment

19. c: Governmental accounting

20. a: Chief financial officer

21. d: Receivable

22. b: Deferral

23. b: Inventory valuation

24. d: Accounting information system

25. a: Error

26. b: Tax deferral

27. b: MACRS

28. c: Cost of goods sold

29. a: Trial balance

30. c: Supply chain

31. a: Equity method

32. a: Cash

33. c: Fund accounting

34. : Revenue

35. c: Free cash flow

36. b: Fixed asset

37. b: Arthur Andersen

38. c: Revenue recognition

39. d: Subsidiary ledger

40. : Balance sheet

41. a: Financial ratio

42. b: Variable cost

43. b: Disability insurance

44. b: Financial Accounting Foundation

45. d: Trueblood Committee

46. c: Permanent fund

47. c: American Institute of Certified Public Accountants

48. : Controlling account

49. : Incentive

50. a: Debt ratio

51. b: Deferred income

52. : Matching principle

53. b: Resource allocation

54. : Encumbrance

55. a: Capital gain

56. c: Subsidiary

57. b: Forensic

58. d: Parent company

59. c: General ledger

CPSIA information can be obtained
at www.ICGtesting.com
Printed in the USA
LVHW011544301019
635718LV00004B/362/P